BRITAIN

ON

B A C K R O A D S

BRITAIN
—ON—
B A C K R O A D S

DUNCAN PETERSEN

300 Raritan Center Parkway,
CN 94, Edison, N.J. 08818

1994 new edition
The routes in this book were first published 1985 by
Pan Books and Ordnance Survey.

This adapted, revised and updated edition first published 1994

in Great Britain by
Duncan Petersen Publishing Ltd
54, Milson Road,
London W14 0LB

ISBN 1 872576 38 9

and in the USA by
Hunter Publishing Inc.,
300 Raritan Center Parkway,
Edison, NJ 08818
Tel (908) 25 1900
Fax (908) 417 0482

ISBN 1-55650-638-4

© Duncan Petersen Publishing Ltd 1994
©Tours text, individual contributors as listed 1994
Maps supplied by European Map Graphics

Conceived, edited and designed by
Duncan Petersen Publishing Ltd,
54, Milson Road, London W14 0LB

Sales representation in the U.K. and Ireland by
World Leisure Marketing,
117, The Hollow, Littleover, Derby, DE3 7BS
Tel (0332) 272 020 Fax (0332) 774 287
Distributed by
Grantham Book Services

Originated in Britain by Modern Reprographics Ltd, Hull
Printed in Italy by G. Canale & C. SpA, Turin

A CIP catalogue record for this book is available from
the British Library

This new edition revised and updated by **Jennifer Grafton**

Original edition edited by Gilly Abrahams

Every mile of **Britain on Backroads** was not only carefully planned, but *driven* by writers and local experts. The editor thanks them for their remarkable local knowledge, painstaking research, and the hours spent at the typewriter, and behind the wheel.

The Land's End and Lizard; Bodmin and Boscastle; Looe, Polperro and Mount Edgcumbe: **David and Hilary Platten**. Totnes and Slapton Sands: **John Weir**. Bude and Bideford; Exmoor: **Brian Pearce**. Dartmoor: **Liz Prince**. Blackmoor Vale and the Dorset Hills: **Gilly Abrahams**. Salisbury, Stonehenge and Wilton: **Andrew Duncan**. New Forest: **Fiona Duncan**. The Weald and the Cinque Ports; Chilterns and Thames Valley; Constable Country; Norwich and the Norfolk Coast: **Richard Beech**. The Surrey Hills and North Downs; Lower Wye and the Forest of Dean: **John Nolan**. Vale of White Horse; Cotswolds: **Linda Hart**. Brecon Beacons and Black Mountains: **Louise Heinemann**. Mid Wales; Cadair Idris and Lake Vyrnwy; Bala and Harlech; Lleyn and Snowdon; Blaenau Ffestiniog and the Conwy Valley: **James Knowles**. The Upper Wye; The Shropshire Highlands: **Harry Baker**. The Malverns: **Wilfred Harper.** The White Peak: **Neil Coates**. The South Pennines; The Dales: **Colin Speakman**. The Lincolnshire Wolds; The North Yorkshire Moors: **Bill Glenton**. Caldbeck, Buttermere and Derwentwater; Windermere, Eskdale and Coniston Water: **Geoffrey Berry**. Scotland all tours: **Leslie and Adrian Gardiner.**

Contents

Thurso

Inverness ●38

Aberdeen

Fort William

Dundee

Oban ● St. Andrews
36 ● Inverary   Perth ●
37
Stirling
Glasgow   Edinburgh
Largs   Dunbar
              Berwick-
Peebles   upon-Tweed
Ayr   Lanark   35
Girvan   Moffat   Jedburgh   Alnwick
Dumfries   Newcastle
Stranraer   Carlisle   Hexham   upon Tyne
                        Gateshead
Keswick ● Penrith   Durham
Whitehaven   29   Darlington   ● Whitby
Isle of Man   28 ● Kendal   27 ●   Scarborough
Northallerton
Barrow-   Ripon   Bridlington
in-Furness   26 ●
Douglas   Lancaster
            25 ●   York   Kingston
Blackpool   Leeds   upon Hull
        Blackburn   Bradford
    Liverpool   Grimsby
Anglesey   Manchester   Sheffield   Doncaster
Llandudno   Lincoln
Holyhead ●   34   Chester   Buxton   24
Bangor   Crewe   23   Skegness
Caernarfon ● 33   Nottingham   Cromer
Pwllheli   32 ● Bala   Stoke-   Boston   22
Dolgellau   on-Trent   Norwich
    31   Shrewsbury ●   Derby   Lowestoft
Aberystwyth   21   Stafford   Leicester
            Birmingham   Peterborough
    Presteigne   Cambridge
Cardigan   Warwick   Northampton   20
    Lampeter   18   Worcester   Banbury   Ipswich
Fishguard   30   19   Luton   Colchester
Carmarthen   Monmouth 16   Cheltenham   Hertford   Chelmsford
            17   Aylesbury
Pembroke   Swindon   Oxford
    Swansea   Cardiff   14   15   London   Chatham   Margate
        Bristol   Newbury   Reading
Ilfracombe   Minehead   Bath   Guildford   13   T. Wells   Dover
    11   ● Wells   12   Winchester   9   10
    5   Taunton   Salisbury   Southampton   Brighton   Hastings
Bude   7   8   Portsmouth   Eastbourne
Bodmin ● 2   Exeter   Dorchester   Bournemouth
Newquay   Launceston   6   Lyme   Isle of Wight
    1   3   Torbay   Regis   Weymouth
Penzance   Plymouth   4

6

The tours are generally arranged in south-west to north-east sequence, beginning in Cornwall and ending in north-east Scotland. Where several tours fall within the same region, for example Wales, they are grouped together, even if it means deviating temporarily from the sequence.

7

Introduction

You only have to do a drive from *Britain on Backroads* to re-discover what you always suspected: Britain is startlingly rich in things to see and do; in history, in quirky fascination, and marvellous, infinitely beautiful and varied countryside. Moreover, Britain's network of country backroads is exceptional in its own right: the perfect partner for, and the key to, that bounty of interest and scenery.

But before being carried away by the prospect, you could do worse than reflect on the experiences of Rat, Mole and Toad, the animal characters in Kenneth Grahame's children's classic *The Wind in the Willows* when they set out one day to sample the joys of the country byways. They were strolling quietly along a country road with their horse-drawn, canary-coloured cart when

'. . . far behind they heard a faint warning hum, like the drone of a distant bee. Glancing back, they saw a small cloud of dust, with a dark centre of energy, advancing on them at incredible speed, while from out of the dust a faint 'Poop-poop!' wailed like an uneasy animal in pain. Hardly regarding it, they turned to resume their conversation, when in an instant (as it seemed) the peaceful scene was changed, and with a blast of wind and a whirl of sound that made them jump for the nearest ditch, it was on them! The 'poop-poop' rang with a brazen shout in their ears, they had a moment's glimpse of an interior of glittering plate glass and rich morocco, and the magnificent motor car, immense, breath-snatching, passionate, with its pilot tense and hugging his wheel, possessed all earth and air . . .'

Wind in the Willows' fans regard this passage as nothing less than prophetic. It sums up, especially for the British, with their deep-rooted feelings about the countryside, the awful impact of the motor car on the sleepy unspoilt world of the horse-and-cart; and it suggests the power of the alien machine to change an old way of life, indeed to alter the delicate natural balance of the countryside.

When the first edition of the *Wind in the Willows* was published, the age of the motor car was still dawning. Over eighty years later, few would deny the truth of Grahame's perception: the motor car has changed the countryside, and, come to that, the world.

However, like any generalization, it is not the full story. The actual outcome of the motor car's impact has, at any rate, been different to Grahame's dark observation about the car possessing 'all earth and air'. Indeed, there are several ways in which the motor car's impact has turned out not quite as badly as it might have done.

When *Britain on Backroads* was being compiled, test-driven and written, the contributors and the editorial team who put the book together talked to dozens of people all round Britain professionally involved in managing the countryside. A broad, but clear, consensus of opinion emerged that although some select country roads, particularly in beauty spots, come under appalling pressure from traffic at peak tourist periods, in general, the lesser A-roads, B-roads and unclassified roads of Britain carry far less traffic than they did before the motorway system reached its present extent.

One other unexpected comment emerged: that easily the worst drivers on backroads today are not the visiting tourists, but the locals: the Mr Toads of the 1990s are, by consent, the 'young farmer' types. As one National Park official put it: 'They pass you at sixty on the narrowest country lane, but you can still identify them because of the sticker in the back window saying "Young farmers do it wearing wellies".'

Visitors are, by contrast, careful, if not dawdling drivers, and that, ironically, is often the greatest source of resentment against them. One of the most irritating, and potentially dangerous experiences of driving along a narrow country lane with poor visibility is rounding a corner to find one must swerve to avoid a car pulled up half-on, half-off the road. No thought has been given to other traffic; the driver, and all the passengers are happily picking flowers, or stroking a pony, or answering the call of nature, oblivious of the frustration and anger they have caused.

Country people, 'professional' and 'non-professional' alike, tend to agree that the most unforgivable – as opposed to the most irritating – crime is feeding animals. In areas like Dartmoor and the New Forest, where ponies and other creatures roam freely, feeding amounts simply to killing. The animals hang about the verges, attracted by the prospect of food. They don't, like humans, have road sense and, inevitably, they lumber into the path of oncoming cars, particularly at night when they are blinded by the headlights. In the New Forest, one pony is killed nearly every night on the roads during summer. If more people could witness the miserable consequences of hitting an animal, there would be fewer such accidents.

There is one other perception of Kenneth Grahame's in *Wind in the Willows* which still has remarkable relevance to driving on country roads. It is, of course, the character of Mr Toad himself: the observation that the excitement of the new, be it a new motor car or a lovely view, simply makes some people behave as if common sense never existed. Carried away by the thrill of discovery, people – responsible ones at that – behave as if they had never considered the possibility of country lanes having poor visibility; or that 20 mph (32 km/h) is fast enough to take blind corners; or that around any corner could be a hedge trimmer or slow-moving tractor into which one could crash, or, swerving to avoid it, collide with an oncoming car. There are times when something of Mr Toad gets into the best of us: when we think it enough to hoot at a blind corner, and carry on without reducing speed; or when we park in a gateway, or in the only passing place on a narrow road; or tow a caravan down a backroad and then complain at being held up for hours when we meet a farm vehicle which is too wide to pass.

The spirit of *Britain on Backroads* is intended to be one of exploration; of discovering Britain's backroads slowly enough to assimilate the mood of a locality, but also alert enough to take in more than the casual passer-by would. Being relaxed – but alert – was, in Kenneth Grahame's view, a great virtue; one which Rat and Mole, as opposed to Toad, possessed in abundance. It is the right approach to using a book such as *Britian on Backroads* safely and considerately.

Touring with *Britain on Backroads*

Happy motor touring depends on three things: planning where to go, and how to get there; actually getting there, with as much enjoyment, and as little frustration as possible; and having fun once you arrive. *Britain on Backroads* has been devised with all these aims in mind.

The routes

Wherever you are staying in Britain, or wherever you live, you will not be far from one of the book's 38 figure-of-eight or circular tours. Most of these have been designed to be driven either in a day if you are content to make only two or three stops including lunch, or in two days at a slower pace, stopping to see more sights.

The tours have been researched, devised, written and driven by local experts all over Britain with the object of giving an in depth introduction to the area. You will find that driving them is a travelling experience in itself, revealing the countryside in a way that will often surprise, and will certainly be of interest. The routes are largely made up of unclassified roads, linked with A and B road sections. Directions are given at key points for easy route-finding.

Around the routes are picked out an extraordinarily wide range of local sights and attractions: castles and great houses, churches and abbeys, pubs and restaurants, views, museums and exhibitions, walks and wildlife, local history and local excursions – indeed anything of interest to the visitor. No one would want, or have the time, to visit them all: the idea is to select, with the help of the text, those which interest you most, and then to explore them in your own time.

Starting points are suggested for each tour, but you can join them and leave them where you wish. However, you are advised to follow the directions in the sequence given.

The roads

Britain on Backroads is about country roads, warts and all: expect some poor surfaces. In upland areas, be prepared to creep around terrifying hair-pin bends, and to edge past unprotected verges, wheels only inches from sheer drops. In some country areas, be ready for blind corners, slow farm vehicles and inadequate signposting.

The maps The routes are featured on the Bartholomew national series of maps: general-purpose motoring maps at a scale of 1:253 440, about four miles to one inch (6 km to 2.5 cm).

The cartography of the Bartholomew maps is continually updated using the latest in computer technology. These maps also carry plenty of helpful extra information for the tourist and road user. The scale allows road bends as close as 200 yards (250 m) apart to show up; the unclassified roads, with no coloured infill, are a faithful representation of Britain's minor roads and country lanes. However, in common with all other maps at this scale, not every single minor road is featured (indeed the tours occasionally use short stretches of unmarked road – see below under **Route Directions**) and the names of some small settlements are omitted.

Hints on map-reading To get the best from the mapping in this book, first familiarize yourself with the symbols, colour coding and other cartographic features. These are given on pages 16-17.

The colour coding makes the different status of the roads particularly clear. The unclassified road network – backroads, byways or country lanes – are of course the key to exploring Britain in depth. They are distinctively marked by simple black lines with no coloured infill, and the book naturally uses them in large numbers for its routes. After them, the B roads (brown) are the most widely used, then A roads with two or more digits. These, in contrast to A roads with a single digit, often offer relatively peaceful driving: they are not main roads, and, now that the motorway system is reasonably complete in Britain, they tend to carry comparatively little traffic. Naturally, there are exceptions: in the mountainous areas of Scotland, all the roads may be A roads, none of them wide enough to allow two cars to pass, and always as quiet as country lanes in the heart of Devon. Conversely, in the West Country at the height of the holiday season, the B3311 between Penzance and St Ives can be bumper-to-bumper.

The Bartholomew mapping used in Britain does not show quite all the unclassified roads, and the names of some small villages and settlements are omitted, In practice, this can be a help to the motorist: too much detail can confuse. On the other hand, it does require active map-reading.

That means, in essence, knowing where you are 'on the map' at any given moment. Understanding the implication of scale is the first step towards this: on these maps, for example, a quarter of an inch (0.6 cm) on the map represents one mile on the ground, and for every mile you travel you should tick off mentally the appropriate portion of the map. To do that, of course, you need a point of reference from which to start. This is generally easy when driving: obvious landmarks continually present themselves in the form of villages, side-turnings and junctions. Not such obvious points of reference are rivers, railways, water and woodland areas.

Perhaps one difficulty in using road maps stands out above all others. You are driving towards what appears on the map to be a crossroads, but on arrival you find that it seems to be a T-junction, with no road continuing straight ahead. You stop, look right and left, and still see no continuing road; and, understandably, suspect you have lost your way.

In fact, you have come to a staggered crossroads. The way ahead lies out of sight no more than 50 or 100 yards (40 or 80 m) down the crossing road, possibly hidden by trees or buildings. The scale of the mapping used in the book can make such staggered crossroads difficult to identify at first glance; but often enough they are just discernible if you examine the mapping closely.

The route directions Printed in italics, these are an aid to trouble-free navigation, *not* a complete set of instructions for getting round the routes. You will find that they are most detailed on tricky backroad stretches, and especially so on the odd occasion where your route follows a road not actually marked on the map. It is, of course, important to follow the directions carefully on such stretches. The text does not always draw your attention to the fact that a road is not marked.

Food Our contributors set out not only to make each tour an interesting drive, but to find a few useful restaurants and pubs on or near the routes. Some areas are not, however, as well endowed with suitable places as others, and this is reflected in the varying number of recommendations.

The restaurants and pubs are not by any means the only ones you will find on or near the routes: but they will be interesting for some or all of the following reasons: value, quality of the food and wine, atmosphere, friendly service and local cooking. They are generally fairly inexpensive and offer good value for money. Although they have been chosen with a lunchtime stop in mind, they are often excellent places for an evening meal as well.

National Holidays   New Year's Day (and an extra day in Scotland); Good Friday; Easter Monday; I May (May Day); Spring Bank Holiday; Summer Bank Holiday (in Scotland the first, in England and Wales the fourth Monday in August); Christmas Day; 26 December (Boxing Day). Please note that the dates of the May Bank Holidays may change in 1995.

Shopping Hours   Generally, shops are open 9-5.30 (not closing for lunch) Mon-Sat; in large cities many small shops are open until 8 in the evening.

In very rural areas, shops close at lunchtime one day a week (usually Wed or Thurs).

Shops are not normally open on Sun, except for some newsagents, tobacconists and supermarkets – alcohol sales being subject to licensing hours, 12-3 pm only.

Time   Britain is on Greenwich Mean Time in *winter* and one hour ahead in *summer*.

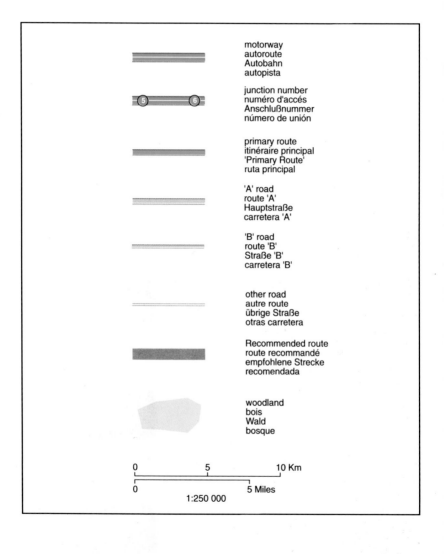

motorway
autoroute
Autobahn
autopista

junction number
numéro d'accés
Anschlußnummer
número de unión

primary route
itinéraire principal
'Primary Route'
ruta principal

'A' road
route 'A'
Hauptstraße
carretera 'A'

'B' road
route 'B'
Straße 'B'
carretera 'B'

other road
autre route
übrige Straße
otras carretera

Recommended route
route recommandé
empfohlene Strecke
recomendada

woodland
bois
Wald
bosque

0   5   10 Km

0   5 Miles

1:250 000

ENGLAND

Land's End and Lizard

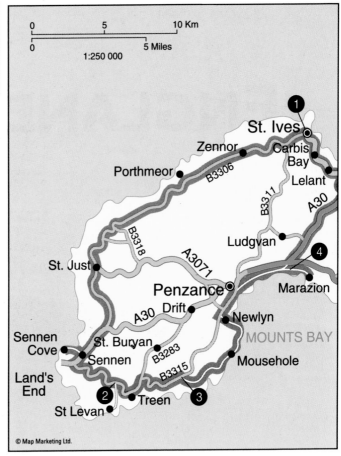

© Map Marketing Ltd.

West Cornwall's interior is surprisingly wild and empty, so Route One follows the coast; granite cliffs constantly buffeted by the Atlantic on the most western stretch contrast with the sub-tropical calm of secluded Penzance. There are over two dozen notably prehistoric sites in Penwith district alone, lending the tour an element of mystery. Dating from much more recent times, the tall chimneys of the disused tin mines, so characteristic of much of Cornwall, can be seen from Carn Brea on Route Two, while Helston's award-winning leisure park brings the visitor face to face with twentieth-century technology.

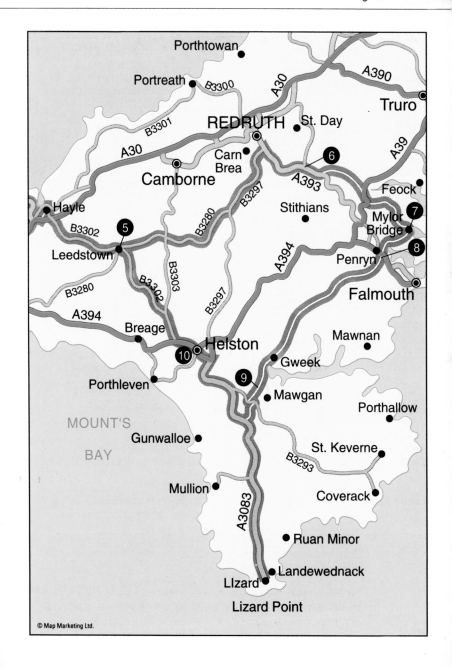

© Map Marketing Ltd.

ROUTE ONE: 45 miles (72 km)

Directions in sequence from: Hayle

Hayle
Paradise Park has an internationally acclaimed collection of rare and exotic birds. Within the park, the Bird in Hand pub welcomes families and serves home-brewed real ale.

St Ives
Twisting streets, granite steps and cobblestones survive from the town's early days as a fishing port. Today, St Ives has a thriving community of artists, attracted by the special qualities of its light. Numerous galleries exhibit paintings and pottery. In the church, the huge *Madonna and Child* is by Barbara Hepworth, whose home was in the town. *Tourist information: tel. (0736) 796297.*

The headland beyond the harbour is known as The Island. This is the best point from which to view the panorama of St Ives Bay and Hayle Beach, with the famous Towan sand dunes behind. ① *Turn left by the tourist information office opposite the church on B3306, signposted Zennor.*

Zennor
Zennor Quoit, an imposing Bronze Age tomb, can be reached easily by a track which leads off left from the road 1 mile (1.5 km) before the village. Large slabs of granite, set vertically, form rough walls surmounted by an even larger cap stone. The chamber thus formed was originally covered with earth. It is thought to be around 4,000 years old.

A museum displaying cremated bones, pottery and other artefacts from Zennor Quoit and other local, ancient tombs lies near the junction of the second turning to the village. *Open daily Apr-Oct.*

St Just
Carn Gluze, just west of the village, is an even more complex chambered tomb than Zennor Quoit.

Sennen Cove
A small fishing community with a pleasant pub, The Success, in a picturesque setting. On the cove, note the old cottages huddled under the cliff.

Land's End
Greatly restored, with all the old unsightly shacks removed, Land's End is now well worth seeing. The Visitor Centre presents two exciting exhibitions illuminating man's relationship with this rocky headland.

Local craftsmen make and sell their wares at Greeb Cottage Crafts. Good meals or light snacks are available in the State House restaurant and bar. Extensive parking.

② *Turn right at Trethewey, signposted Porthcurno, and follow signs for Minack through the village and up the hill to the theatre car park.*

Minack
(Not on map.) The open-air theatre enjoys a magnificent setting on the

● *The sands of Sennen Cove, NE of Land's End. The cove is reached down a narrow road from the village of Sennen, noted as the westernmost village on the English mainland.*

cliffs. Performances of plays and concerts are given throughout the summer and prove an unforgettable experience.

Minack – Mousehole   At Boleigh, the road passes between the Merry Maidens and the Pipers (Bronze Age long stones). Legend has it that the 19 maidens and the two pipers who played for them were turned to stone for dancing on the sabbath. ③ *After passing the Merry Maidens, turn right down lane for the picturesque harbour of Lamorna; follow signs for Mousehole.*

Mousehole   With its tiny harbour and colourful fishing boats, the village (pronounced 'Mowsal') is one of Cornwall's most attractive ports.

Mousehole – Newlyn   The coast road affords continuous magnificent views of Mount's Bay with St Michael's Mount (see below) on the far side.

Penzance   Elegant terraces, palm trees and idiosyncratic Egyptian house (Chapel St.)

23

all help to illustrate why the town was known as Cornwall's 'Brighton'. *From the centre, follow signs for Hayle round the one-way system.*

Marazion   St Michael's Mount, 2 miles (3 km) round the bay, is where Phoenician tin traders used to load their cargoes, two centuries BC, because the local inhabitants did not trust them enough to let them on to the mainland. The castle, dating from the 14thC, is still lived in but is *open to the public: tel. (0736) 710507 for times.* From its ramparts there are superb views of the Cornish coast. To reach the Mount, either walk across the causeway or, if the tide is in, take a ferry *(regular service in summer).*

④ Turn right on B3310 immediately after crossing the railway bridge; return to Hayle via A30.

◼︎◼︎◼︎◼︎◼︎ ROUTE TWO: 56 miles (90 km)
Directions in sequence from: Hayle

⑤ Leave Hayle on B3302, signposted Helston. After turning left at Leedstown, follow signs for Redruth on B3280 and then B3297. After 2½ miles (4 km), turn left along unclassified road signposted Carnkie and head towards the prominent radio mast. The track to the summit is in 1½ miles (2.5 km) on the right.

Carn Brea   From the top of this long granite outcrop there are wide-ranging views of Camborne and Redruth. To the south can be seen over a dozen old mine pump houses with their characteristic chimneys. The southern slope is the site of what is perhaps the oldest factory in Britain. Here men of the New Stone Age re-worked Old Stone Age tools to a new standard of polished efficiency.
    The castle, which once served as a lighthouse, is now a restaurant, which serves lunches, dinners and summer cream teas.

⑥ Two miles (3 km) past Fox & Hounds Inn (excellent food and real ale) turn left on to unclassified road signposted Perranwell and Bissoe. Turn right at sign for Perranworthal. At crossroads, turn right, signposted Falmouth. Turn right again at T-junction and after ½ mile (0.8 km) turn left, following signs for Mylor.

Mylor   A popular yachting centre where there are many small craft moored in the sheltered creek, or laid up in the boat-yards. *⑦ From the harbour, return up the lane and take the second turning on the right, signposted Penryn.*

Falmouth   A busy port with active dockyards, the town is also a popular seaside resort and has a long stretch of sandy beach. *Tourist information: tel.*

(0326) 312300.

Pendennis Castle, reached along the lovely Castle Drive scenic route, was built by Henry VIII, *c.*1540, with revenue obtained from the closure of the Cornish monasteries. *Open daily Apr-Sept; Tues-Sun, Oct-end Mar.*

⑧ *Returning up A39, turn left on B3291 signposted Gweek.*

Gweek

At the Cornish Seal Sanctuary, which cares for stranded and injured seals, knowledgeable staff guide visitors round the five special pools. The seals are victims of pollution and bad weather. *Follow signs from bridge, through housing estate.*

Lizard
(detour)

⑨ *For this diversion, cross the bridge and turn left on B3293 signposted St Keverne and Mawgan. In 2 miles (3 km) turn right on unclassified road, then left on A3083.*

Lizard is the southernmost point of Britain; but Kynance Cove, with its curiously coloured serpentine cliffs and fascinating rock formations, is of greater interest and worth the short walk from the car park. Housel Bay has a fine, safe bathing beach and makes a very attractive picnic spot. *Follow the signs from village.*

Helston

Helston Flora Day is on 8 May, when the locals dress up and dance in procession through the streets, and in and out of the houses, to the famous 'Furry Dance' tune.

The Aeropark (aircraft exhibition) and Flambards Village (reconstructed village) are on the Helston side of Culdrose Airfield. *Open Easter-Oct.*

⑩ *Turn left at the roundabout to town centre, then take A394, signposted Penzance. Once through the town, turn right on B3302.*

Bodmin and Boscastle

Along the north coast, the scenery is rugged and wild between the thriving little fishing ports nestled in sheltered coves. From here the tour passes through the strange and ever-changing landscape of the china clay country, where Cornwall's major industry can be seen at work from close quarters. Then follows the tranquil woodland beauty of Luxulyan Valley and Bossiney (both seen at their best from April to June when the hedges are filled with bluebells and campion), the grace of old stately manor houses and the isolated farmsteads and open country of Bodmin Moor.

ROUTE ONE: 52 miles (83 km)

Directions in sequence from: Wadebridge

Wadebridge   The multi-arched bridge over the River Camel is said to have been built with bales of wool in its foundations, to represent the source of the town's prosperity in medieval times. ① *Turn left at traffic lights on the west end of the bridge, into The Platt. Then first right into Polmorla Rd. and follow signs for Padstow.*

Tredinnick   *At St Issey turn left opposite the Ring o' Bells pub* for the Shire Horse
(detour)   Centre, Trelow Farm, Tredinnick.

Little   Beautifully restored in the latter half of the last century, the church of St
Petherick   Petroc Minor, on the right at the bottom of the hill, is worth a visit for its medieval font, old bench ends and unusually fine vestments.

Padstow   Originally called Petrocstowe after St Petroc, a Welsh Celtic missionary who arrived from Ireland c.517 AD, this is a busy fishing port and popular holiday resort, which nevertheless manages to retain its old character. Extensive car parking at top of town and down by the harbour.

For the May Day Obby Oss festival the town is decked with spring greenery and the local people, dressed in white, sing the age-old May Song and dance in company with the Oss, a weird black monster which parades round the town.

The tropical bird gardens at the top of the town house many exotic species in beautiful garden surroundings. There is also an extensive display of butterflies. Close by is Prideaux Place, an Elizabethan manor house still occupied by the same family. *Open afternoons, Easter to Sept..*

Amongst the many attractions of the town there are several good restaurants. Try The Seafood Restaurant, on the Quay, for special occasions, or The Taste Bud in Market St. for salad lunches.

② *From the main car park above the town, turn right and follow*

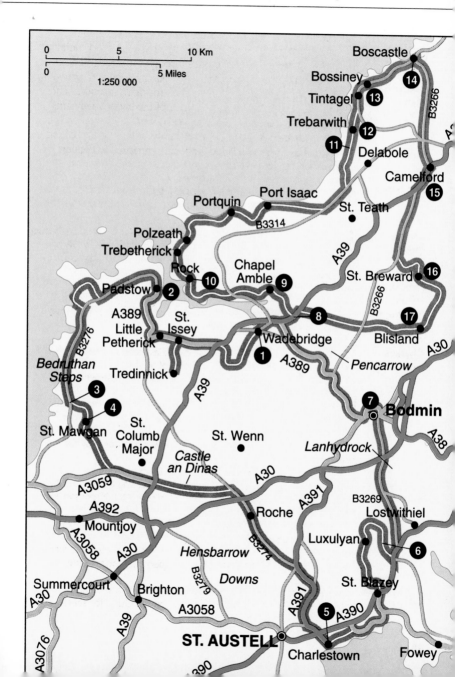

signs for Newquay. Popular bathing beaches, a fine golf course and Trevose Head with its lighthouse, *open in summer to the public*, are all signposted off to the right along this road.

Bedruthan
Steps

Fine views of the coast down to Newquay may be had from various points along this part of the road.
    ③ *At Mawgan Porth, just before the bridge, turn left along the Vale of Lanherne towards St Mawgan Village.*

Pub
(St Mawgan)

The Falcon Inn serves good food outdoors in summer, or beside a log fire in winter. ④ *To leave the village, proceed up the hill keeping the church on the left. At St Mawgan airfield, turn left, and left again on to A3059. At roundabout, take exit signposted Castle-an-Dinas.* This Iron Age hill fort with its massive triple ramparts, makes an excellent picnic spot.

Roche

On leaving the village, note the ruins of the old hermitage on the prominent outcrop of Roche Rock, to the left.

Hensbarrow
– Penwithick

Here the route passes through the strange white landscape of the clay workings. The Wheal Martyn China Clay museum, which traces the history of the industry, is reached by a 2-mile (3-km) diversion along the A391.

Charles-
town

On the far side of St Austell, this harbour is a rare survival of a Cornish Georgian village, and was the setting for the *Onedin Line* television series. The Visitor Centre contains museums of shipwreck and rescue, with audio-visual presentations of the town's history. ⑤ *From the harbour, follow signs for Par along A3082 (A390) to St Blazey. At traffic lights, turn right past the church, following signs for Liskeard, then turn left, just before level crossing, on to unclassified road signposted Luxulyan. After ½ mile (0.8 km) turn right, following sign to Prideaux and Luxulyan valley.*

Luxulyan
Valley

The woodland drive is particularly beautiful in spring, when bluebells carpet the ground. From next junction beyond the aqueduct there is easy access to woodland walks along canals and on to aqueduct.
    ⑥ *Keep right, following signs for St Blazey and Fowey. Turn left at junction with A390, signposted Liskeard, and left again on to B3269, signposted Bodmin.* About 1 mile (1.5 km) along this road a lay-by on right affords wonderful views of Lostwithiel and the Fowey river valley.

Lanhydrock
House

A 17thC manor house with fine gardens. The Long Gallery has a magnificent ceiling depicting Old Testament scenes. *Open daily Apr-Oct.*
    ⑦ *Follow signs through Bodmin to Wadebridge, forking right on to A389 by the clock tower at the end of the town.*

Pencarrow   In the grounds of this Georgian house you may pick your own soft fruit in season. The Cornwall Crafts Association has a gallery and shop in the stables. *Gardens open daily Easter-Oct; house open Sun-Thurs, Easter-Oct.*

▬▬▬ ROUTE TWO: 38 miles (61 km)

Directions in sequence from: Wadebridge

⑧ *Take A39 signposted Camelford and after 1½ miles (2.5 km) turn left on to unclassified road signposted Chapel Amble.*

Pub
(Chapel
Amble)

A good pub, the Maltsters Arms, serving meals and bar food in a pleasant village. ⑨ *Turn left just past the post office, and follow signs to Rock.*

Rock   This is the premier sailing centre for north Cornwall. The Quarry car park at the end of the road gives access to the beach and walks among the dunes. A passenger ferry service to Padstow operates from the beach during daylight hours. ⑩ *Returning up lane from car park, turn left at sign for Polzeath and keep to coastal road at each junction.*

Daymer
Bay
(detour)

At Trebetherick turn left for Daymer Bay. Large car park at end of lane. Charming, half-hidden St Enedoc church, burial place of Sir John Betjeman, lies a short walk across the golf course. Daymer Bay is a delightful family beach. Watching the windsurfers negotiate the breakers is an absorbing pastime for a windy day.

Polzeath   *Drive through Polzeath and up hill. After ½ mile (0.8 km) turn left, and at next junction, left again to New Polzeath.* From car park, walk out to Pentire Head, where Rumps Point affords magnificent cliff scenery.

Portquin   The legend is that when all the fishermen from the village were drowned in a storm, their distraught widows deserted the village, leaving their houses with dinner still on the tables. Ruins of fishermen's cottages can still be seen.

Port Isaac   Unlike Portquin, this fishing village, with its picturesque harbour and narrow streets, still thrives. Parking is available on the harbour beach, depending on the tide. The Port Gaverne Hotel, just beyond the village, has a fine restaurant.

Delabole   Famous for high quality roofing slate, the Delabole quarry is claimed to be the biggest man-made hole in the country. ⑪ *On entering the village, turn left at the sign for Trebarwith Village (not on map). The lane beyond the village is steep and narrow with a hairpin bend, left, at the bottom, for Trebarwith Strand (not on map).*

● *'The Hurlers', one of the ancient stone circles on Bodmin Moor.*

Pub
(Trebarwith Strand)

The Mill House Inn serves excellent food all year round. ⑫ *Turn left by the Mill House Inn, up the steep lane signposted Treknow, and left at the T-junction on to B3263).*

Tintagel

Although famous for its associations with King Arthur, the castle on the headland is actually Norman and was previously the site of a Celtic monastery. The extensive ruins are worth visiting. Notice also Old Post Office, a well-preserved example of a 14thC manor house. ⑬ *To leave Tintagel, turn right at the T-junction opposite King Arthur's Hall and follow B3263.*

Bossiney

From the car park, walk down to spectacular Rocky Valley with its ruined mill house and Phoenician rock carvings in the cliff behind the building, or up through the woods to St Nectan's Kieve – a curiously formed waterfall.

Boscastle   The narrow twisting inlet protects Boscastle's harbour from storms, but must have proved a dangerous entrance for the old sailing luggers that used this coast. The Witches' Museum beside the harbour displays a macabre exhibition of the history of witchcraft. *Open Apr-Oct.*
⑭ Leave Boscastle by returning up the hill round the hairpin bend. Turn left at the junction with B3266 signposted Camelford. On entering the town, turn left to remain on B3266.

Camelford   The North Cornwall Museum and Gallery, passed on the left, houses a number of agricultural exhibits from the 19thC and earlier. The Camel Art Society also exhibits paintings by local artists. *⑮ At the main road, turn right along A39 signposted Wadebridge. On reaching the Camelot Garage, fork left along B3266, signposted Bodmin. After 3 miles (5 km) turn left following signs for St Breward.*

St Breward The maze of lanes criss-crossing this part of Bodmin Moor are all well signposted, making it possible to explore some attractive moorland scenery without getting lost. The area is dotted with lonely farmsteads and wild ponies can often by seen. *⑯ After driving through the village, turn right at the telephone kiosk, following signs for Blisland.*

Blisland   This claims to be the only Cornish village with a proper green.
    Do not miss the church of St Protus and St Hyacinth which has a carved wagon roof, granite columns which lean at astonishing angles and a highly decorated screen. *⑰ Passing the Royal Oak pub, fork left at the post office and continue down the hill, following signs for St Mabyn and Wadebridge, over a level crossing and bridge.*

Looe, Polperro & Mt. Edgcumbe

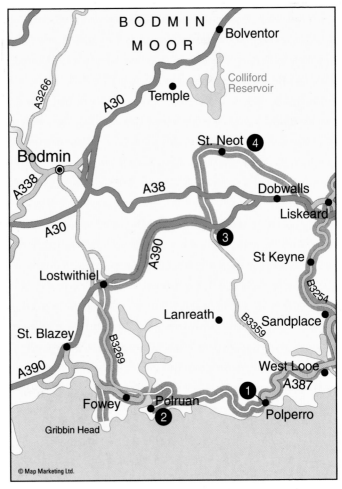

© Map Marketing Ltd.

South-east Cornwall has a colourful past. Towns pillaged and burnt in the Hundred Years War with France, spectacular Plymouth Sound where the great Elizabethan fleets of Drake and Raleigh found shelter, the rich estates of the great mansions, and the fishing villages such as Polperro, Cawsand and Kingsand.

Both routes offer glorious views from the headlands but explore inland too. Route One takes in the lush Fowey valley, while both routes touch on the edge of the wild Bodmin Moor.

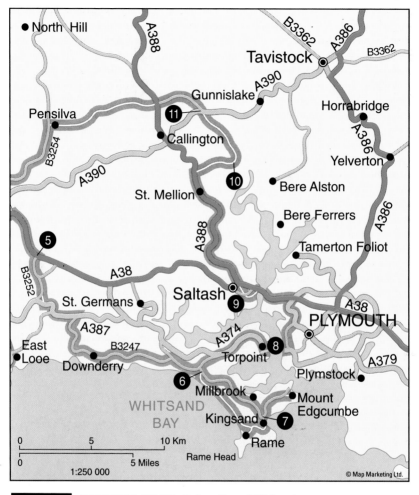

ROUTE ONE: 34 miles (55 km)

Directions in sequence from: Liskeard

Liskeard   A market town with narrow, steep streets and several handsome buildings which have survived in spite of the developers. One of Cornwall's 'Stannary' towns.

St Keyne   The Paul Corin Musical Collection, near the station, features fair ground and street organs in working order. *Open May-Sept.*

33

Looe   A tourist-oriented town with excellent facilities and beautiful surrounding countryside. *Tourist information: tel. (0503 622072.*

On the outskirts, the Woolly Monkey Sanctuary (follow signs on approach to town) accommodates a colony of monkeys breeding in near-natural conditions.

Polperro   Shoals of visitors come to photograph this picturesque fishing village, where the local industry is much in evidence. At the centre of the village, in the Old Forge, the model village depicts in miniature many traditional features of old Cornwall. *Open mid-Mar to Oct.* ① *From the village, keep left, following signs to Polruan.*

Polruan   Worth pausing in the main car park to take in the view of Fowey harbour and the ruined castle. ② *Turning right from the car park, follow signs for Pont. At village, turn left, following signs for Lanteglos Highway and Bodinnick Ferry. This service operates daily until dusk throughout the year.*

Fowey   Pronounced 'Foy', this attractive town surrounds a busy harbour used by fishermen and yachtsmen, as well as by larger ships loading china clay for export. Regatta and carnival in mid-August.

The diversion to Gribbin Head is clearly signposted and passes Menabilly House, once home of Daphne du Maurier.

Gribbin Hd.   Park in designated field at the end of the lane for a short walk to
(detour)   Gribbin Head with panoramic views of St Austell Bay.

Restaurant   The Cormorant Restaurant offers a wide variety of dishes in luxurious
(Golant)   surroundings. Gentlemen will need ties.

There is riverside parking in this area.

Lostwithiel   Once the capital of Cornwall, this ancient riverside town has a church with a remarkable Breton-style spire, and a main street lined with buildings dating from medieval times to the 18thC.

Situated above the town (follow signs to Ancient Monument), Restormel Castle was built by Robert of Mortain, the stepbrother of William the Conqueror, in an attempt to control the local populace.

From the ramparts at the top of the castle's circular stone keep there are views of the surrounding countryside.

③ *Turn left off A390 on to unclassified road signposted St Neot.*

St Neot   The most outstanding aspect of this typical moorland village is its church: the stained-glass windows, dating from the 14thC, are renowned for their brilliant colour and quality. ④ *On leaving the village, follow the signs through narrow lanes for Dobwalls.*

● *Looking seawards from the estuary of the Fowey – the busy harbour is a haven for craft large and small.*

Dobwalls   The Old Slate Caverns are still lit, as they were when being worked, by burning tapers supported on wall brackets. Warm clothing is required for the underground tour.

The Tridle Theme Park is well signposted from the village. Model locomotives take visitors over miles of track; *open daily Easter to Sept.*

35

ROUTE TWO: 48 miles (77 km)

Directions in sequence from: Liskeard

⑤ Two miles (3 km) along A38, turn right on to B3252 signposted Looe. After 2½ miles (4 km) turn left at sign for Hessenford and Widegates. Follow signs for Hessenford on to A387.

Downderry After leaving the village, the road follows the line of the cliff top, giving sweeping sea views.

Millbrook From the village there are superb views of Plymouth Sound.

⑥ Turn right off B3247 on to unclassified road signposted Freathy Cliff.

Rame Head A clearly signed diversion from the cliff road gives access, through
(detour) narrow lanes, to the church and coastguard station with parking area adjacent. Electricity has not yet been brought to the church, which is still lit entirely by candles.
 Records show payments of watchmen at the headland as early as 1486, and it was used as a point for warning and celebratory beacons in Tudor times.

Cawsand Twin villages, but until 1844, Kingsand was in Devon – the boundary
and stone can still be seen outside the Halfway Hotel. There is traditional
Kingsand rivalry between the villages, both of which were established in Elizabethan times, when Plymouth merchants built pilchard cellars along the beach and caused an influx of people into the area. Later, smugglers prospered in both villages.
 Before Plymouth's breakwater was built, the bay provided anchorage for the Fleet. *⑦ On leaving the village, turn right at the junction signposted Maker, Mount Edgcumbe and Cremyll.*

Maker The 15thC church tower has a varied history: during the Civil War it was fortified and captured by Parliamentary forces in 1644. In the 18thC the tower was used as an Admiralty signalling station.

Mount The estate is best known for its extensive gardens, formally planted with
Edgcumbe ornamental trees and rhododendron walks. Extensive views of Plymouth Sound and Drake's Island enhance the beauty of the park, which is open all year and especially attractive in spring and autumn.
⑧ The ferry runs 24 hours a day all year. After crossing, follow signs to Saltash.

Saltash On crossing the Tamar suspension bridge (without having to pay the toll when driving in this direction, as only those leaving Cornwall are charged), note Brunel's 19thC railway bridge to the left. Warships of the

Royal Navy can occasionally be seen at anchor in the estuary below the bridge.

⑨ *Avoid turning into Saltash itself. One mile (1.5 km) after crossing the bridge, turn right on to A388, signposted Callington. This is an inconspicuous turn with no advance warning.*

Shortly after passing St Mellion golf course, turn right at sign for Cotehele House and Quay. Follow signs for house, through narrow lanes.

Cotehele House

Little has been altered at this splendidly atmospheric medieval house which was begun in the 15thC. Even the furniture, armour, tapestries and needlework have always been here.

There is also much to see in the extensive grounds including unusual shrubs, a medieval dovecot, the old manorial waterwheel restored to working condition, a blacksmith's and a wheelwright's shop. *House open daily Apr-Oct; gardens open all year.*

At Cotehele Quay, there are 18th- and 19thC bridges, a shipping museum and a restored Tamar sailing barge.

⑩ *turn right from the car park by the house and left at the T-junction, following signs for Harrowbarrow.*

Pub (Harrow-barrow)

Good food in pleasant surroundings at the Carpenter's Arms. ⑪ *Turn left on to A390 and then right on to B3257 signposted Launceston.*

At Kelly Bray turn left, then almost immediately right, following signs for Golberdon. After passing through Meaders, take left fork signposted Pensilva.

Pensilva

On leaving the village the route passes over open heathland, typical of Bodmin Moor, with distant views of Liskeard.

Totnes and Slapton Sands

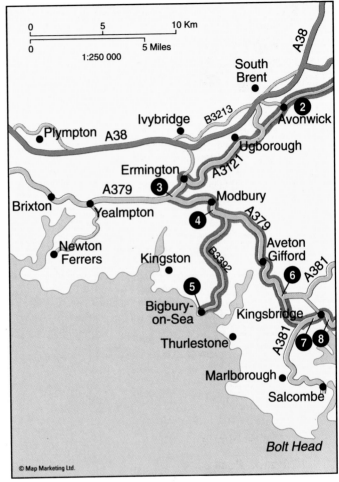

The heart of south Devon is an area of great beauty, diversity and interest; the roads follow the gentle folds of the landscape which give way to moors to the north and sea and estuary to the south and east. This part of Devon is a very rich farming area, but the pattern of the landscape is still much as it was in the fifteenth century. The tour includes extensive views of the countryside as well as the coast, and involves a 1½-mile (2.5-km) drive along a pebble ridge road, literally at sea level.

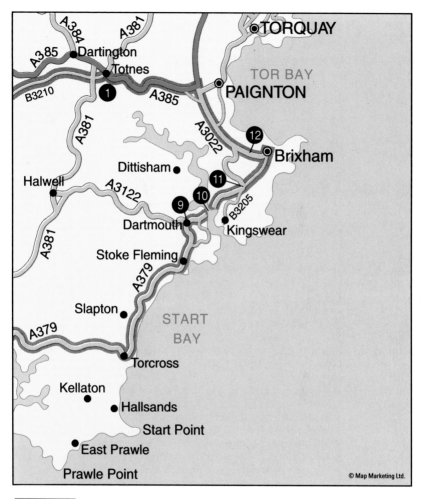

© Map Marketing Ltd.

ROUTE: 85 miles (136 km)

Directions in sequence from: Totnes

Totnes   The core of this pleasant town (one of the oldest municipal boroughs in England) has a wealth of interesting buildings. Worth parking and strolling up the main street to the Butterwalk (antiques and craft shops). *Tourist information: tel. (0803) 863168.*

Overlooking the town is the circular Norman keep of Judhael's Castle which stands on the site of a much older motte and bailey. *Open daily.*

39

The Elizabethan House contains a museum that, in addition to the usual displays, has a computer exhibition. *open Mon-Fri, Easter-Oct.*

① Starting from The Plains, on the west bank of the river at the end of the town, follow signs to Buckfastleigh and Kingsbridge for ½ mile (0.8 km). At traffic lights, just beyond railway, bear left (A381 to Kingsbridge) and after a short while, first right (signposted Avonwick) along B3210.

Totnes –
Avonwick
The road follows a ridge above the valley of the Harbourne river, a valley of gentle slopes overshadowed in the distance by the southern flanks of Dartmoor with Beara Common rising to 1,020 feet (311 m).

Ugborough
(detour)
② Just after crossing the bridge spanning the river, bear left at garage and follow signs to Ugborough. A quiet village with slate-hung houses, gospel hall, and a large and interesting church which occupies the site of a prehistoric camp. The short detour to the village is recommended, if only for the view over the rooftops from the churchyard.

Ugborough –
Ermington
Just before Ermington, after crossing the bridge over the River Erme, bear right to the church, then turn right for Mill Leat Trout Farm. Fresh and smoked trout can be bought here, and visitors have the option of catching their own fish. Choose between a fly lake and ½-mile (0.8-km) stretch of river. Tackle for hire. *Open Mon-Sat.*

Ermington
Nestling against the hillside, the village is worth a visit for its crooked and twisted church spire. *③ Continue along this scenic valley to Hollowcombe Cross. Turn left here for Modbury (A379) and left again at T-junction. The entrance to Flete House is opposite.*
Flete House, surrounded by woodland, stands in a commanding position above the river. Originally an Elizabethan manor house, it was much altered in the 19thC, but retains a Gothic style. During World War II the house became a maternity home for the Plymouth area, and around 10,000 babies were born here. *Open Wed and Thurs afternoons (2-5) summer only: by appointment: tel. (0755) 30308*

Modbury
'Even when Plymouth was a furzy down, Modbury was a busy town.' Today, Modbury has a main street that goes down one hill and up another: an unspoilt vista with touches of Georgian elegance. The 20thC is represented by the conspicuous television aerials mounted on long poles to obtain better reception in this area of hill and combe. The road out of town offers a fine view of St George's church and, eventually, of the South Hams on the right and Dartmoor to the left.

④ Follow A379 for 1½ miles (2.5 km) then bear right at crossroads for Bigbury-on-Sea (B3392).

Bigbury-on-Sea
Worth looking inside the church to see the unusual and long commemorative verses to John and Jane Pearse, who died in 1612 and 1589 respectively.

Much holiday trade paraphernalia here, but Burgh Island is of considerable interest. At low tide it can be reached across the sand; when the tide is in, a 'sea tractor' runs a ferry service. The building on the crest of the island was once a huer's hut for the lookout who raised the hue and cry when a shoal of pilchards was in sight. There are superb views from the island, of the mouth of the River Avon and dramatic cliff scenery.

Burgh Island's pub, The Pilchard, is reputed to be one of the oldest in Devon; the food here is excellent.

⑤ Retrace route along B3392, and follow road to Aveton Gifford. (The short cut along unclassified road from Bigbury looks tempting but is a tidal road and can only be used at low tide. If at all in doubt, use B3392.)

Aveton Gifford
Pronounced 'Orton Jifford', the village has one of south Devon's oldest churches. Although modernized after being hit by a bomb during World War II, the church merits a visit for its two-storeyed 13thC porch.

Aveton Gifford – Kingsbridge
Just past the village, the A379 crosses the water meadows of the River Avon on a medieval causeway. *⑥ Two miles (3 km) from the village, at roundabout, carry straight on taking B3197 (signposted Salcombe) for a further 2 miles (3 km). At major junction bear left, following A381 through West Alvington to Kingsbridge. ⑦ On entering the town, turn left at bottom of hill (signposted Plymouth/Totnes) and continue up the main street (Fore St.). Car park half-way up on left.*

Kingsbridge
The main feature of the town is The Shambles, a fine market arcade supported on broad granite pillars and dating, in part, from 1585.

⑧ To return to route, follow one-way system, bearing right at Duncombe St. (signposted Salcombe/Dartmouth) and then left for Dartmouth (A379) at junction.

Torcross
From here the view is unique, with lake, reed bed and shingle ridge in the foreground and sea beyond. Torcross lies at the southern end of the long (2½ miles/4 km) pebble ridge known as Slapton Sands, and is set perilously close to the sea.

Slapton Sands
Trapped behind the ridge are the waters of Slapton Ley, the largest natural freshwater lake in Devon. A lane leading to the village of Slapton separates the open lake from a silted-up area which is a valuable habitat for wetland and other bird species. A field centre in the village provides information on local walks and wildlife.

● *Lower Ferry, Dartmouth: this lovely estuary is one of the best protected on the south coast – all but completely landlocked.*

A tall stone obelisk on the right of the ridge commemorates the use of the area in late 1943 and early 1944 for beach landing practice prior to the Normandy invasion.

Dartmouth   ⑨ *Bear right at junction with A road and follow into the town centre.* The town has many interesting buildings, in particular the merchants' houses (1635-40) in the Butterwalk.

Not surprisingly, in a town dominated by the Royal Naval College and with a long history as a port, the museum (in the Butterwalk) contains many maritime exhibits. *Open Mon-Sat, Easter-Oct; Mon-Sat afternoons, Nov-Easter.* Newcomen, inventor of the atmospheric steam engine, was born in Dartmouth and one of his original engines can be seen working at the Newcomen Engine House (adjacent to the Butterwalk). *Open daily, Easter-mid-Oct.* The castle, 1 mile (1.5 km) south of the town, is a 15th-16thC coastal fort. *Open daily.*

⑩ *Follow signs to Kingswear and Paignton and road markings to Higher Ferry and Paignton (A379). The ferry runs a continuous daily service. Closed to vehicles first two weeks in March.*

Dartmouth – Half-way up the hill (A379) look to the left: glimpses of the deep cleft of
Brixham the River Dart can be seen through the woods of Waterhead Brake.
(Ⅰ) *At the top of the hill, just past the garage, bear right. Follow B3205 to
Brixham.*

Brixham A fishing town of largely unspoilt character. The harbour dominates the
scene and numerous boat trips are available from here.
For an unrivalled view of the harbour, visit Breakwater Beach on the
north-western edge of the town. *To reach the beach, bear left at
T-junction at bottom of hill, and follow the waterfront for ¼ mile (0.5
km).* Car park on left.

(ⅠⅠ) *From the town centre, take the A3022 to Paignton. After 3 miles (5
km) ignore right turn to Paignton and continue along A3022 for about
2½ miles (4 km). At major junction, bear left for Totnes (A385).*

Bude and Bideford

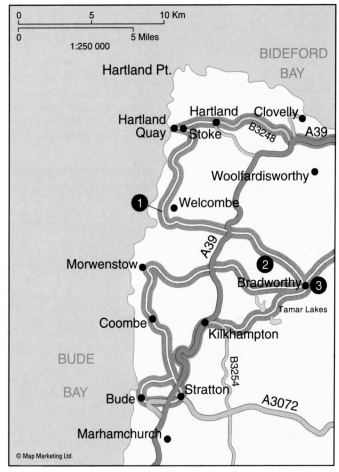

0   5   10 Km
0   5 Miles
1:250 000

Hartland Pt.

BIDEFORD
BAY

Hartland   Clovelly
Hartland
Quay   Stoke   B3248   A39

Woolfardisworthy

1   Welcombe

Morwenstow   A39

2

Bradworthy   3

Tamar Lakes

Coombe   Kilkhampton

BUDE

BAY   B3254

Stratton

Bude   A3072

Marhamchurch

© Map Marketing Ltd.

In terms of distance from cities and public services, this is one of the most remote corners of England. The coastal area has some busy tourist attractions, but for the most part this region is quiet and unspoilt. Inland there are peaceful villages, lush pastures and leafy lanes. The north-facing coastline has little fishing villages and wooded cliffs. The west facing coastline, however, faces the full onslaught of Atlantic gales. It is a dramatic coast of contorted rocks and bracing winds, and a walk along the coast path between Hartland and Bude is guaranteed to be memorable.

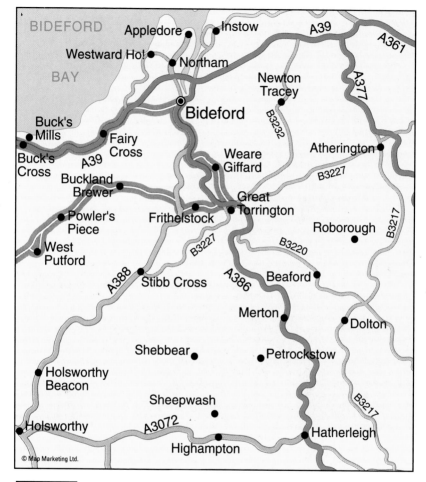

ROUTE ONE: 54 miles (86.5 km)

Directions in sequence from: Bideford

Bideford   This historic port on the River Torridge was prominent in Tudor times, and has many associations with the Grenville family. Little to see of its history except the remarkable medieval bridge with its 24 arches of different spans. There are pleasant sloping streets with some elegant houses and the tree-lined quay still handles some coastal trade. The beach is not particularly remarkable – rather pebbly – and, like many English beaches, is often not as clean as it ought to be.

45

• *The North Devon coast at Hartland – its ruggedness an appropriate match for the treachery of the local waters. This grandiose scenery runs more than ten miles (16 km) from Hartland Point to Lower Sharpnose Point.*

Fairy Cross The 17thC mansion of the Pyne-Coffin family is now the Portledge Hotel, where restaurant or buffet meals may be followed by a stroll.

Buck's Mills Just north of Buck's Cross, an attractive group of thatched cottages borders a stream running to the cliff edge. The village lacks the harbour and cobbled street of Clovelly, but is more peaceful.

Clovelly The main street of this utterly charming village is traffic free: cars must be left at the cliff top, so be prepared for a steep walk down to the harbour. (The return journey can be made by Land-Rover.) Avoid peak periods; Clovelly is the area's chief tourist attraction.

Stoke

St Nectan's church has the highest tower in Devon, a fine Norman font and a delicately carved medieval screen.

Hartland Quay

A small museum of shipwrecks *(open daily Easter week; from Whitsun-Sept)* is appropriately sited on this rugged coastline of jagged rocks.

A pleasant 1-mile (1.5-km) walk leads to Speke's Mill Mouth waterfall and nature reserve. This can also be approached from Kearnstone, 1½ miles (2.5 km) south of Stoke.

The Hartland Quay Hotel, converted from the Harbour Master's house and workers' cottages, has shipwreck relics in the Green Ranger bar. Bar food and dinner, *Mar-Oct.*

Welcombe Mouth

(Not on map.) A rough and narrow track from crossroads ½ mile (0.8 km) north of Mead and ¾ mile (1 km) west of Welcombe leads to a small car park beside a waterfall dropping to a pleasant beach.
① *Continue uphill, following the coast to Mead. The roads to Welcombe are difficult and it is advisable to avoid the village.*

Pub
(Darracott)

(Not on map.) The Old Smithy Inn, dating from medieval times, has much atmosphere and is said to be haunted by a man in armour. Real ale, bar food only.

② *After Meddon take the second turning on right for Loatmead. Here turn left and then first right for Dinworthy and straight on through this hamlet for Bradworthy (see Route Two).*

West Putford

St Stephen's church escaped Victorian restoration and has retained the atmosphere of the 18thC. It has uneven walls, a chancel floored with Barnstaple tiles and a rare, oval Norman font.

The Gnome Reserve has a remarkable collection of garden gnome figures, most of which are for sale. Not everyone's taste, but different. *Open daily, Easter-Oct.*

Powler's Piece

Crossroads where detours can be made ¾ mile (1 km) to south-east for Common Moor, an attractive area of heath and scrub, and ¾ mile (1 km) north-west for Melbury Woods, a Forestry Commission plantation with picnic area and nature trail.

Frithel-stock

Adjoining the church are the peaceful and beautiful ruins of a medieval Augustinian priory.

Great Torrington

Apart from a few elegant houses, it is a rather dull-looking town in a grand setting. From the central car park (where once a castle stood) there is a splendid view of the River Torridge far down below, and of the strip fields which were originally part of a leper colony.

One mile (1.5 km) south-east on B3220 the Rosemoor Garden Trust has several types of gardens, a semi-natural woodland area and an arboretum, all part of the grounds of a small 18thC house. Unusual plants, including old-fashioned roses, are on sale. *Open daily.*

From Dartington's modern, ugly factory comes high-quality, stylish, hand-blown glassware. Interesting displays and guided tours. Factory shop and pleasant cafeteria. *Open Mon-Fri except Bank Hols.* The factory is off School Lane, which is opposite the parish church.

Weare Giffard Strange to think that this attractive, straggling town on the east bank of the Torridge was once a busy port, the only signs of which now are the rows of lime kilns on the riverbank. The big house seen from the road is Weare Giffard Hall (private), famous for its great hall.

Bideford Half a mile (0.8 km) from the outskirts of town, a lay-by on the right affords a fine view down the Torridge estuary to Bideford Long Bridge.

ROUTE TWO: 27 miles (43 km)

Directions in sequence from: Bude

Bude Small seaside resort with several large hotels and guest houses, good sandy beaches, popular with surfers, and many other sporting facilities. There is an old canal, formerly used for carrying beach sand inland for agricultural purposes. *Tourist information: tel. (0288) 355366.*

On the wharf by the canal, Bude and Stratton Historical and Folk Exhibition is worth a visit; it has many nautical displays. *Open daily, 11-4, Easter-Sept.*

Restaurant (Stratton) At The Tree Inn, the 13thC Galleon room (à la carte menu) has beams made from timbers of wrecked ships. There are several bars serving excellent food.

Kilk-hampton St James's church has a richly-decorated Norman doorway and exceptional 15th- and 16thC woodwork in the roof timbers and bench ends. There are also monuments to the Grenville family,

Tamar Lakes Two modern reservoirs formed by damming the River Tamar, which divides Cornwall from Devon. The upper lake has facilities for sailing, board-sailing, canoeing and fly fishing. The lower lake is quieter, more attractive and good for bird-watching.

Bradworthy This old village is built round a large square, once used for fairs and markets. From the outskirts of the village there are views across to Dartmoor and Bodmin Moor. ③ *Turn right at the top of the square,* *then fork right and straight on for Blatchborough and Youlstone.*

Morwen-stow

The 19thC theologian, poet and eccentric, the Revd R. S. Hawker, lived here. His rectory has chimneys shaped like the towers of his churches. It is worth the walk to Vicarage Cliff where his hut, made of driftwood, can still be seen.

St Morwenna's church is not to be missed. Its special features include a Norman doorway, superb Norman arches (one of which has a weird 'beak-head' ornament), and a Saxon font. In the churchyard, the figurehead of the *Caledonia* marks the grave of her shipwrecked crew.

The Bush Inn serves real ale, bar food only. *Closed Sundays.*

Morwen-stow – Coombe

Just to the east of Lower Sharpnose Point is the Composite Signals Organization Station, a satellite tracking station with several dish-shaped aerials. Fine view south along Cornish coast beyond Bude to Tintagel, Pentire Point and Trevose Head.

Coombe

Attractive ford with thatched cottages can be reached by turning left at the bottom of the hill. Return and continue on previous road. *Turn first right for Duckpool with its car park and pebbly beach (detour of one mile/1.5 km). Return and continue across bridge.*

After ¼ mile (0.5 km) turn left for another short detour to Stowe Woods, where there is a car park, picnic area and nature trail.

Dartmoor

T hree distinct areas are explored on this tour. Route One goes through the rich red land of the Exe Estuary. From Exeter, the road leads back inland across the tree-capped Haldon Hills; here are splendid views and forest walks. Route Two crosses the eastern part of Dartmoor, which offers the most spectacular tors (outcrops of rock) and the moor's best-known village. Although this tour ventures into some fairly out-of-the-way places, it avoids the very narrowest lanes that are difficult for drivers to negotiate.

ROUTE ONE: 38 miles (61 km)

Directions in sequence from: Bovey Tracey

Bovey Tracey

Climbing the hillside above the River Bovey, this little town has a church that is notable for its 15thC stone and wood carving. The screen, with its painted birds and grapes, is delightful. Note also the fox and duck misericord, and the south porch boss of four heads joined together at the neck.

Chudleigh

① *In Chudleigh, turn right just past the zebra crossing, down Clifford St., signposted Ugbrooke House, Ideford and Teignmouth.* At the bottom of Clifford St., The Wheel craft centre is *open daily.*

Ugbrooke

The stately home of the Cliffords was originally built around 1200, but was redesigned by Robert Adam. Visitors see fine furniture, paintings, embroideries, a dolls' house, and a collection of early gramophones. *Open afternoons, end May; Tues-Thur and Sun, end July-end Aug.*

② *Continue along the same road, beneath the separate carriageways of A380, and through Ideford and Luton. At Little Haldon, turn sharp left (signposted Exeter) and left again on to B3192.*

Little Haldon

Park on the brow of this hill, then walk a short distance away from road for a worthwhile view of the sea near Dawlish.

③ *Cross one carriageway of the A380 on the bridge, then follow directions on to the Exeter-bound carriageway of the A380. A few hundred yards along the road, turn right again across the other carriageway on to B3381, signposted Starcross.*

Starcross

Here, Isambard Kingdom Brunel tried out an astonishing engineering concept: locomotives driven by atmospheric pressure. The idea was a failure, but the pumping house survives.

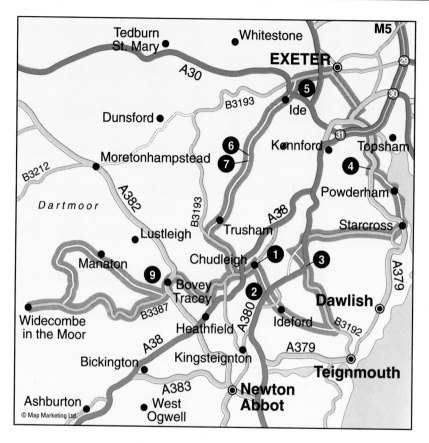

© Map Marketing Ltd.

Powderham Castle Grandiose seat of the Earls of Devon, this 14thC castle has been much altered over the years, resulting in a curious mixture of strength (four of the original towers still stand) and decoration (the music room is by Wyatt). The deer park has a fine avenue of cedars leading up to the castle. *Open daily. Easter-Oct, except Sats.*

④ *Continue along the same road for about 2 miles (3 km), then turn right on to A379. Follow signposts to Exeter.*

Exeter A bran tub of a city: dip in and beyond the busy centre (rebuilt after extensive bomb damage in 1942), discover buildings, alleyways and even underground passages from many parts of its history which goes back to Roman times. *Tourist information: tel. (0392) 265700.*

The lovely Gothic cathedral offers a satisfying unbroken vista down

Dartmoor Past and Present

Dartmoor is the nearest thing to a wilderness in southern England, but it abounds in traces of man and his work. Isolation has preserved an unusual number of prehistoric remains – stone circles, standing stones, burial chambers and hut circles, dating from as early as 1800 BC, litter the whole area. From more recent times, there are the spoil heaps and gulleys left by the tin miners who operated here from the 12th to the 15thC.

Today army firing ranges make large tracts of northern Dartmoor inaccessible at certain times. If you plan to wander in the vicinity of the Okehampton ranges, check firing times first by ringing Plymouth (0752) 701924, or enquire at a local post office.

● *Powdermills Farm, Dartmoor, with Higher White Tor in the background.*

the long, rib-vaulted nave. Amongst a wealth of interesting details, note the minstrels' gallery with its carvings of musical angels, and the much-pinnacled, 14thC bishop's throne, which has nothing whatsoever to do with humility.

Down by the waterfront, the wonderfully imaginative Maritime

Museum has the world's largest collection of working boats, many of which can be explored. The collection is displayed indoors (in Victorian warehouses), on the shore and afloat. A fine place for children. *Open daily. Apr-Sept; Sat and Sun, Oct-Mar.* The High Street was largely rebuilt after German bombing during the Second World War.

Pubs
(Exeter)

Two old and attractive pubs which serve good food are The White Hart in South St., and The Ship in Martin's Lane, just off Cathedral Close.

⑤ From the Exe Bridge take the Moretonhampstead road (B3212). Not far out of Exeter, turn left on to a road marked for the A30, M5 and Ide. After ½ mile (0.8 km), turn right to Ide.

Ide

As an instant contrast to the city, this long village has a ford, a 13thC bridge, some genuinely old cottages and a delightful fake called Tudor Cottage.

⑥ Park at the Forestry Commission Belvedere car park on left. To see Lawrence Castle (see below), walk back a short way along the road and turn right up the drive.

Lawrence Castle

(Not on map.) Known locally as Belvedere Tower, this 70-foot (21-m) folly was built in 1788 as a monument to Major-General Lawrence, founder of the British Empire in India. The incredible view from the top encompasses nearly the whole of Davon. *Open summer afternoons and weekends Oct–Apr – but subject to note on the gate!*

Haldon Forest

(Not on map.) A picnic site about 1 mile (1.5 km) further along this ridge-top road is also the starting point for a variety of walks – the shortest is 2½ miles (4 km) laid out by the Forestry Commission.

⑦ From Belvedere car park, take the little road opposite, leading down off the ridge. The road winds down into the pastoral Teign Valley. Follow signs for Trusham.

Trusham

Worth pausing here to look inside the church, which has two unusual monuments. The Staplehill family are commemorated by a painting on wood (16thC), while John and Mary Stooke are shown in two painted medallions (1697).

⑧ In the middle of Chudleigh Knighton take a right fork. This is still the B3344; continue along it to Bovey Tracey.

◼◼◼◼ ROUTE TWO: 17 miles (27 km)
Directions in sequence from: Bovey Tracey

⑨ Drive through the town to the lower end where a road turns off right for Haytor (B3344.)

Parke Rare Breeds Farm

(Not on map.) A ¼ mile (0.5 km) along this road is the entrance to the farm and an information centre run jointly by Dartmoor National Park and the National Trust. The farm contains rare and traditional breeds of

sheep, cows, pigs and poultry in a fine setting. *Open Easter-Oct.* There are in addition woodlands and riverside walks accessible at all times of the year.

Haytor

A grassy slope leads to the actual tor, standing at 1,490 feet (454 m). The Dartmoor tors are composed of granite, which formed 295 million years ago, firstly as molten magma. Gradually eroded by rain and frost, their weird shapes are the moor's most characteristic feature. Haytor is one of the easiest to reach.

The Rock Inn, below Haytor in Haytor Vale, serves excellent food and has a pleasant garden.

Dartmoor

This open, rolling land, dotted with prehistoric remains, all belongs to somebody. Most of it is also 'common land', which means that the commoners (usually local farmers) have the right to graze their sheep, cattle and ponies here, and over all of it is legal public access.

Widecombe in the Moor

The first view of this famous village is from the top of Widecombe Hill on the approach road. Widecombe Fair, as celebrated in the song, is still held on the second Tuesday in September and does indeed attract 'Uncle Tom Cobleigh and all'.

The church, known as the 'Cathedral of the Moor', is an imposing reminder of the wealth and piety of the medieval tin miners who lived and worked in the area. Note also the 16thC Church House with its granite pillars, and the charming village sign.

Hound Tor

(Not on map.) Only ¼ mile (0.5 km) from the road on the right hand side, this rocky viewpoint is easily accessible.

Jay's Grave

(Not on map.) Less than 1 mile (1.5 km) from Hound Tor a little grave can be seen by the roadside. This is the grave of a young girl who hanged herself and was buried at the parish boundary in the early 19thC. There are often flowers at this lonely little mound, placed by unknown hands.

Manaton

Just south of this old moorland village is Bowerman's Nose, a curious pile of rocks resembling a man in a hat.

Becky Falls

On the far side of Manaton, the Becky (or Becka) Falls tumble down over 70 feet (21 m) of granite boulders. Well worth taking the short path down to the Falls – a popular spot.

Blackmoor Vale & Dorset Hills

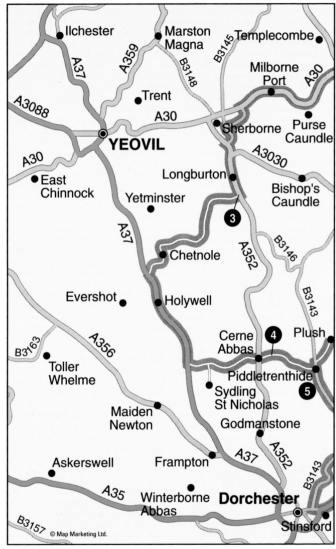

Each of the four towns included in this tour has something different to offer: Shaftesbury is visited for its views; Sherborne's abbey is one of the glories of southern England; Dorchester has associations with Thomas Hardy; and Blandford

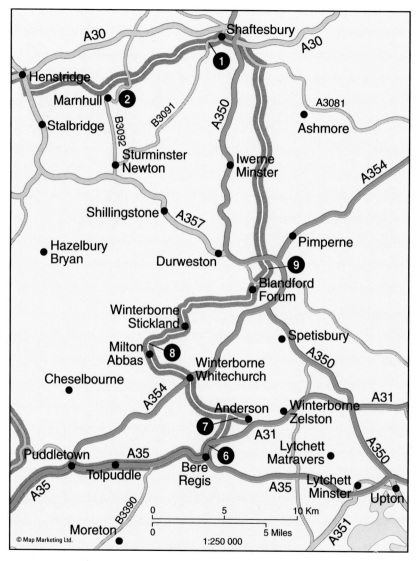

Forum has many Georgian buildings.

In between there are ancient churches, lovely manor houses and charming villages. There are also a few surprises, such as the interior of Bere Regis church and the astonishing Cerne Giant.

● *Milton Abbas, model village on the site of a former market town. Even the church is designed to harmonize with the village.*

ROUTE: 104 miles (167 km)

Directions in sequence from: Shaftesbury

Shaftes-bury

Panoramic views of the Blackmoor Vale, from this windy, hill-top town of ancient origin, put the first lap of the tour into perspective. The best look-out point is from Park Walk, beside the Abbey ruins *(open daily, Easter-Oct, strictly for those with the imagination to flesh out excavations). Tourist information: tel. (0747) 53514.*

At the same end of the town, Gold Hill, a steep old street with cottages and cobblestones, starred in a television commercial for a brand of brown bread.

① Leave town on B3091, then turn right on to unclassified road sign posted to Stour Row and Marnhull. At Todber turn left for Marnhull.

Marnhull

This smart village with a handsome church was Marlott in Thomas Hardy's *Tess of the d'Urbervilles*. Near the church, the Crown pub, offering a set-price menu or bar meals, was the model for The Pure Drop in *Tess*. *② Leave village on Fifehead Magdalen road. At T-junction, turn left then continue on to Henstridge.*

Purse Caundle

Only minutes from the A30, yet a secret, quiet place with a 15thC manor house visible from the main street. *The house is open* afternoons, Thurs, Sun and Bank Holidays, Easter Mon–Sept.

Sherborne An appealing atmosphere pervades this small, neat town of predominantly yellow-ochre stone buildings. In the main street, good quality shops include food stores selling Dorset knobs (crisp little rolls delicious with butter and cheddar or Dorset blue cheese), and new and second-hand bookshops. Allow time in the abbey church to absorb not only the exquisite richness of the fan vaulting (15thC), but also the medieval carved and painted nave bosses depicting humans, animals, birds, a mermaid and a dragon. The abbey, founded in 705, also has several striking monuments. Note in particular the pun of the horses' heads on the Horsey tomb.

Sherborne School, next to the abbey, occupies some of the old monastic buildings. Known by locals as the 'King's School', its pupils are easily recognized in term by their straw boaters.

To the east, the town has two castles. The Old Castle (12thC) is now a ruin. The New Castle, built by Sir Walter Raleigh, has fine furniture, Old Masters, gardens laid out by Capability Brown and a 50-acre lake. *Open Thurs, Sat, Sun and Bank Holiday Mon, afternoons, Easter–Sept.*

Longburton Worth fetching the key from the address on the door, to see the painted canopied tomb in the church of St James. ③ *A short distance from the church, turn right, follow signpost to Leigh* (once famous for witches). *At Leigh, follow signpost to Chetnole. At Chetnole, take Evershot road to T-junction, and left on to A37.*

An even more attractive route is from Leigh to Batcombe, but only drivers prepared to tackle an extremely steep road culminating in a T-junction should attempt the drive.

Sydling St Nicholas A tucked-away village that has much to offer including a smithy dating from 1800 (in the main street), a church known for its gargoyles and monuments, and a flint-walled Elizabethan tithe barn, splendid still in spite of the corrugated-iron roof.

Cerne Abbas The Cerne Giant, conspicuous from the road, is a vast, chalk-cut pagan fertility figure flaunting its masculinity. The Church objected strongly when it was weeded in the late 19thC, on the grounds that local morality would deteriorate.

The village of Cerne Abbas (Tudor houses, duckpond, remains of a 10thC abbey) boasts several pubs, including the ancient-looking New Inn. ④ *On leaving the village, turn right just past the church, and follow signposts to Piddletrenthide.*

⑤ *At Piddletrenthide, turn left on to B3143, then almost immediately turn right on to unclassified road if in search of a good lunchtime stopping place.*

Pub
(Plush)
Worth a short detour is the Brace of Pheasants, a deservedly popular pub-restaurant, beautifully situated.

Pub
Alternatively, another excellent pub can be found by continuing on to the Thimble at Piddlehinton.

Dorchester
Thomas Hardy's Casterbridge has commemorated the author with a statue at Top o' Town and a reconstruction of his study in the County Museum, High West St., *open Mon-Sat.*

Also in High West St., Judge Jeffreys' Restaurant occupies the site where the infamous judge lodged during the Bloody Assize of 1685. The town is built mainly in grey Portland stone, but has an air of bustling activity that defies gloom, especially on Market Day, Wed.

Just south-west of the town, Maiden Castle, the largest and most elaborate prehistoric earthworks in Britain, looks impressive from A354, but walkers will want to explore its ditches and ramparts, some of which rise to around 89 feet (27 m).

Nearby, at Poundbury Farm is the site of Prince Charles' proposed new town, designed by architects Chapman Taylor.

Stinsford
Hardy's heart was buried in St Michael's churchyard, although his ashes were buried in Westminster Abbey. However, local wags used to say that the surgeon's cat ate the heart and another had to be substituted.

At nearby Higher Bockhampton *(not on map, but follow signpost from A35)* the thatched cottage where Hardy was born and lived for many years can be seen *from the outside daily. Apr-Oct.* (There is a 10-minute walk from car park. *Interior seen by appointment only (except Thurs). Tel. (0305) 262366.*

Puddletown
First, feast your eyes on the fine tombs of the Martyn family in the village church, then travel a short way down the A354 to Athelhampton, much of which was built by Sir William Martyn in the 15thC. *House open afternoons, Wed, Thurs, Sun and Bank Holidays, mid-Apr to mid-Oct; also Tues, May-Sept; Mon, Fri in August.*

The partly battlemented house has a superb great hall with an open timber roof, and lovely grounds divided into several gardens, each suiting a different mood.

Tolpuddle
The 'martyrs' who made this village famous (in 1843 they were transported to Australia for joining a trade union) used to meet under the spreading sycamore tree that still stands, propped up but healthy, on the green.

Bere Regis
At the far end of the village, just before the Royal Oak pub, turn right down lane to St Peter's church, to see an astonishing carved and painted roof – almost life-size apostles jut out from the walls and look down on

the congregation. ⑥ *Returning to main road follow signs to Winterborne Kingston at two roundabouts. At village, turn right to Winterborne Tomson (not on map).*

W'borne Tomson

Just beyond the manor house at Winterborne Anderson, turn left to discover a rare gem of a church. Tiny, round-ended and built of stone and flint, it was saved from dereliction around 50 years ago through funds raised from the sale of Hardy manuscripts. ⑦ *Return to Winterborne Kingston and follow signposts to Milton Abbas. Turn left into village.*

Milton Abbas

In the late 18thC, Lord Milton 'moved' the old village of Milton Abbas out of sight of his grand new home. However, posterity has benefited from his ruthlessness; the 'new' village with its almost identical thatched cottages survives very much as he built it, with not a TV aerial in sight. His house, now a public school, *is open during spring and summer school holidays,* and the magnificent abbey church, 14th-15thC but much restored, *is open daily.*

The thatched Hambro Arms pub serves real ale, and fits neatly into this 'model' village. ⑧ *Return to road at top end of village, turn left then first right to Winterborne Stickland.*

Blandford Forum

The deep-red bricks of the beautifully proportioned Georgian buildings, particularly in the Market Place, give this town a welcoming warmth. The town has a small but lively contemporary art gallery showing changing exhibitions (Hambledon Gallery, Salisbury St.), and good bookshops. ⑨ *Leave the town on the Salisbury road, A354. While still in the built-up area, take left turn along unclassified road signposted to Shaftesbury. Go across roundabout signed Melbury Abbas.*

Blandford – Shaftesbury

Green, gently rolling Dorset countryside gives way to spectacular views at Fontwell Down, before the road plunges down Spread Eagle Hill back to Shaftesbury.

New Forest

Take care when driving on Forest roads, especially at night, when ponies are difficult to spot. If you find an animal in trouble, contact the police, who will alert an agister (Forest wildlife warden).

The Forestry Commission, which manages the New Forest, both commercially and for the pleasure of visitors, has done more or less everything possible to accommodate the motorist (and camper) without spoiling the place's natural beauty: picnic places, tent and caravan sites proliferate.

ROUTE ONE: 30 miles (48 km)

Directions in sequence from: Lyndhurst

Lyndhurst Chief town of the New Forest, with a long-winded, one-way system; interesting food shop, Strange's, speciality local venison. *Tourist information: tel. (0703) 282269.*

The 17thC hall attached to Queen's House at the top of the High Street is the meeting place of the ancient Verderers' Court, which meets to administer Forest affairs. The stirrup over the fireplace once measured the size of Foresters' dogs – those too big to pass through were considered a danger to game. William the Conqueror took over the New Forest as a royal hunting ground – the meaning here of the word 'forest'.

St Michael's church, next to Queen's House, is 19thC with fine stained glass by William Morris. Buried in the churchyard is Alice Hargreaves, Lewis Carroll's inspiration for Alice.

Leaving the town, notice the extensive 'lawns' left and right. Cropped short by the ponies, these expanses comprise, with heath and woodland, the main elements of the Forest's scenery – a remarkable survival of a medieval landscape into the 20thC.

Butterfly farm
(detour)

About 1 mile (1.5 km) on left along unclassified road, signposted Beaulieu from the A35, is the New Forest Butterfly Farm at Longdown. Fascinating world-wide collection of butterflies and the like in an indoor tropical garden; *open daily Apr-Oct.*

Denny Lge.
(detour)

The forest road to this keeper's lodge, signposted from the B3056, provides excellent chances of seeing fallow or even roe deer.

Beaulieu Whatever your feelings about the razzmatazz of the stately homes business, seeing the ruins of the Cistercian abbey, founded by King John in a fit of conscience, is worthwhile. Lord Montagu admits that Palace House, purchased in 1538 by his ancestor, the Earl of Southampton, and originally the gatehouse to the Abbey, is undistinguished, but it stands in an exceptional position at the head of the Beaulieu River.

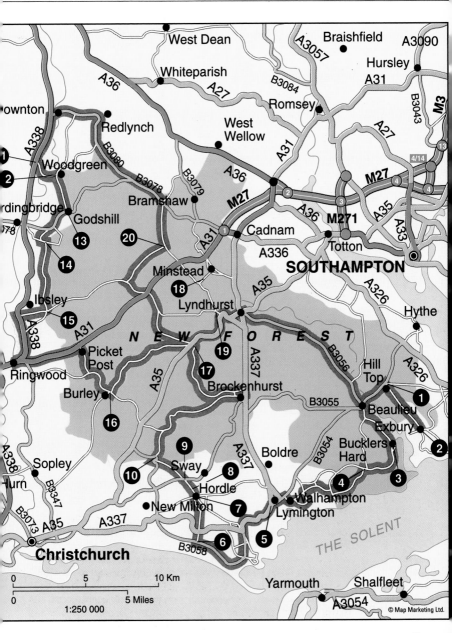

West Dean
Braishfield
A3090
Whiteparish
A3057
Hursley
A31
A36
A27
B3084
B3043
M3
ownton
A338
Redlynch
West Wellow
Romsey
A27
A31
13
B3080
A36
A31
4/14
Woodgreen
B3078
B3079
A36
M27
2
M27
4
Bramshaw
M27
1
Cadnam
A36
M271
1
dingbridge
Godshill
A31
SOUTHAMPTON
13
A336
Totton
A35
A33
14
Minstead
18
A35
A326
20
Lyndhurst
Hythe
Ibsley
N E W
F O R E S T
15
A31
A338
19
B3056
Hill Top
A326
Picket Post
A337
17
Ringwood
A35
Brockenhurst
Beaulieu
1
Burley
B3055
Exbury
16
Bucklers Hard
2
Sopley
9
Boldre
B3054
3
10
Sway
8
A337
4
urn
B3347
Hordle
7
Walhampton
New Milton
A337
Lymington
5
Christchurch
B3073
A35
A337
6
B3058
THE SOLENT
B3054

0   5   10 Km
0   5 Miles
1:250 000
Yarmouth
Shalfleet
A3054
© Map Marketing Ltd.

The National Motor Museum is arguably the best of its kind in the world, and superbly laid out: the complete history of motoring in a collection of more than 200 vehicles. Monorail; veteran car and bus rides; model railway; restaurant; café. *Open daily.*

Exbury and ① *If detouring to Exbury, be ready for the double right turn here.*
Lepe Beach Clearly signposted just before Exbury village is the famous Rothschild
(detour) collection of over 250 acres of rhododendrons and azaleas, glorious during early summer. *Open daily, mid Apr to early June, closed Sat, also July–mid Oct, but telephone enquiry is advised. Tel (0703) 891203.*
② *For Lepe beach, continue straight on following the sign to Inchmery:* car park, Country Park and shingle beach in 2 miles (3 km); fine view across Solent; café.

Bucklers In the 18thC great warships, including Nelson's Agamemnon ('Am and
Hard Eggs' to her crew) were built and launched between the two rows of pretty labourers' cottages. Despite summer crowds, an evocative place, and a popular yachtsman's port.
The Maritime Museum relates the village shipbuilding story. *Open daily.*
The tiny chapel, half-way up the 'street', was once a cobbler's shop, with a cellar beneath used for storing smuggled goods.

Hotel The Master Builder's House Hotel was the home of famous shipbuilder
(B'klers Hd.) Henry Adams. Relaxed public bar; buffet bar; restaurant.

River trips Half-hour cruises can be had along the Beaulieu River in summer. For
(B'klers Hd.) departure times go to Pier Kiosk; well-signposted riverside walk from Bucklers Hard to Beaulieu.
③ *Leaving car park turn immediately left on to unsignposted minor road. At T-junction turn left, signposted East End.*

Bucklers Hard At St Leonards *(not on map)* are the substantial remains of an extremely
– Lymington large medieval tithe barn. Soon after the tithe barn a lovely view to the Isle of Wight opens out, left.

④ *At signpost 'Sowley 1 mile' turn left.*

Lymington Still a strong sense of the 18thC in this pleasant sea-faring town – imposing Georgian houses in the High St., from the bottom end of which a cobbled alleyway leads to the Town Quay. Street market on Sat; ferry to IOW. ⑤ *Follow signs for A337, towards Bournemouth.*

Keyhaven At T-junction in Keyhaven village turn left for ferry to Hurst Castle (signposted) or right for a bracing walk along the shingle spit out to Hurst Castle. This was one of Henry VIII's coastal forts; Charles I was

● *Wide open areas of heath rub shoulders with the great woods of the New Forest.*

held here briefly *en route* for execution; *open daily, Good Fri-end Sept; weekends Oct-Maundy Thur; regular ferries to Castle from Keyhaven.*

Milford Beach *(detour)*

In Milford on Sea, take the road signposted 'Beach'. This is a steep, shingled beach with a marvellous view of the Needles. *Return to the B3058 and follow the signs for Christchurch/Bournemouth.*

⑥ *In about 1 mile (1.5 km) watch carefully for this right turn after a corner: you want Downton Lane; it should (if the signpost is intact) be signposted Hordle.*

Pub *(Downton)*

The Royal Oak pub: home-cooked food and Pompey Royal bitter.
⑦ *Keep left at this fork, ambiguously marked 'Stopples Lane'.*
⑧ *At the next T-junction turn right, then in 100 yards (91 m) left, signposted Tiptoe and Sway.*

⑨ *At the next junction (with the B3055) turn right and in 100 yards (91 m) left for Tiptoe and Wootton.*

⑩ *Just before the junction with the B3058 (beside The Inn), turn right, signposted Brockenhurst.*

Wootton –
Brockenhurst
Sweeping views of the heath, with its lovely colouring, especially at Hinchelsea Moor picnic area.

Brockenhurst
– A35
Past Rhinefield House, the road enters Rhinefield Ornamental Drive, an 1859 plantation of magnificent tall trees, mainly conifers, with many interesting foreign species. Walks from Blackwater car park.

ROUTE TWO: 20 miles (32 km)

Directions in sequence from: Downton (Wiltshire)

Breamore
Signposted from the A338, Breamore House is an Elizabethan mansion dating from 1583; interesting furniture; authentic Great Kitchen; carriages on display. *Open afternoons Tues, Wed, Sun, April, and Easter hol; daily except Mon, Fri, May, June, July, Sept; daily Aug.*
In Breamore village ⑪ *take minor road left signposted Woodgreen.*

⑫ *In Woodgreen turn right signposted Godshill.*

⑬ *At T-junction with B3078 turn right signposted Fordingbridge. In a third of a mile (0.5 km), turn half left down a very minor road at the corner signposted Stuckton.*

⑭ *At this unsignposted T-junction turn left. Then at the North Gorley junction keep left, signposted South Gorley.*

⑮ *Reaching Moyle's Court, follow signs for Ellingham and Ringwood.*

Burley
Popular New Forest centre; strong smuggling associations. *After left turn by shops,* ⑯*, continue straight ahead, along Chapel Lane, signposted 'Burley Church'.*

⑰ *Soon after joining A35, turn left on to the unclassified road marked 'Bolderwood Ornamental Drive'.* This runs through woodland containing superb beeches. Look for the pollards.

Minstead
(detour)
The simplest approach is via Lyndhurst. The village's cottage-like church contains an extremely rare 17thC triple-decker pulpit, a Norman font, intriguing galleried pews and a luxury family pew with its own fireplace. Conan Doyle is buried here. Also at Minstead (signposted) is Furzey Gardens: an authentic forester's cottage, dating from 1560, surrounded by gardens. *Open daily, except Christmas and Boxing Day.*

⑱ *To rejoin the route, keep left at this unmarked fork, and left again at the T-junction ½ mile (0.8 km) on, which is also unmarked. At Emery Down, turn sharp right* **⑲** *by The New Forest Inn, signposted Bolderwood and Linwood.* Expect a superb drive through incomparable New Forest scenery; there is a deer sanctuary at the left end of Bolderwood car park. *Soon rejoin marked route.*

Rufus Stone   **⑳** *Having crossed the war-time airfield of Stoney Cross, turn right at the T-junction if you wish to visit the Rufus Stone (later left on to the A31, and first left again signposted Brook and Downton).* The stone, a popular but rather disappointing spot, marks the place where William Rufus, second Norman king of England, is supposed to have met his death in a hunting accident. *If continuing the route, turn left (unmarked).*

South Downs

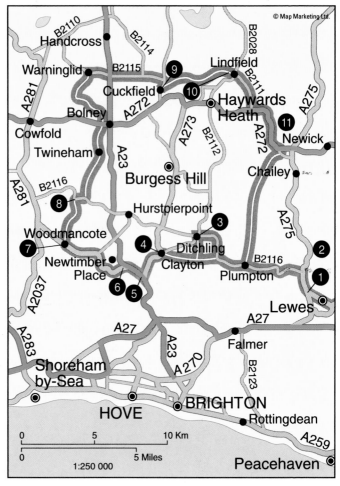

Together, these two loops encompass almost every type of Sussex scenery. You sample the highest points of the South Downs – surprisingly lonely in parts – and the secluded villages of the Weald, typically set in woodland. There are numerous opportunities to leave the car and have a short stroll; those who stay inside all the way round really do miss the flavour of this area. There is nothing quite like a warm summer's day on the tops of the downs, with a cooling wind blowing in from the sea.

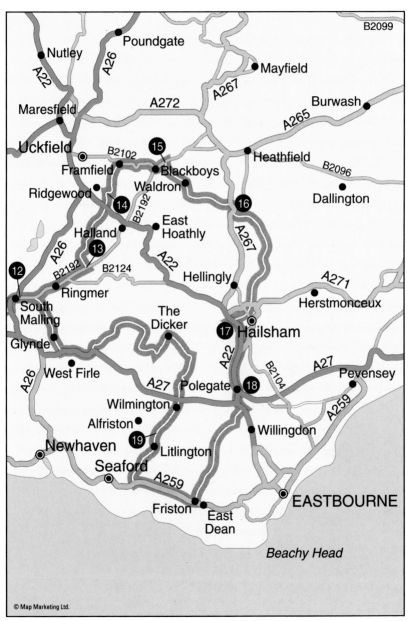

ROUTE ONE: 39 miles (64 km)

Directions in sequence from: Lewes

Lewes A county town full of interest, standing in a hollow and sprawling up a hill alongside the River Ouse. It began life as a Saxon trading centre, gaining in prestige after the Norman Conquest with the building of the castle and of the most important Cluniac priory in England. The town still retains much of its medieval character and architectural interest. 'Lewes Town Walk' published by East Sussex County at 50p is useful.

Of the Norman castle built on a high mound in the centre of the town, the keep (magnificent view over the town from the top) and the barbican remain. Close by, Barbican House is a Georgian building housing a museum of local archaeology. *Castle and museum open Mon-Sat, also Sun, Apr-Oct.*

South of the castle stands Southover Grange, an Elizabethan manor house built with Caen stone taken from ruins of the nearby St Pancras Priory (demolished in 1539 as a result of the Dissolution of the monasteries). The diarist John Evelyn (1620-1706) lived here as a boy and the Prince Regent often stayed in the 1790s. *The gardens are open to the public daily. Tourist information: Lewes House, 32 High St. Tel. (0273) 471600.*

- *The Seven Sisters – a magnificent view from above Cuckmere Haven.*

① *Leave Lewes by Offham Rd. At the junction with the A275 turn right towards East Grinstead.*

② *Turn left on to the B2116 signposted Hurstpierpoint.* From this road under the Downs there are many fine views over the Weald of Sussex.

Ditchling Use the car park so that you can stroll round this attractive village. Near the Early English cruciform church and the village pond stands a Tudor manor house, with an interesting outside staircase, which belonged to Anne of Cleves. ③ *From Ditchling village, turn left at crossroads just after village car park on to B2112. For Beacon, after 200 yards (183 m) take left fork on to unclassified road.* The Beacon is 813 feet (248 m) high; you can take a bracing walk along the South Downs Way from the car park. ④ *Return to the B2112, turning left on to it and left into Clayton at junction with A273.*

Clayton The Saxon church with its perfect plain chancel arch, and above it, well preserved 11th-12thC wall paintings, is on the left just before A273. Up above, on the downs, are two landmarks, a pair of 19thC windmills known as 'Jack and Jill'. Note folly on right of junction.

⑤ *Turn right at junction of A273 and A23 (traffic lights).* The village of Pyecombe was once famous for its shepherds' crooks.

⑥ *Turn left on to A281 (Horsham road).*

Newtimber Place A moated Jacobean house which contains Etruscan style wall paintings. *Open Thurs afternoons, May-Aug. By appointment only; tel. (0273) 833164.*

⑦ *At Woodmancote turn right on to unclassified road, which will be signposted for Blackstone.*

⑧ *At the B2116 turn right and in 600 yards (549 m) turn left on to unclassified road to Twineham.*

Warninglid – Lindfield The route passes through Cuckfield and then on to Lindfield, both of which manage to retain their their village atmosphere, despite urban encroachment.
    Short distances to the north of this area are four very fine gardens: Nymans *(off map)*, Sheffield Park *(indicated)*, with the famous Bluebell Railway, Wakehurst Place and Borde Hill *(not indicated)*. They are all intriguingly different. ⑨ *A quarter of a mile (0.5 km) after joining the B2036, turn left at the roundabout into Ardingly Rd. (signposted 'Hospital'). Follow signs for Lindfield, turning left at Hickmans Lane, then right into Lindfield High Street.*
    ⑩ *Turn left in Lindfield, just before the village pond.*

*Chailey –
Plumpton*

⑪ *From the A272 turn right for Lewes, then in 50 yards (46 m) right again, signposted Plumpton Green.* The road crosses Chailey Common Nature Reserve with tremendous views of the downs and several opportunities for parking.

ROUTE TWO: 54 miles (87 km)

Directions in sequence from: Lewes

⑫ *Leave Lewes on the A26, Tunbridge Wells road, turning right at the top of Malling Hill on to the B2192, signposted Ringmer.*

⑬ *One mile (1.5 km) after the B2192 and B2124 join, turn left on to unclassified road, signposted Bentley Wildfowl and Motor Museum.* This is a useful stop for children; *open daily Easter-Oct; weekends only Nov, Dec, Feb.*

⑭ *After Bentley join the A22, going north for ½ mile (0.8 km), then turn right on to unclassified road for Framfield. Go straight over the next crossroads and through Framfield, then take the B2102 in the direction of Heathfield. Keep left at the junction with the B2192.*

Pub
(Blackboys)

Excellent 14thC pub with extensive garden and a wide range of food. ⑮ *Take the first right outside Blackboys, down the unclassified road for Waldron and Horam.*

Waldron

A pretty, tree-shaded village which has a vineyard and a shop where you can taste the local wine.

⑯ *In Horam take the minor road on the left opposite Merrydown Wine & Cider Works for Hellingly and Hailsham. In Hailsham* ⑰ *follow through-town traffic signs to the A22 and there turn left.*

*Polegate –
Friston*

⑱ *Just after traffic lights at junction with A27 at Polegate, turn right at next set of traffic lights on to minor road for Wannock.* A beautiful, downland dry valley road leads through the tiny village of Jevington to Friston where the church, with its charming beamed roof is approached by a revolving tapsell gate. There is in addition a fine walk on to the Seven Sisters cliffs from Crowlink car park, which is signposted from the village pond.

*Friston –
Exceat*

(Exceat not on map.) A high, downland road with superb views. At Exceat, the Seven Sisters Country Park, on the southern edge of Friston Forest, encompasses 692 acres of the Cuckmere valley and part of the Seven Sisters chalk cliffs.

Litlington

Charming village with typical flint buildings. On the left is The Plough and

Harrow, which serves real ale and good pub food; garden. There is an interesting nursery almost opposite.

Alfriston
(detour)

⑲ *Just after Lullington Court, turn left, signposted Alfriston, then left at next junction, over narrow bridge and left at next junction to Alfriston.* This is a busy tourist village, but well worth visiting. The 17thC Star Inn was probably a smugglers' haunt, and certainly sheltered pilgrims on their way to Canterbury. Have a look at the rather imposing church which is often called 'The Cathedral of the Downs'. Nearby stands the 14thC rectory, The Clergy House, bought in 1896 for £10 by the National Trust – their first property. *Retrace route to Litlington road, then turn left to Wilmington.* In 600 yards (549 m) is Lullington church, said to be the smallest in the country. In late winter the roadsides here are a mass of snowdrops.

Wilmington Priory and The Long Man

The famous Long Man of Wilmington, a long staff in each hand, looks down from the side of Windover Hill on which he was carved, no one knows when. He is a 231-foot (70 m) figure cut in the Downs and is best viewed from the priory car park on the left near the remains of a 13thC Benedictine priory.

Michelham Priory

Much restored moated 13thC priory, with Tudor barn, gatehouse and working water mill selling flour. Lunches and teas are available and there are various exhibitions on display, including tapestries, furniture and miniature musical instruments. *Open daily Mar-Nov.*

Firle Place

Home of the Gage family since the 15thC, containing notable paintings, furniture and porcelain. *Open Sun, Wed and Thurs, Apr-Sept; also Bank Holiday afternoons, Easter-Aug.* Nearby, Firle Beacon is 713 feet (217 m) high with extensive views, another in the chain of warning beacons.

Glynde

Glynde Place, home of the Hampden family, is a fine Elizabethan manor with some interesting works of art inside – a charming house which still feels very much like a home. *Open Wed, Thurs, Apr-Sept; afternoons first and last Sunday of every month.*

Along the road is Glyndebourne, the famous opera house.

The Weald and the Cinque Ports

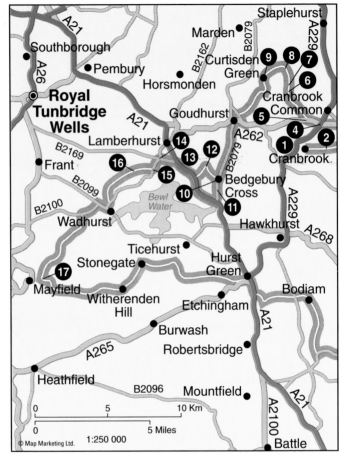

Here are two areas in close proximity, yet strong in contrast. The hilly, enclosed countryside of the Weald remains one of the most thickly wooded areas of lowland England. It is also a region of orchards and of hop gardens: the oasts of Kent are one of the county's defining features, and in winter the poles and wirework of the hop gardens rise starkly above the hedges. Altogether different are the levels around Winchelsea and Rye: once marshland, but now drained, they are an open, flat and sometimes mysterious landscape of sheep pasture and tillage with only the occasional up-standing feature.

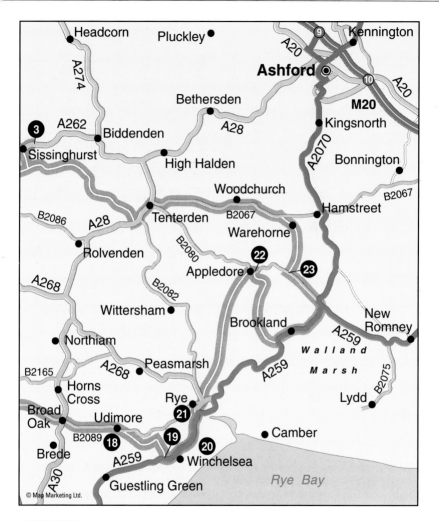

© Map Marketing Ltd.

ROUTE: 80 miles (128 km)

Directions in sequence from: Cranbrook

Cranbrook ① *In the town free car park to right off St David's Bridge (the road to the mill).* Cranbrook opens up into an attractive, typically Wealden high street with upper storeys clad in white-painted weather-boarding or hung with decorative tiles. Walk from the church along Stone St. with its curious side alleys and jettied upper storeys towards Union Mill, a smock

75

mill dating from 1814, still in excellent condition. *Open Sat afternoons, Easter-Sept, and Bank Holiday Mon.* The bend on Mill St. is a perfect example of an old Kentish street. *Tourist information: tel. (0580) 712538.*

② *Leave town on the road past Union Mill.*

Sissing- ③ An optional, but strongly recommended detour; *turn right at the*
hurst *A262 and then first left along the lane to Sissinghurst Castle* (sign
(detour) posted). Arguably one of the most beautiful gardens in England, and certainly one of the most famous, Sissinghurst was created in the 1930s by Vita Sackville-West and Harold Nicolson amongst the remains of what had been one of the most splendid Elizabethan houses in Kent. Also visit the tower where Vita had her study. *Open Tues-Fri after noons and all day Sat and Sun, Apr-Oct.*

Cranbrook ④ *At this deflected junction, follow the signs for Tunbridge Wells*
Common – *(A262).* ⑤ *Turn right here, along a lane signposted to Colliers Green*
Curtisden *(not on map). Take it slowly: there are few useful signposts.* ⑥ *At*
Green *unsignposted junction turn right, then first left, following the sign for Marden.* This is orchard country, and the low, squat trees, trained to easy picking height, can be seen growing in disciplined rows. Go there in mid-to-late April for blossom time. ⑦ *At this junction fork right.* ⑧ *Turn left here to Curtisden Green.*

Curtisden Here the Revd Kendon set up a mission to improve the working
Green conditions of hop pickers during the 1880s. ⑨ *Take the left fork signposted to Cranbrook, then go immediately right at a small triangle of grass with a converted oast on your left (junction unsignposted).* Here are sweeping views of a typical Wealden valley filled with orchards and hop gardens.

At the T-junction following immediately, turn right along the A262 to enter Goudhurst.

Goudhurst A picture-postcard hilltop village, though somewhat marred by main road traffic. It is best seen starting at the bottom end, by the duck pond. The church, entered via a marvellous yew arch, has notable painted wood tombs of the Colepepper family: one shows father, mother and 18 children at prayer. The Star and Eagle, next to the church, is a 14thC heavily beamed inn. The quaint former Hughenden Tea Room is now a restaurant.

⑩ *Just before a telephone box on B2079, take the unsignposted lane to your right.*

Bedgebury ⑪ *For another worthwhile detour carry on along the B2079 for about*
Pinetum *¼ mile (0.5 km) to explore this outpost of Kew Gardens.* The pinetum
(detour) consists of over 200 species of conifer; *open daily.*

● *Scotney Castle, near Wadhurst, is 14thC with 17thC additions.*

Scotney Castle Garden

⑫ *Fork left here.* ⑬ *Make the difficult right turn at the junction of B2169 and the A21.* This leads to another romantic garden, with a 14thC moated castle ruin at its centre. *Open Wed-Fri and Sat and Sun afternoons, Apr-Oct.*

⑭ *Follow the B2169 into Lamberhurst, and then turn left on to the B2100.* ⑮ *After passing the county boundary sign into East Sussex, take the first (unsignposted) right turn down a single-track road; a narrow and very bendy lane.* ⑯ *After a sharp right hand bend, take a sharp left at this unsignposted T-junction. Then ignoring all right and left turns including two signposted to Wadhurst, keep going straight on in the direction of Wadhurst.*

Wadhurst –
Mayfield
Here you pass through one of the Wealden 'holloways', cut down into the soft yellow sandstone by centuries of erosion by horse, bullock and foot traffic. ⑰ *Fork left at the steep triangular green, following the signpost for Witherenden.*

Mayfield –
Witherenden
A lane characteristic of many in the Weald which run along the top of ridges, with river valleys out of sight on either side. You have to stop and peer over gates to see the views.

Stonegate –
Hurst Grn.
Good views, or rather glimpses, over the pretty, rolling country of the Linden valley.

Bodiam
The 14thC castle owes much of its beauty and popularity to the fact that its moat is still in water. *Open daily Apr-Oct; Mon-Fri, Nov-Mar.*

Udimore
⑱ *Turn right here along a lane marked 'Winchelsea, Narrow Road' – a warning worth heeding.* Along it you will drop off the ridge into the flat-bottomed and formerly marshy valley of the River Brede. After turning right towards the level crossing you will be travelling at only a little higher than sea level. Look out for the thick-fleeced Romney Marsh sheep, a feature of this area.

Winchelsea
⑲ *At this junction in Winchelsea climb the hill, bear right immediately after the fortified entrance gate and then turn left at sign indicating the way to the church.* Perched on its hilltop like a demure English equivalent of some Italian fortified town, Winchelsea has an atmosphere entirely of its own. The broad, straight streets are the result of a very early piece of town planning: Edward I began to rebuild here on the French 'gridiron' pattern after Old Winchelsea had been swallowed by the sea, but the town never grew to the extent planned, ironically enough since gradual silting up put paid to its prospects as a port. Today the whole place seems fast asleep.

Like the town, St Thomas's 14thC church is only a fragment of the building first intended, but it is impressive, with striking modern stained glass and interesting wall tombs.

⑳ *Leave the town keeping the church on your right hand side, and follow the road through the Strand Gate and down the hill. At the bottom take a right turn to follow the A259 to Rye.*

Rye
The 'Cinque Ports' were a confederation of five harbours grouped together for defence by Edward the Confessor. Originally the five were Hastings, New Romney, Hythe, Sandwich and Dover, but *c.*1156

Winchelsea and Rye were also included. The ports supplied the crown with fighting ships and with skilled seamen. As at Winchelsea, the sea gradually retreated from Rye, although the town still retains a river channel that is navigable by small boats. Walk down the splendid cobbled Mermaid St.; like the church square it is lined with buildings of all periods.

The Mermaid Inn (rebuilt much as it now stands, in 1420) is known through the novels of Russell Thorndike, who used it as a setting for his 'Dr Syn' smuggling stories; the interior is genuinely ancient.

Rye –
Appledore

(21) *Leaving Rye on the A268 turn right immediately after the railway bridge.* This is a causeway road, with the Royal Military Canal on the right. Planned as a strategic alternative to Martello towers in defence against Napoleon, the 23-mile (37-km) long canal was built between 1804 and 1809 at vast expense. Militarily it proved worthless.

(22) *Cross the canal and take an immediate right turn.* This lane will lead you into the heart of marshland. Only the reed-filled drainage channels could qualify as 'marsh' nowadays and, sadly, field drainage is enabling farmers to put vast areas into intensive agricultural use. But to date enough of the old pastures survive to give this flat landscape a character of its own.

Brookland St Augustine's church has a uniquely-shaped steeple clad with wooden shingles, and a powerful sense of the past.

(23) *Half a mile north of the leaning tower of Snargate church, take a right turn along a single-track causeway road to the pretty village of Warehorne.*

Tenterden Peggoty's Tea Shoppe at 122 High St. has home-made cakes that are indeed what they claim to be.

Exmoor

Glorious views dominate this tour which begins with a sprinkling of seaside resorts, goes westwards for the thrill of Atlantic surf, then extensively explores the beauty of Exmoor. Perhaps seen at its best in late summer, when the deep purple of the heather near the coast mixes with the bright yellow of the western gorse, the moor and its villages inspired such poets as Samuel Taylor Coleridge and Robert Southey. It is a splendid area for exploring on foot, and both routes include several opportunities for easy or strenuous walks; those who stay in the car will, however, still be rewarded by the charm and diversity of the landscape.

ROUTE ONE: 55 miles (88 km)
Directions in sequence from: Lynton

Lynton and Lynmouth   The largest settlement in Exmoor National Park, these twin villages are connected by a cliff railway and steep Lynmouth Hill. The buildings are

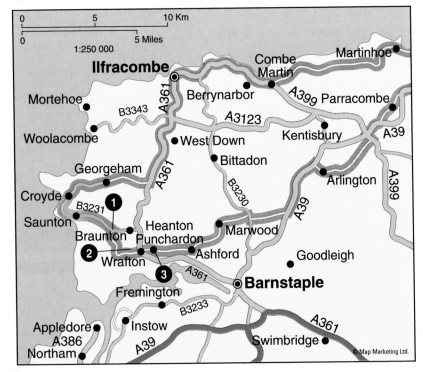

largely Victorian with Swiss-style architecture and some older thatched cottages.

Lynmouth At the Exmoor National Park information centre, on the Esplanade, an interesting display concerning famous 19thC sea rescues includes an early life boat. *Open Easter-Oct.*

From the harbour, motor-boat trips along the coast are best in late spring and early summer, when nesting sea birds can be seen.

Valley of Rocks This dry valley has curious rock formations, many with associated legends. Picnic area, wild goats and spectacular cliff walk.

Lee Bay A sheltered bay offering a nature museum, walks and tea gardens (summer only). A beautiful toll road leads to Woody Bay.

Hunters' Inn *(Not on map.)* Heddon's Gate Hotel has panoramic views over lush Heddon Valley. In the restaurant local specialities include venison and salmon. *Open all year.*

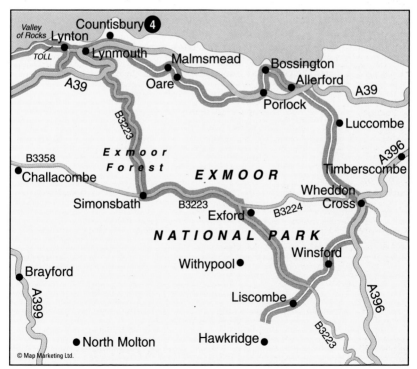

Knap Down (Not on map.) Fine views over Combe Martin and westwards along the coast.

Combe Martin Seaside resort with several interesting buildings including the eccentric Pack of Cards Inn, built by a gambler in the 18thC, and the church of St Peter ad Vincula, which has a fine tower and painted screen.

Water-mouth (Not on map.) Landlocked harbour with caves and a peculiar 19thC mock castle.

Ilfracombe The main tourist resort of the area has large Victorian hotels and a picturesque harbour with hilltop mariners' chapel. *Tourist information: tel. (0271) 863001.*

　　Chambercombe Manor, a medieval manorial farmhouse in the south-eastern outskirts of the town, has an intriguing secret room, a vast cider press in the kitchen, and a water garden. *Open Mon-Fri, and Sun afternoons, Easter-Sept.*

Georgeham Henry Williamson, author and naturalist, lived here and is buried in the churchyard. The Rock Inn serves traditional ales and inexpensive meals.

Croyde Attractive village of thatched cottages, somewhat spoiled by holiday camps. Sandy beach suitable for surfing, and exhilarating walks to Baggy Point. The Gem Rock and Shell Museum has shells, minerals and semi-precious stones, and a shop. *Open Mar-Oct, and in winter by appt.*

Saunton Down (Not on map.) Lay-bys provide fine views across Saunton Sands and Braunton Burrows to Taw and Torridge estuary, Westward Ho! and Hartland Point. ① *Take first turning on right after village (signposted Braunton Burrows). Then take second unsignposted road to the left.*

Braunton Burrows Large area of sand dunes, famous for wild flowers including orchids in early summer. Nature trail from Sandy Lane car park or board walk to Airy Point from end of toll road.

Braunton Great Field (Not on map.) One of two remaining medieval open fields in England. The strip cultivation pattern contrasts with grazing land of adjacent Braunton Marsh, where medieval barns and linhays (animal shelters) can be seen.

② *At Braunton, turn right at T-junction (unsignposted), continue through Wrafton and straight across A361. Then turn right after The Williams Arms.*

Pub *(Wrafton)* The Williams Arms, a busy thatched inn, has several bars and a restaurant offering a wide variety of dishes.

Heanton Punchardon Fine view from the church over RAF Chivenor to Taw Estuary and Appledore. ③ *After leaving village, continue straight ahead at two crossroads, avoiding the main part of Ashford. At Guineaford, take left turning on road signposted to Marwood church.*

Marwood The 12-acre garden at Marwood Hill has lakes, a 'bog' garden, camellias, rhododendrons and a collection of Australian plants. *Open daily.*

Arlington The Regency home of the Chichester family retains the atmosphere created by its last owner, Miss Rosalie Chichester (*d.* 1947), an inveterate collector of small items. The coach house contains a collection of horse-drawn vehicles. Extensive grounds with nature walk and lake with bird-watching hide. *Open Sun-Fri, Apr-Oct and Bank Hol Sat.*

Parracombe St Petrock's church (made redundant when a new church was built nearer village centre in Victorian times) has fascinating interior, unaltered from 18thC. *Closed in winter,* but key obtainable in village.

◼ ROUTE TWO: 45 miles (72 km)

Directions in sequence from: Lynton

Countis-bury Small hilltop settlement. Short walks to Foreland Point for views back to Lynton and Lynmouth, and to Iron Age fort on Wind Hill for views over East Lyn valley. ④ *On leaving village take first turning on right for Brendon. At Brendon, cross the bridge and turn left.*

Malmsmead A beauty spot with an old bridge over Badgworthy Water, Malmsmead is the centre for exploring *Lorna Doone* country. Large car park, picnic area, gift shop and riding stables.

 The Natural History Centre has wildlife displays and organizes guided walks. *Open Wed, Thurs, May-Sept; Tues, Aug.*

 About 2 miles (3 km) of delightful walking along Badgworthy Water takes you deep – and high – into Exmoor. The country is ideal for the walker who wants to improvise: paths are well signposted and the bogs are harmless. But take the appropriate Ordnance Survey *Landranger* (1:50 000) map, which shows public rights of way as dotted magenta lines.

Oare The small, rather plain church of St Mary is famous nonetheless. It is the setting for the marriage and shooting of R. D. Blackmore's heroine, Lorna Doone.

Porlock Delightful village at bottom of notoriously steep Porlock Hill, which can be avoided by a tollroad affording magnificent views. Worth pausing in the village to look at the medieval Doverhay Manor House (now a museum and information centre), and the 13thC church of St Dubricius, which has interesting monuments.

● *Double-arched pack-horse bridge, Allerford.*

Pub
(Porlock)
The thatched Ship Inn is known for its associations with the poets Coleridge and Southey. Bar meals are available.

Bossington
Footpaths lead from the village to the beach and to Selworthy Woods. Good views from Bossington Hill, which are particularly spectacular at sunset.

Somerset Farm Park is an old manorial farmhouse with a medieval chapel of ease. Visitors see the farm at work and the farm animals, including the only historical exhibition in the country of working donkeys. Displays of farm crafts. *Open Sun-Fri, afternoons only, Easter-Sept,* although the farm's future is uncertain at the time of writing.

Allerford
Attractive village with medieval pack-horse bridge and ancient Pyle's Mill, *open daily. To reach the mill, turn left on to A39, then right on to minor road.*

Webbers Post   *(Not on map.)* Good views over Horners Woods. There is also a nature trail to Cloutsham and back (3 miles/5 km), through old woodland rich in wildlife, including red deer.

Dunkery Hill   Lay-bys afford fine views over Avill Valley to Brendon Hills and Quantocks. Short walk to summit of Dunkery Beacon, Exmoor's highest point at just over 1,700 feet (518 m), with even more extensive views including large areas of Exmoor, the Vale of Porlock and over Bristol Channel to the Welsh coast.

Winsford   Charming village on River Exe with many small bridges. At the 14thC Royal Oak Inn excellent salads are served in the bar.

Tarr Steps *(detour)*   *(Not on map.)* From Spire Cross, a 1½-mile (2.5-km) detour (plus short walk from car park) leads to an ancient clapper bridge, said to be Britain's oldest bridge although its date is unknown. The wooded valley of the River Barle provides a beautiful setting.

Winsford Hill   Extensive views from summit at Wambarrows (Bronze Age burial mounds). Much of south-east Exmoor can be seen as well as beyond to Blackdown Hills and Dartmoor.

Waters-meet   *(Not on map.)* At the junction of the East Lyn and Hoaroak rivers there are waterfalls, wooded gorges and a 19thC hunting lodge, now an information centre and tea garden.

Salisbury, Stonehenge and Wilton

Salisbury's cathedral and Cathedral Close can claim to be respectively the most haunting, and the most charming examples of their kind in England; Stonehenge is the most numinous prehistoric monument in Europe; Wilton House combines literary associations with fine architecture as perhaps no other country house in Britain. Each is conveniently close to the other, and as this circuit proves, can be linked by some unforgettable country roads: you sail the tops of the downs, with astonishing views, then dive down through pretty valleys with charming settlements along their chalk streams.

ROUTE: 45 miles (72 km)

Directions in sequence from: Lyndhurst

Stonehenge ① *Coming from Amesbury on the A303, be ready to fork right on to the A344 after the dual carriageway ends – clearly signposted Stonehenge. In about 800 yards (730 m) turn right into the car park.*

You go down some steps to a refreshment counter, bookshops and ticket booth, all turfed over at the rear, in an attempt not to spoil the site with unsightly protrusions. Here is your first hint that you are visiting not just a stone circle, but an outdoor temple, observatory, ceremonial meeting place and burial ground covering several acres. *Open 10.00-6.30 Good Friday-Sept 30; 9.30-4.00 Oct 1-Maundy Thursday; closed Dec 24, 25, 26 and Jan 1.*

Stonehenge – phase one With officialdom behind, the power of the grey stones in their simple setting starts to strike home. You will notice the sheer number of earth mounds – barrows – scattered over the surrounding downland: graves of the people who inhabited the area, and built the monument. In addition to the barrows, you should notice the vestiges of a great circular earthwork about 100 feet (30 m) outside the stone circle, with an opening in the north-east marked by a stone – the Slaughter Stone. A hundred feet outside this entrance is another large stone, the Hele Stone; and inside the earthwork's inner bank is a circle of 56 holes, known as the Aubrey Holes, after the antiquarian who first observed them. These are the first phase of Stonehenge.

Stonehenge – phases two and three As a second phase, 82 'bluestones', brought all the way from the Preseli Hills in south-west Wales, were placed in concentric circles. The stone avenue was probably built at this time, too: it continues north-east, past the Hele Stone, then veers towards the River Avon, pointing the way the stones came from Wales. Archaeologists are certain they were loaded on boats at Milford Haven, sailed round the south coast and finally up the Avon to be disembarked nearby at Amesbury.

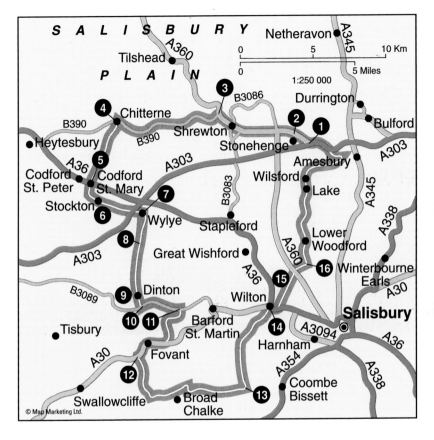

The third phase seems to have been the addition of the largest stones – the Sarsens – brought overland from the Marlborough Downs. The work could have been done with primitive bone tools: but you still strain to imagine the organization and discipline of the workforce.

Stonehenge – the theory That, extremely simplified, is the story of Stonehenge; it spanned about eight hundred years, from around 2800 to 1400 BC; refinements may have continued another nine hundred years. What kept them at it for so long?

The most intriguing of modern theories is that the process of *continued* construction enabled the priests and rulers of those early people to time and again impress, and therefore control, their subjects. It is well known that the Slaughter Stone – Hele Stone axis is aligned with the midsummer sunrise; but archaeologists have recently worked

● *Stone circle, outdoor temple, ceremonial meeting place and burial ground, Stonehenge is unique of its kind.*

out that most of the other features, including the Aubrey Holes, would have enabled its architects to predict, and demonstrate to credulous witnesses, a whole range of grand, sometimes frightening, phenomena such as solar and lunar eclipses. The growing complexity of the monument could well reflect the rulers' perennial need for new tricks to persuade the ruled who should remain master.

② *From Stonehenge continue west on the A344.* Fine rolling views soon open up over Salisbury Plain, heartland of the 'Wessex Culture' of agriculture and crafts which flourished during the Stonehenge period. There is strong evidence that these people had links with the Mediterranean, for Stonehenge is on a former trade route linking the Mediterranean and Ireland; in fact it runs through the Preseli Hills in south-west Wales from which came the smaller stones for Stonehenge.

The Stonehenge area is best avoided 20th-22nd June when armies of 'hippies' may arrive to celebrate the summer solstice.

③ *As the village of Shrewton comes to an end, turn left on to the B390, signposted 'A36 (B390)'.*

Shrewton –
Chitterne

You now run through typical Salisbury Plain country: this used to be grassland, but ploughing-out and Ministry of Defence operations (witness the tank tracks) have mostly eaten it up; however, enjoy the views.

④ *Turn left signposted Codford.*

⑤ *In Codford St Mary ignore side turnings and continue straight ahead to meet the A36. Turn left and in 150 yards (137 m) turn right signposted Sherrington and Stockton.*

⑥ *Having crossed the River Wylye turn left at the T-junction signposted A303, Stockton and Wylye.*

Stockton

A view of the 'big house' soon opens up on the left: the original structure was put up by a wealthy Elizabethan cloth merchant, John Topp, who also endowed the Topp Almshouses in the village. A side-turning leads to the impressive Norman church and some other interesting buildings. *Continue straight ahead, under the A303, into Wylye.* ⑦ *Entering Wylye take the first right, signposted Great Wishford and go along Teapot St., soon continuing ahead into Fore St. In 200 yards (183 m) look carefully for the right turn, signposted Dinton. Immediately cross the railway line and enjoy an airy ride over the downs with more views.* ⑧ *Go through the sharp left and right turns following the sign to Dinton.* ⑨ *Continue straight on down 'Steep Hollow', signposted Dinton.*

Dinton

The village has several interesting houses; Philipps House, built by James Wyatt in 1813-16; Hyde's House, near the church, perhaps on the site of historian Edward Hyde's birthplace; Little Clarendon (late 15thC) and the adjacent cottage; *Philipps House shown by appointment with the Warden, telephone Teffont 208; Little Clarendon (apply at the house).* ⑩ *Continue on St Mary's Rd. past the church, to meet the B3089, where turn left.*

⑪ *Soon after The Penruddocke Arms turn right, signposted Compton Chamberlayne. To shorten the drive continue through Barford St Martin to join the A30 to Wilton.*

Pub

The Green Dragon at Barford St Martin is a welcoming pub with a fair range of dishes available over the bar.

Compton
Chamberlayne
– Fovant

Having turned right on to the A30, watch out left for the famous regimental badges carved on the chalk down. A noticeboard explaining them is on the left of the road by three large beeches, with a side-turning where you can pull up.

⑫ *This is the first major left turn after Fovant, signposted Broad Chalke and Bowerchalke.*

Fovant – Chiselbury Camp, out of view to the left (access on foot by track at top
Broad Chalke of hill), is a fine Iron Age hill fort, excellent for a stroll, views all round.
There is a remarkable view to the right after passing the quarry.

Broad John Aubrey, the Wiltshire antiquarian, (see under Stonehenge), lived
Chalke here. Take a look at the wonderfully mellow pink-brick-and-moss north
front of Reddish House, a small but grand 18thC manor house.

⑬ *Turn left signposted Wilton opposite the large house.* This
unclassified road, leading north-west to Wilton, can claim to be one of
the best backroads of southern England: it is boldly engineered,
astonishingly wide in parts for a minor road, and much of it is through
tunnels of magnificent pollarded beeches.

⑭ *At the traffic lights in Wilton turn right and continue on the A30 to
the roundabout, passing Wilton House on the right.*

Wilton One-time capital of Wessex, Wilton had a great abbey whose heyday
was in Saxon times, and whose eclipse was during the general
destruction of the monasteries under the Tudors. The confiscated abbey
and lands were given to Sir William Herbert, first Earl of Pembroke, a
powerful courtier.

SALISBURY CATHEDRAL

Many people consider that this building, wholly consistent in its Early
English design, has the most beautiful exterior of all the cathedrals in
Britain.

From whichever direction you view the spire, it seems equally
impressive – though a particularly memorable approach is up St
Ann's Gate. It is the highest spire in England, and while there are
some on the Continent which are taller, none manage to soar quite as
this one does.

The spire rests on the great central tower. Part-way through
construction, the marble pillars supporting the tower began to buckle.
In panic, the masons fitted two great reinforcing arches. They held,
and the spire continued upwards, ton upon ton.

But the weight has pushed part of the cathedral foundations into
the earth, so that today the spire leans some 29 inches (737 cm) out of
the perpendicular. A costly restoration programme was still
incomplete in 1989, and the spire's future will probably always be
uncertain. *Tourist information (0722) 334956*

Wilton House

Sir William pulled down the abbey and used its stones to build himself a mansion – the first Wilton House. The present house is much altered and rebuilt, but still shows something of the original. Famous features are the porch possibly designed by Holbein, the south and west fronts by Inigo Jones, the Double Cube Room, and, outside, the Palladian Bridge.

It is all the more splendid because of its status as a cultural hot-house. The second Earl married the sister of Sir Philip Sydney, who wrote *Arcadia* here. Shakespeare is supposed to have visited with his company; Christopher Marlowe, Edmund Spenser, Ben Jonson, Izaak Walton and many others came in their time: as a diarist wrote, 'Wilton House was like a college, there were so many learned and ingeniose persons'. *Open 11-6, daily, Apr-Oct 14, last admission 5.15.*

The Royal Wilton Carpet Factory (a short walk from Wilton House) was started by the ninth Earl of Pembroke with the help of French weavers – then the acknowledged masters – poached from France, much to the displeasure of the French king.

⑮ *At the roundabout take the unclassified road signposted Amesbury.*

⑯ *Turn right for a detour to Old Sarum, left to continue.*

Old Sarum

Here, just off the route (well signposted), a medieval town grew up inside the earth fortifications of an Iron Age camp. Remnants of a castle and cathedral can be seen in the innermost ring. The place was the precursor of modern Salisbury, and long after its decay and de-population remained a 'Rotten Borough' – represented, until the Great Reform Bill, by two members of Parliament.

Lower Woodford

The Wheatsheaf is a serviceable pub with a reasonably priced menu and plenty of seating space.

Wilsford Cum Lake

The big house on the right must be one of the best exponents in the county of decorative chequered stonework characteristic of Wiltshire.

The Surrey Hills and North Downs

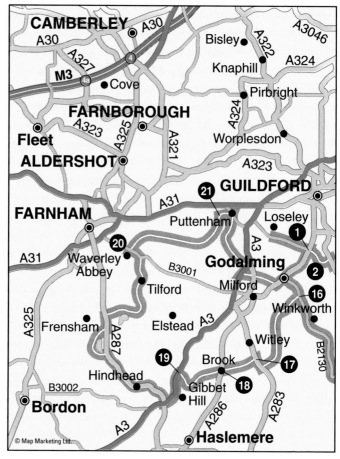

Dormitory towns and 'Tudorbethan' houses in a tame and boring landscape: that for many people means Surrey, but the reputation is unfair. The route passes through scenery that is at once spectacular and intimate; not large-scale, but with great variety of height and landscape. It encompasses panoramic view points, enclosed and mysterious lanes, famous beauty spots – Box Hill, the Devil's Punchbowl, Frensham Ponds – and historic houses. It explores in depth the stretch of the North Downs around Box Hill and the parallel greensand hills, from Leith Hill to Hindhead, which comprise most of the 'Surrey Hills'.

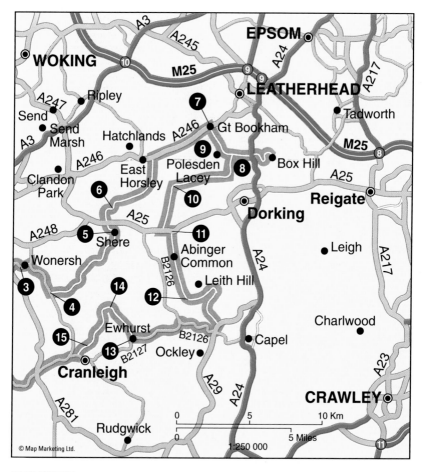

© Map Marketing Ltd.

1:250 000

ROUTE ONE: 75 miles (121 km)

Directions in sequence from: Godalming

Godalming The town is dominated by its Norman church, and boasts attractive half-timbered 17thC houses.

Loseley Park (detour) ① *Turn left on to the B3000 and in ½ mile (0.8 km) right (signposted) for a short detour to Loseley Park.* This is an Elizabethan manor house with paintings, furniture and 'Nonsuch' panelling. The estate's dairy produce may be familiar from the shelves of health food shops or supermarkets. *Open (and farm tours) afternoons, Bank Holiday Mon,*

93

Wed-Sat late May-Sept. Return to the A3100, turn right ② then first left, just before garage, signposted Bramley and Cranleigh. At junction with A281 turn right. ③ At Wonersh turn right (no sign). ④ Turn left, signposted Shere.

Shere

One of Surrey's prettiest villages: willows weep by its river; there are old houses, narrow streets and a charming greystone church.

Pub
(Shere)

The White Horse has a warm atmosphere and serves good food.
⑤ In Shere turn left at T-junction and at junction with A25 cross over, signposted East Clandon.

Clandon Park
(detour)

⑥ After steep uphill bend, turn left at top of hill (poorly signposted) for a detour to Clandon Park at West Clandon. The 18thC Palladian house has a rich interior which includes the Gubbay collection of Chinese porcelain birds. *Open afternoons Mon-Wed, Sat and Sun, late Mar to mid-Oct; restaurant.*

Hatchlands
(detour)

Return to A246 turning left for East Clandon if you wish to continue the tour to visit Hatchlands, a handsome 18thC mansion. Open afternoons Tues-Thurs, Sun and Bank Holiday Mon, late Mar to mid-Oct; Sat afternoons in August.

⑦ In Great Bookham turn right off A246, signposted Polesden Lacey.

Polesden Lacey

A Regency mansion (signposted from road), whose heyday was the Edwardian era when it was the home of society hostess Mrs Ronald Greville. *Open Sat and Sun afternoons Mar and Nov; afternoons, Wed-Sun, Apr-Oct; all day Easter Sun and Mon, Bank Holiday Mon and preceding Sun.*

Great Bookham – Box Hill

⑧ At the A24 turn left, following signs at roundabout for Box Hill, and turn right off the road leading past Burford Bridge Hotel. At the bottom of the zig-zag road, notice pretty Flint Cottage, from 1867 the home of writer George Meredith, and later of Max Beerbohm.

Box Hill

A splendid downland area with woodland and walks and majestic views southwards; named for its fine box trees. *⑨ Turn left for Ranmore, signpost difficult to spot amidst hedge.*

Ranmore

(Not on map.) The common commands far-off views and the Victorian church with its striking octagonal tower is a landmark for those walking the North Downs Way.

Ranmore – Abinger Common

⑩ Turn left, signposted Abinger. ⑪ Turn right off A25 for Abinger Common. On the corner note the house of the 17thC diarist, John Evelyn; he is buried in the church just north of the A25.

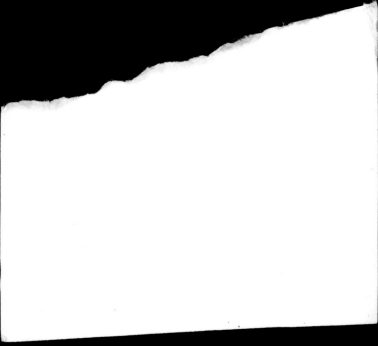

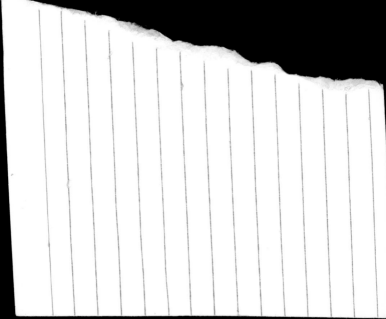

● *There are sweeping views across the Weald from Box Hill.*

Abinger Com. The route follows mysterious lanes under canopies of foliage so dense
– Leith Hill   that on a dull day you could need to use your headlights.

Leith Hill ⑫ *Bear left at fork, following sign for Coldharbour.* Rhododendrons and
unusual trees make this National Trust area (750 acres) a delight; at 965
feet (294 m) it is the highest spot in south-east England; St Paul's
Cathedral and the Channel can be seen on a clear day. There are views
southwards from the road, but it is best to pause and park (eg just
before Coldharbour). *No admission to the fine Anstiebury prehistoric
camp; turn right on to A29 for Ockley.*

⑬ *In Ewhurst turn right at sign for Peaslake, Shere, Gomshall.* ⑭ *Turn
left at signpost for Winterfold (not on map);* the windmill *(marked on*

95

map) is not visible from the road. ⑮ *Fork right signposted Wonersh and Guildford. At next T-junction, turn left signposted Cranleigh.*

Winkworth Arboretum Signposted 300 yards (274 m) before, but not at, car park (on right); a hillside covered with rare trees and shrubs sloping down to a lake; teas.

██ ROUTE TWO: 48 miles (77 km)

Directions in sequence from: Godalming

⑯ *Turn left off the B2130 on to Home Farm Rd. (signposted Hambledon), then immediately left again, on to Hambledon Rd.* ⑰ *Take second left off the A283, signposted Sandhills and Brook, immediately after the turning for 'British Rail Station'.* ⑱ *Continue straight over the A286 at Crossways Cottages.* ⑲ *An attractive wooded lane runs alongside Forestry Commission land, with a tricky and dangerous exit on to the A3 (fast traffic is just leaving a dual carriageway section).*

Gibbet Hill Views to north-west over the famous Devil's Punchbowl, a large depression to the north of the road.

Hindhead There is likely to be heavy traffic here at weekends.

Frensham Pond *Turn left at the signpost for 'Frensham Pond Hotel', and right at the Hotel,* to skirt this expansive and picturesque pond.

Frensham Little Pond *Turn right at signpost for this pond,* perhaps even more attractive than its neighbour. Parking on right amidst delightful woods. Drive slowly over this surprisingly poorly-surfaced road.

Tilford A picturesque village. *Turn right at the Green, by the attractive Barley Mow pub, and follow sign for Elstead, Milford, Godalming, over bridge.*

Waverley Abbey The ruins of England's earliest Cistercian house (13thC) and Park (where Jonathan Swift worked as secretary to William Temple) are closed to the public; but both can be glimpsed from the entrance to Waverley Abbey House, just over the bridge on the left. Stella's Cottage, home of Esther Johnson (associated with Swift) can be seen further on to the north of the road.

⑳ *From Waverley Abbey House take the turning northwards opposite, signposted Aldershot and Guildford, then right up Botany Hill and follow signs for Puttenham; from the top are panoramic views.* ㉑ *Turn right on B3000, then right again after 100 yards (91 m) signposted Shackleford.*

Guildford *(detour)* Make a detour to Surrey's county town to see the High Street studded with historic buildings, notably the Jacobean Archbishop Abbot's hospital (with 17thC oak carvings, stained glass windows and pictures) and 17thC town hall; view from the top of the remains of the Norman castle's keep; modern cathedral (finished 1964); rowing boats for hire on the Wey. *Tourist information: tel. (0483) 444007.*

Vale of White Horse

The mysterious figure of the White Horse, cut into the chalk hillside, not only gives its name to the vale it overlooks but also symbolizes this area's ancient history.

Starting in an important Saxon town, the route goes across the Vale to the Ridge Way, one of the oldest roads in Europe. Walks along this historic track high up on the Downs lead to the White Horse itself and the ramparts of a hill fort occupied around two thousand years ago. The tour also includes a Bronze Age burial site and some charming villages of medieval origin.

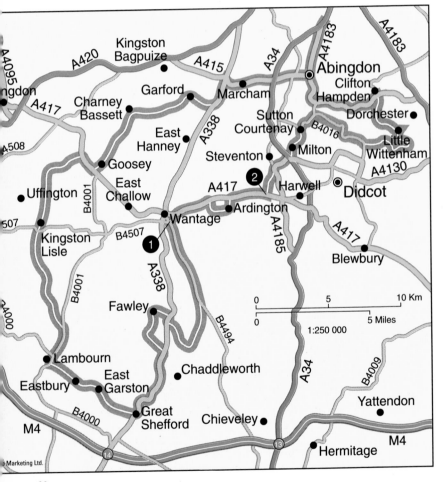

Kingston Bagpuize
A420
A415
A34
A4183
A4183
Abingdon
Clifton Hampden
Garford
Marcham
Charney Bassett
A417
A4095
ngdon
A417
Sutton Courtenay
Dorchester
B4016
East Hanney
A338
Little Wittenham
A4130
A508
Milton
Steventon
Goosey
A417
2
Harwell
Didcot
Uffington
B4001
East Challow
Ardington
A4185
507
Wantage
1
Kingston Lisle
B4507
A417
Blewbury
A338
B4001
Fawley
0   5   10 Km
0   5 Miles
1:250 000
B4494
A34
B4009
Lambourn
Chaddleworth
East Garston
Eastbury
Yattendon
B4000
Great Shefford
Chieveley
M4
14
13
Hermitage
M4
000
Marketing Ltd.

ROUTE: 60 miles (96 km)

Directions in sequence from: Abingdon

Abingdon
For 900 years an important town where the Rivers Ock and Thames meet. Its abbey, one of the richest in Britain, owned more of Berkshire than anyone except the king. The 17thC County Hall towers over the market-place, where huge fairs were held until 1968. There are public gardens, riverside walks, an open-air swimming pool, golf and tennis. Boats for hourly hire near the 500-year-old bridge spanning the Thames. *Tourist information: tel. (0235) 522711.*

The abbey buildings, Thames St., include interesting 12th-14thC remains. *Open daily in Summer and afternoons in Winter, but enquiries should be made before visiting: tel. (0235) 532181/553701.*

St Helen's church, majestic with its tall spire and five aisles, is a most unusual shape, being wider than it is long. Picturesque almshouses and 17th-18thC cottages nearby contrast with its grandeur.

The old Gaol, an imposing riverside building constructed by Napoleonic prisoners of war, was used for a time by a corn merchant until its recent conversion to a leisure centre.

Marcham
The manor house is now a college owned by the National Federation of Women's Institutes.

Garford
Just before the turning to the village, the route crosses the River Ock. The line of the Downs soon comes into view to the south.

Charney Bassett
The church's Norman door has a frieze of fierce faces, and a chancel doorway carving – possibly Saxon – shows two dragons biting a man.

Goosey
'Goose Island' has a huge village green where cattle were kept until a generation ago. Stray animals were put in an enclosure on the site of the Pound Inn.

Kingston Lisle
The Blowing Stone sits under an old oak tree by some cottages. It is a 3-foot (1-m) high, perforated sandstone sarsen; blowing into the top

---

OXFORD

With its wealth of splendid buildings, its museums and churches, its bookshops, covered market and historic pubs, Oxford, which is 7 miles (11 km) north of Abingdon, demands at least one whole day to itself. Of the 35 colleges, Christ Church, Magdalen and New College should not be missed; nor should the Radcliffe Camera, the Bodleian Library, the Sheldonian Theatre or the Ashmolean. *Tourist information: tel. (0865) 726871.*

---

hole can produce a trumpet-like sound which can be heard a couple of miles away. Many legends exist, one being that King Alfred used it to summon his troops to battle.

Ridge Way   An ancient track that once stretched from the Dorset coast to East Anglia. Here you can walk in the footsteps of Bronze Age and Iron Age man, of the Romans who buried their dead on Whitehorse Hill, and the Saxons who called it a 'herepath', meaning war road. Today The Ridge Way is a signposted long-distance footpath.

Whitehorse Hill   A ½-hour walk to the west along the Ridge Way leads to the oldest hill figure in the country – a vast white horse carved in chalk. Its origins remain a mystery; some experts believe it is Iron Age, others say it is Saxon. Particularly baffling: why is this the only hill figure to face right?

Uffington Castle   Eight acres surrounded by bank and ditch, on the hillside above the horse. Pottery finds show it was occupied around 300 BC; splendid views.

Lambourn Downs   Spread out along the road is an extraordinary Bronze Age cemetery. Although traditionally called Seven Barrows, there are more than 35 here, with examples of almost every shape.

Lambourn   This is racehorse country and training gallops have replaced the sheep that grazed here for centuries. The River Lambourn rises in pools near the village and flows 12 miles (19 km) south-east to Newbury. The route follows it for almost half that distance. *Turn left in Newbury St.*

Eastbury   Picture-postcard cottages along either side of the river. In the church, a window dedicated to the memory of poet Edward Thomas (1878-1917), and his wife Helen, was engraved by Laurence Whistler.

East Garston   Thatch and tile roofs, timber-framed and brick-infilled cottages, make this another attractive riverside village. There is no West Garston; the name comes from 'Esgar's tun' – Esgar being a Lambourn tenant at the time of Domesday.

Great Shefford   The name comes from 'sheep ford', a reminder of how important sheep once were here (Lambourn means 'river for dipping lambs'). Today large areas of the down have been made arable.

Hungerford *(detour)*   A 4-mile (6.5-km) detour leads to this busy market town which has unusual customs. A constable for the Manor, who is elected annually, summons his court by horn; the Town Clerk reads the Ancient Customs granted by John of Gaunt, and two tithing men – who distribute oranges to young and old – can kiss the lady of every house they visit.

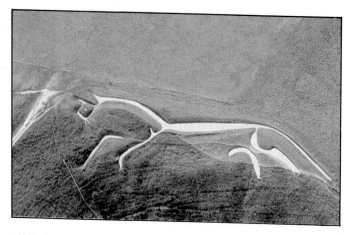

● *Whitehorse Hill: when the horse was carved, and how, remains a mystery.*

The town has much Georgian architecture and is noted for its antique shops. It is also a base for fishing along the River Kennet.

Fawley

The village where Thomas Hardy's grandmother lived was the model for Marygreen in *Jude the Obscure*. Hardy also gave Jude the surname Fawley. This detour adds about 4 miles (6.5 km) to the tour.

Ridge Way

Park just beyond 'Hill 1:10' sign. Walk east for ten minutes to the monument to the local landowner, Lord Wantage.

Wantage

① *On entering Wantage, turn left at T-junction or town car park.*
Wantage was an important Saxon town where Alfred the Great was born in 849. Today all roads lead to his market-place statue.

There are many 17th-18thC buildings of warm local red brick with blue-glazed bricks for decoration. In the large medieval cruciform church, look for the oldest brass in England behind the north-east pillar of the tower.

The Vale and Downland Museum, Church St., has purpose-built galleries explaining the surrounding land and landscape, and man's life here from prehistoric times. Especially interesting exhibit on how enclosures created unemployed landless labourers as well as the hedges-and-fields landscape. *Open Tues-Sat; afternoons on Sun.*

Ardington

This estate village, built by Lord Wantage in the 1860s, has undergone a planned revival. New craft businesses welcoming visitors include a pottery, a picture-framer, a leather worker, a jeweller, a cane-chair maker, a printer, a mason and furniture-makers. *Open daily.*

● *Day's Lock, Little Wittenham.*

② *Take turning to left (signposted Steventon). At junction with A4130, turn left again then follow signs to Milton.*

Milton   The Manor (17thC with Georgian wings) is as demure as a dolls' house from the outside. Inside, the Strawberry Hill Gothic Library is quite a surprise. *Open afternoons only, Easter and Bank Hol weekends; Tues-Fri, Jun-Aug.*

Sutton Courtenay   Follow signs to car park to explore rich architectural scene and Thames meadows on foot. Eric Arthur Blair (George Orwell) and former Prime Minister H. H. Asquith are buried at the 12thC All Saints' church.

From the church turn right and continue to end of street where path follows millstream to weir and Sutton Pools. A 35-minute circular walk is well worthwhile; look out for kingfishers and grebes.

Just beyond the village, the Sinodun Hills, crowned by the Wittenham Clumps, come into view. *To reach this well-known landmark above the Thames take second turning to right after Appleford (signposted Brightwell), then the second turning to left (no signpost) to car park.*

Wittenham Clumps
Best views (as far as the Chilterns) are from the more northerly hill, while the one nearer car park has earthworks of an Iron Age hill fort.

Little Wittenham
Park by church for a stroll to Day's Lock, a bustling place on summer weekends. (Footpath continues to Dorchester's famous Abbey Church).

Pub
(Clifton Hampden)
The 14thC Barley Mow Inn (just before bridge) was described by Jerome K. Jerome in *Three Men in a Boat*: 'It is . . . the quaintest, most old-world inn up the river. Its low-pitched gables and thatched roof and latticed windows give it quite a storybook appearance, while inside it is even still more once-upon-a-timeyfied.' All still true, but today cordon bleu meals are served in the bar, restaurant or garden.

It takes six arches to span the Thames here at Clifton Hampden, but the bridge has only one lane. In 1844 Sir Gilbert Scott restored the 12th-14thC church and designed the manor house, on a cliff above the river.

Chilterns and Thames Valley

Between London and Oxford the gentle landscape is interrupted by the long arc of the Chiltern Hills, stretching from the Thames valley into Hertfordshire. Avoiding suburban areas, the tour explores this area of outstanding natural beauty, where innumerable winding combes – some still cloaked with the famous Chiltern beech woods – lead from bare downland ridges to secluded villages.

Several large houses and churches deserve attention along the routes, but plenty of time should be reserved for West Wycombe, one of the strangest places in Britain.

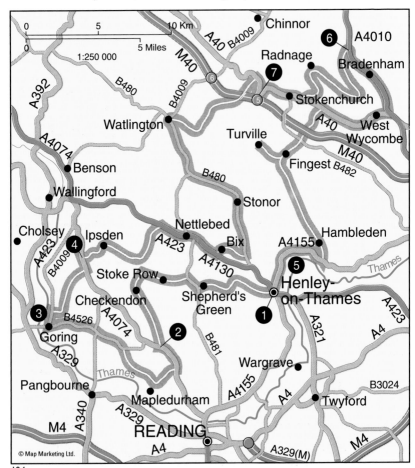

⏳ rE ONE: 30 miles (48 km)

⏳irections in sequence from: Henley-on-Thames

⏳ey-on-Thames

By far the most handsome of the old Thames Valley towns, Henley is best seen first from the stately river bridge of 1786, which is flanked by a pub on one side and a grand hotel and church on the other. The centre of the town has a wealth of half-timbered and Georgian buildings. *Tourist information: tel. (0491) 578034.*

For the connoisseurs of beer, Henley is a place of pilgrimage. Brakspear's ambrosial Henley Ales, brewed in New St., can be consumed in no fewer than 14 hostelries in the town, including The Angel on the bridge, and The Three Tuns in the Market Place. When available, try the dark, wine-like Old Ale. ① *Leave town along the road that climbs the hill beyond the market-place, signposted to Peppard.*

Greys Court

Perched on a knoll overlooking a lovely combe, this Jacobean manor house is worth visiting for its garden, set amongst the ruins of a 15thC fortified house. *Open afternoons only, Apr-Sept; house: Mon, Wed, Fri, garden: Mon-Sat; closed Thurs.*

Shepherd's Green

Small but typical Chilterns 'green' village, with thatched or pantiled houses nestling around a triangle of rough grass.

Stoke Row

Amid the suburban blandness of Stoke Row the Maharajah's Well comes as a delightful surprise. The oriental-style well cover, complete with golden elephant, was donated to the village in 1864 by the Maharajah of Benares. Note also the tiny hexagonal 'pepper-pot' cottage nearby.

Checkendon

Pretty village with lovingly restored brick and timber cottages. Worth looking inside the church to see the medieval frescoes.

② *At Cane End go straight ahead at crossroads and then turn left immediately along A4074.*

Maple-durham

Perfect example of a small Thames Valley village; attractive flint and brick houses, with no hint of 20thC infilling to destroy its architectural unity. Mapledurham Lock, with its mill (see below), was inspiration for E.H. Shephard's delightful illustrations in Kenneth Grahame's *The Wind in the Willows* (see the introduction to this guide, page 8).

Sixteenth-century Mapledurham House is perhaps most impressive from the outside but fine plaster ceilings may lure visitors inside. The best view is from the churchyard, through rusty ornamental gates. There is also a working watermill nearby. *Open afternoons only, Sat, Sun and Bank Holiday Mon, Easter Sun to Sept.*

Goring and Streatley   Twin villages on either side of the Thames, linked by a wooden bridge. The public bar of The Swan Hotel in Streatley has arguably the best armchair view of the Thames anywhere.

In Goring, access to the riverside is by the slip road alongside the fine old mill. The locks are to the right, but the most attractive walk, with good views of the weir and the church (set virtually at the water's edge), runs in the other direction.

③ *Go back through the village to the railway bridge, then turn left along B4009. After ½ mile (0.8 km) turn right and then left almost immediately, following signs for Ipsden.*

Ipsden   On entering the village note the fine brick and tile barn on the left, and on the right the small corn store raised on staddle stones to keep the rats out. ④ *At T-junction at end of village turn left, then turn right almost immediately at the crossroads.*

Nettlebed   The short, narrow main street is lined with brick and timber houses and old coaching inns. *Just past junction with B481 take unsignposted turning to left.* To the left of the road a well-preserved 18thC bottle-kiln, incongruously surrounded by modern houses, is all that remains of a once thriving brick and pottery industry. *Ignoring the first turning to the right, take the unsignposted right fork almost immediately after it.*

Crocker End   *(Not on map.)* A particularly perfect example of a Chilterns 'green' village, larger than Shepherd's Green, with its cottages dotted randomly about.

ROUTE TWO: 40 miles (64 km)

Directions in sequence from: Henley-on-Thames

⑤ *Leave Henley on the A4155.*

Hamble Brook Valley   Surely one of the prettiest valleys in the Chilterns accessible by car. It is also one of the few with the pleasant distraction of a stream flowing through it.

Hambleden   *After village name sign, turn right.* Attractive, carefully preserved settlement of flint, brick and timber cottages grouped around a small square next to the churchyard. *To return to the valley road, take lane leading off west side of the village square, past the church tower.*

Pub
(Skirmett)   In spite of some rather tacky suburban appendages of recent years, Skirmett is still graced by the presence of a pub that has retained the atmosphere of an untouched village 'local'. Known in the area simply as 'Lil's', after its former proprietor of long standing, The Old Crown has soggy old armchairs in its low-ceilinged saloon, a staircase in a cupboard

● *Henley: the handsome bridge and ever-popular Angel Hotel.*

and no bar – the beer is served from a brick-floored cellar at the back.

Turville

An irresistibly picturesque village, much used by film makers. The Bull and Butcher serves Brakspear's ales, good inventive quiches, and a traditional roast on Sundays in winter.

The church has an impressively massive 14thC tower. Amongst several other interesting features are two wooden screens decorating the north aisle, erected *c.*1737 to create a separate seating area for the Lord of the Manor, and a beautiful, semicircular stained glass window, designed by John Piper.

A signposted footpath leads up a steep hill to the windmill *(not open to the public)*. The glorious view makes the short climb worthwhile.

Fingest

The church has an unusual saddleback roof on its roughcast Norman tower.

● *West
Wycombe
Park.*

**West
Wycombe**

This is an unspoiled village of 16th-18thC houses, saved from demolition by the National Trust in 1929. West Wycombe Park, the 18thC Palladian mansion to the west of the village, was built by the notorious Sir Francis Dashwood. Its grounds include a lake in the shape of a swan. *Open afternoons only, Mon-Thur, June-Aug; Sun and Bank Hol Mon.* The natural caves were extended manually in the 1750s and may have been used for meetings of Dashwood's Hell Fire Club. *Open pm, Sat, Sun, Nov-Mar; weekdays Mar and Apr; Mon-Sat, May-Oct; Sun Bank Hols.*

The gold ball on top of the tower of St Lawrence's church can seat eight people, and used for distinctly un-religious purposes by Dashwood and his eminent friends. Next to the church is the sinister Mausoleum, with its single tomb.

Bradenham

Turn off the A4010 to see this village where church and manor stand imposingly at the head of a long green.

The village is preserved against change by the National Trust, who recently made the controversial decision to allow an underground NATO command bunker to be built under the wooded hill nearby.

⑥ *Take left turning signposted to Saunderton Bottom. At junction about 2 miles (3 km) further on take the road signposted to Radnage.*

Radnage

Turn right and right again to reach the secluded church with its squat tower, Saxon font and 15thC timber roof.

(7) *At the motorway junction, follow the sign indicating the A40 to Oxford, then take first turning left, signposted to Christmas Common.*

Cowleaze Wood
Signposted footpaths (starting a short distance south of car park and picnic area) lead out on to the escarpment spurs of Bald Hill and Shirburn Hill. The views from both hills are inconceivable from the road.

Watlington Hill
National Trust viewpoint. On the lower slopes, note the dark clumps of yew, indigenous to these hills.

Stonor Park
Characterful old house which has evolved over many centuries, and is set in lovely parkland. *Sun afternoons, Apr-Sept; Bank Hol Mon; afternoons only, Wed, May-Sept; also Thurs Jul-end Aug; and Sats in Aug.*

Lower Wye & Forest of Dean

The Wye Valley is one of the loveliest areas in Britain. The high ground on either side of the river offers views which are often fine and occasionally almost theatrically dramatic – witness the famous double bend at Symonds Yat. Several towns owe their charm to the Wye, but the valley's most romantic spot is undoubtedly Tintern Abbey, which even the crowds and coaches cannot spoil.

Although the Forest of Dean is geographically close to the Wye, its unique atmosphere created by the close-knit, fiercely independent community of foresters and miners (there are iron and coal mines in the Forest) can still be felt.

████ ROUTE ONE: 50 miles (80 km)

Directions in sequence from: Monmouth

Monmouth
Charming and restful county town, where the River Monnow flows into the Wye. Thirteenth-century Monnow Bridge, with its two-storeyed fortified gate-house, is the only one of its kind in Britain. In Agincourt Sq., the 18thC Shire Hall is fronted by a statue of Henry V, who was born in Monmouth in 1387. Another statue commemorates Charles Rolls, co-founder of Rolls-Royce. Nelson's fighting sword is the prize exhibit at the Nelson Museum, Priory St. This and other mementoes of the admiral were collected by Charles Rolls' mother, Lady Llangattock. *Open Mon-Sat and Sun pm. Tourist information: tel. (0600) 713899.*

① *Drive north through town (signposted Ross) to roundabout at Dixton. Return south for ½ mile (0.8 km) along A40, then turn first left at traffic lights, to reach A4136.*

The Kymin
Steep 1½-mile (2.5-km) drive up to the pavilion built in the 18thC by the Kymin Club, whose upper-class members met here once a week in summer. They also erected a temple commemorating the Battle of the Nile in 1798. The marvellous view to the west was praised by Nelson when he breakfasted here in 1802. Now owned by the National Trust.

The Buck Stone
Once a rocking-stone, it is now cemented in place, having been rolled down to the road below by some touring actors in 1885. To reach the Stone, park in lay-by on left and walk short distance up steep path (not signposted).

Staunton
After leaving village, note standing stone on left, immediately before fork.

Symonds Yat
The exceptional view of the River Wye, snaking its way through a thickly wooded gorge, attracts too many admirers in high summer. Out of season it is magnificent. 'Yat' is an old local term for gateway, and Symond was a High Sheriff of Herefordshire in the 17thC.

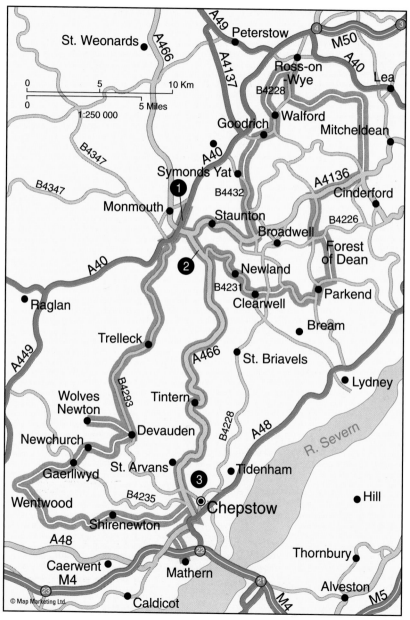

Goodrich The 12th-14thC castle has been described as the noblest ruin in Herefordshire, its moat hewn like a precipice out of solid rock. *Open daily (but closed Sun morning in winter.)*

Buried under the church altar is Jonathan Swift's grandfather, Thomas, who was responsible for the village's whimsical, Y-shaped vicarage. To the left, immediately before the bridge, the remains of the 14thC Flanesford Priory can be seen.

Walford Hill Court, a monumental mansion of 1700, is approached by an impressive avenue of elms, said to have been planted by philanthropist John Kyrle, the 'Man of Ross', in the 18thC. *The house is not open to the public, but visitors can go up the avenue to the Garden Centre.*

Note the picturesque black-and-white Old Hall opposite.

Ross-on-Wye In the centre of this delightfully situated town, the 17thC stone market house stands on rows of open arches. Nearby, St Mary's church (mostly 13th and 14thC) has some good 15thC glass and a monument to John Kyrle (1637-1724) who lived in Ross and became its most famous benefactor. Outside the church, the plague cross records the 315 deaths here in 1637.

Forest of Dean The old court room of the Restoration-style Speech House, now an inn, is the meeting place for the ancient Verderers' Court, which meets to administer Forest affairs. The arboretum behind the inn has 300-year-old holly trees.

To the east, there are superb views across the forest.

Parkend The track to the left of the road belongs to the Dean Forest Railway; *steam trains run every Sun, June-Sept; also every Wed, Jun-Jul and Bank Hols*, from the Norchard Steam Centre on B4234 near Lydney, about 3 miles (5 km) to the south.

Clearwell At the ancient iron mines, eight caverns house geological samples and mining equipment. *Open daily, Mar-end Oct.*

Clearwell Castle, England's first neo-Gothic mansion, built in the mid-18thC, was badly damaged by fire in the 1920s but has been restored in recent years and is now a hotel.

The Wyndam Arms, dating from the 14thC, serves real ale and delicious light lunches.

Newland All Saints' church has been called the 'Cathedral of the Forest'. The 13th-14thC tower has five elaborate pinnacles. Inside there are grand effigies and a 15thC monument to the Forest's Free Miners who had the right to claim ownership of a pit if they had worked in the mines for more than a year and a day.

A row of attractive almshouses lies to the south of the church.

ROUTE TWO: 45 miles (72 km)

Directions in sequence from: Monmouth

② *Leave Monmouth as for Route One, but keep on A466 after crossing bridge at traffic lights.*

Wye Valley
The road follows the meandering course of the Wye through a variety of river valley landscapes perhaps unequalled in Britain. The scenery is not large in scale, but its special quality has been celebrated by writers and painters alike.

Tintern Parva
The old railway serving local industries (iron, wireworks, paper mills) is no longer in use, but the station has been preserved as a visitor centre, with a café serving home-made refreshments, and exhibitions in the railway carriages.

The splendidly-sited abbey was founded by the Cistercians in 1131, but most of the extensive and elegant ruins date from the 13th-14thC, when it was almost entirely rebuilt. The spirit of the place, celebrated by Wordsworth in his famous poem, still shines undimmed through the tourist industry surrounding it. *Open daily, Mon-Sat and Sun afternoon except Sun mornings in winter.*

Wyndcliff
(Not on map.) The rewards of a bracing climb up 365 steps, many of them hewn out of the cliff-face, are panoramic views over the Wye and Severn. Poorly signposted car park off road to right, opposite unsignposted picnic area on left immediately before 'bend in the road' sign. Another car park is further on, turning right signposted to Wyndcliff.

Chepstow
③ *On entering Chepstow turn left. Go through the old West or Welsh Town Gate to the High St. Continue down Middle St. to car park in Bridge St.*

The impressive castle, stretched out along the cliff top, was one of the first Norman fortifications to be built in stone instead of wood. *Open daily (but closed Sun morning in winter).* Nearby, in Bridge St., is Stuart Glass, where visitors can purchase glass and watch it being engraved. Chepstow Museum is a good local museum. *Tourist information: tel. (0291) 623772.*

Mathern
(detour)
A 2-mile (3-km) detour *(take Newport exit at Mounton roundabout)* leads to this old village, with its 15thC church.

Wentwood
The reservoir has a pleasant picnic site with good views. For a more impressive 180° panorama taking in the Severn Estuary and Black Mountains, climb Gray Hill, opposite. There are tumuli and a Neolithic stone circle on the east side of the hill.

● *The Wye Valley – beloved of salmon fishermen and connoisseurs of landscape.*

Pen-y-cae-mawr This is a short detour, but the fine views to the west on the descent are worth it.

Gaerllwyd   Neolithic tomb in semi-wrecked condition. The huge broken c
has five supporting stones *in situ*. Tucked behind hedge along B-1235, it is
visible from the road.

Newchurch   From the road, there are superb views across to the Bristol Channel.

Devauden   Beaufort Aviaries (entrance on the green next to the pub) have rare
pheasants, tropical birds and peacocks. *Open daily.*

Wolves   A 3½-mile (5.5-km) drive leads to the Model Farm. Built at the end of
Newton   the 18thC, it has a unique, cross-shaped barn, housing a Folk Collection
(detour)   and Craft Centre. At the time of going to press, the Centre's future is
uncertain. For further information: tel. (02915 231). *To reach the farm,
go up signposted lane on left, ¾ mile (1 km) past Wolvesnewton church.*

Trelleck   Harold's Stones – three mysterious, aligned standing stones – are
signposted (for pedestrians) on right, just before left bend into village.
Named after King Harold, they date from Neolithic times. The village
also has a reputed healing well, Virtuous Well, and Terret Tump, an
early Norman motte and bailey site. The church's sundial features the
stones, well and tump.

Beacon Hill   On a clear day this short detour leads to an exhilarating view of the
Black Mountains and Brecon Beacons to the west. Popular picnic spot
with excellent forest walks. Best views are from the road.

Lydart   Fine views of mountains to the west, and of Monmouth to the north,
enfolded in its circle of hills.

Raglan   A visit to Raglan Castle (8 miles/13 km) south-west on the A40) should
Castle   not be missed if time allows. Raglan stands on the site of a Norman
(detour)   keep but the present building dates from the 15th-16thC, when military
castles were developing into Tudor palaces. The detached, hexagonal,
five-storeyed tower or keep, which is surrounded by a moat, is the
most interesting part of the defences. Inside the castle, the grand
staircase, niches and fireplaces show the transition taking place. *Open
daily (but closed Sun morning in winter).*

he Cotswolds

The Cotswolds are part of a limestone belt that crosses England from Dorset to Humberside and is especially prominent between Bath and Chipping Campden. The tour begins on the gentle side of the Cotswolds, where the land rises gradually, and crosses to the steep western escarpment with its wooded combes. Note how the limestone appears everywhere – on ploughed fields, in dry-stone walls, but best of all in the vernacular architecture that gives a simple but dignified unity to the entire area. Sheep have been the other major influence on Cotswold life – and this is evident all along the route.

▄▄▄▄ ROUTE ONE: 48 miles (77 km)

Directions in sequence from: Bourton

Bourton-on-the-Water
A wealth of natural and man-made attractions in main Cotswold tourist centre. River Windrush, spanned by five graceful bridges, flows crystal-clear between shops and impressive houses. Be sure to use the car park as parking is usually difficult otherwise.

The Motor Museum, in an old mill, houses a superb display of vintage cars and related collectors' items, as well as an exhibition of vintage advertisement signs, a Father Christmas's workshop, and the Childhood Toy Collection. Upstairs, the Village Life Collection includes a re-creation of a Victorian shop. *Open weekends, Feb; daily Mar-Nov.* The Model Railway layout covers more than 400 square feet (37 sq. m); visitors can operate the trains with push-buttons. *Open daily Apr-Sept; rest of year weekends, Bank Holidays and school holidays only.*

Guiting Power
The church, down the lane from the village green, has Norman doorways, nave and priest's door. ① *At crossroads beyond the village turn left to Roel Gate for descent from Cotswold escarpment.*

G'ting – Winchcombe
Splendid view of Winchcombe and Severn vale with Malvern Hills in the distance. This road was an old salt way from Worcestershire.

Winchcombe
The King of Mercia founded an Abbey here in the 8thC and this was the 'county town' of Mercia until the Norman invasion. It retains a prosperous look and much traditional Cotswold architecture.

Elizabeth I, Anne Boleyn and Charles I all spent time in historic, and less than tranquil, Sudeley Castle. Catherine Parr (widow of Henry VIII) died here; her tomb, designed centuries later by Victorian architect Gilbert White, is in the chapel. Excellent collection of paintings and furniture. Delightful grounds with Elizabethan garden. *Open Apr-Oct.* The tourist information office *(tel. (0242) 602925),* folk history museum and Simms' Museum of Police Memorabilia are all in the Town Hall. *Open Mon-Sat, Apr-Oct.*

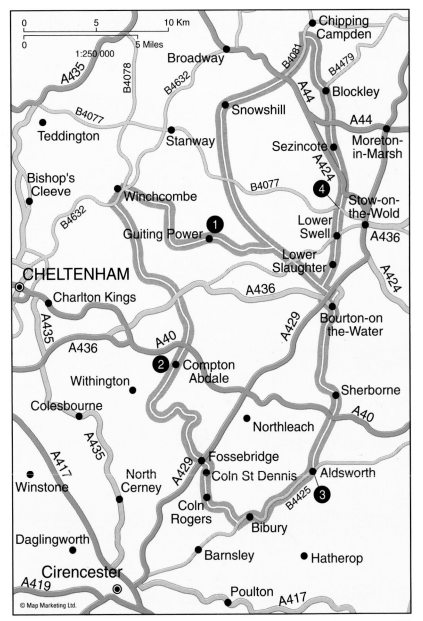

Belas Knap Neolithic burial mound 1,000 feet (304 m) above sea level. From road side, follow yellow arrows for 1 mile (1.5 km) to reach this well-preserved long barrow.

A short way along the road from Belas Knap there are fine views to the west. Note how the road follows the contour of the hill alongside Humblebee Woods.

Compton Abdale Charming village lying in a steep fold of the hills. At the crossroads note the stream tumbling into an old stone trough. St Oswald's church, high on a cliff, has a Perpendicular tower bedecked with strange gargoyles. ② *Follow signs for Roman Villa, and descend into the valley of the River Coln, which rises in hills near Sevenhampton. The route follows the river for almost 10 miles (16 km).*

Chedworth Roman Villa Well-preserved remains show how elegantly some Romans lived. There are three beautiful mosaic floors and the best surviving example of a bath suite with choice of Turkish or Swedish-style baths. The museum shows smaller finds. *Open Tues-Sun and Bank Holiday Mon, Mar-Oct; Wed-Sun, Nov and Dec; by appointment, Feb.*

Chedworth – Fossebridge *On leaving villa follow sign marked Yanworth* (good views south over Coln Valley to Chedworth Woods) *but turn right before village.* The valley soon begins to open out, the hills becoming less steep as the road approaches Fossebridge.

Fosse-bridge One of the Romans' most perfect roads, the Fosse Way, crosses the River Coln here, on its direct route from Exeter to Lincoln.

Coln St Dennis The Norman church has a marvellous central tower overlooking Coln water meadows.

Coln Rogers Named after Roger of Gloucester who gave 'Colne in the Hills' to the monks of Gloucester in 1150. Fine church with Saxon nave and chancel.

Bibury One of the prettiest Cotswold villages, much visited for its row of picture-postcard stone cottages where 17thC woollen weavers lived, drying their cloth beside the Coln. Village houses and 'wool church' display a wealth of architectural detail. Parking space is short in summer.

The Trout Farm, which has 40 rearing ponds covering eight acres, supplies a quarter of a million trout to our fishing waters annually. Visitors may feed and purchase fish. *Open daily.* In a 17thC corn mill, the Arlington Mill Museum has a countryside collection; *open daily Easter-Oct.*

③ *At Aldsworth, turn left into village, then immediately right, signposted Bourton-on-the-Water.*

Sherborne   The 4,000-acre Sherborne estate is situated on the River Windrush. The land belonged to the Dutton family from 1551 to 1982, when it was bequeathed to the National Trust. The most famous member of the family was 'Crump' Dutton, renowned locally for being a gambler and a hunchback.

- *Guiting Power; 'Guiting' derives from the Old English, 'God's forest'.*

● *Typical Cotswold landscape and architecture – the village of Naunton.*

Sherborne – Bourton   Views across the Windrush valley to Little Rissington's disused airfield, now a medical centre for US forces.

Lower Slaughter   This classic Cotswold village beside the River Eye (babbling to the Windrush under clapper bridges) is almost too good to be true; inhabitants sitting in the sun outside their houses look like actors on a film set. The name comes from 'sloe-tree' which abounds locally. *Turn right, then left, then right again through village, then follow signpost to Lower Swell.*

◼ ROUTE TWO: 32 miles (51 km)

Directions in sequence from: Bourton

Lower Swell   Just beyond the village, there are views across the valley to Stow-on-the-Wold, once renowned for its sheep fairs.

④ *At junction with B4077 turn left (signposted Tewkesbury), then right (signposted Longborough). At T-junction, turn right then immediately left (signposted Stow). At next T-junction turn left, then take turning to right (signposted Sezincote) beyond pub.*

Sezincote   An astonishing mansion (remodelled 1805) combining Hindu and Muslim architecture, with equally impressive gardens a mix of classic English landscape design and concepts brought back from India. *Open afternoons only: house, Thurs, Fri, May-July, Sept; garden, Thurs, Fri, Bank Holiday Mon, Jan-Nov.*

Chipping Campden
The English historian G. M. Trevelyan called the High Street 'the most beautiful village street in England'. Campden's former wealth – it was the centre of the wool trade from the 13thC to the 17thC – can be seen in its splendid houses and inns, but most of all in its church.

The Cotswold Games were held annually on nearby Dover's Hill from 1612 to 1852 – a sort of English Olympics, famous for sports such as shin-kicking. The Games, revived in 1963, take place on the first Friday after the Spring Bank Holiday.

The Badger Inn serves excellent home-cooked food.

Snowshill Manor
An eccentric collector of model ships and telescopes, bicycles and sedan chairs, Samurai armour and old farm implements, toys and clocks and much more, left his collection and this charming manor house to the National Trust. His own quarters, in a converted outhouse, underline his unusual way of life. *Open Wed-Sun and Bank Holiday Mon, May-Sept; Sat, Sun and Bank Holiday Mon, Apr and Oct.*

Snowshill
Soon after leaving the village the route crosses exposed, treeless uplands, illustrating why the Cotswolds are sometimes described as 'bleak'.

Cotswold Farm Park
The most complete collection of rare British farm animals, including Old Gloucester cattle (their milk is used to make Double Gloucester cheese). *Open late Mar to Sept.*

The Upper Wye

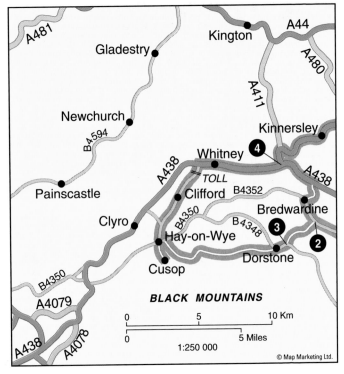

Whitney ④

TOLL

Kinnersley

A438

Bredwardine

③

②

Dorstone

BLACK MOUNTAINS

| 0 | | 5 | | 10 Km |

| 0 | | | 5 Miles |

1:250 000

© Map Marketing Ltd.

Cascading down from its source in mid-Wales, the River Wye loops eastwards into England along a valley that quickly tames it into huge meanders – a transformation that is one of the main pleasures of this tour.

Starting in Hereford, the route follows the Wye through lush water-meadows surrounded by wooded hills, before climbing to wind-swept heights reached along steep and narrow (but well-maintained) roads. Along the way there are remarkably unspoiled half-timbered villages, several Norman churches and a small town with an outsize reputation for second-hand bookshops.

ROUTE: 59 miles (95 km)

Directions in sequence from: Hereford

Hereford   Although the city dates back to Saxon times, there was much rebuilding in the 18thC. However, several buildings have survived from earlier

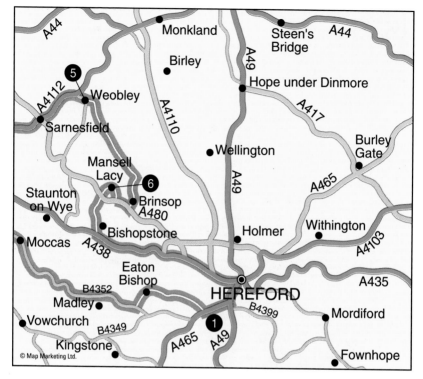

© Map Marketing Ltd.

days, notably the cathedral with its splendid Norman nave (and rare, medieval map of the world); the half-timbered, 17thC Old House in High Town; and 14thC All Saints' church, easily recognized by its crooked spire. *Tourist information: tel. (0432) 268430.*

① *Leave Hereford on A465 (signposted to Abergavenny). After about 2 miles (3 km) turn right, signposted Belmont Abbey.*

Belmont Abbey
(Not on map.) The Roman Catholic church (formerly a cathedral) was built in 1850. Worth going inside to see the excellent Victorian architecture. *Continue along Ruckall Rd., which becomes a pretty undulating lane.*

Eaton Bishop
The Norman church is well worth a visit for its fine, 14thC stained glass windows, chiefly browns, yellows and greens. *Continue along the deep-set lane. At T-junction turn right on to B4352.*

Madley
Down a lane to the left of the straggling main street, the exceptionally

123

● *Hereford landscape; distant Brecon Beacons.*

large church (built to accommodate travelling pilgrims) has what is claimed to be the second largest font in England.

Pub
(Madley)

The impressive python skin tacked to a ceiling beam in the lounge of the Red Lion, was brought back from Africa by one of the pub's customers.

Moccas

A 6thC Celtic saint established a monastery here after seeing a white sow with piglets (an old religious sign of good fortune); hence the village name, which is Welsh for 'pig's marshy meadow'. The monastery has gone but the small Norman church is worth seeing.

Turn right to Moccas Court, a Georgian mansion designed by Adam and set in a park laid out by Capability Brown. The main feature of the house is a circular room that has never had a fire lit in it for fear of damaging the 200-year-old French wallpaper. *Open Sun afternoons only, Apr-Sept.*

Bred-wardine

Francis Kilvert, the famous Victorian diarist, was vicar here from 1877 until his death two years later. (He died from peritonitis ten days after returning from honeymoon.) His grave in the churchyard is identified by its white marble cross, to the left of the giant yew under which the Kilvert Society have placed a seat. Monuments inside the church include one to a knight killed defending Henry V at Agincourt. Just past the church, there are glorious views from the 18thC brick bridge.

② Anyone wishing to shorten the tour should cross the bridge and continue to junction with A438. One mile (1.5 km) beyond Letton's Norman church (with its 800-year-old iron door-hinges) turn right on to A4111 and right again almost immediately on to A4112 (signposted to Leominster). Continue to Kinnersley (see below).

For the complete tour, return towards Moccas on B4352 for ½ mile (0.8 km), then take turning to right, signposted to Dorstone, along a narrow, steep lane (1:4, but with passing places). Turn right for short detour to Arthur's Stone.

Arthur's Stone

(Not on map.) This Bronze Age burial chamber (reached along a rather bumpy lane) consists of a huge slab of sandstone some 20 feet (6 m) long and nearly as wide, perched on stone uprights. Superb views over the Wye Valley nearly 1,000 feet (304 m) below.

Dorstone

Approached down a steep hill (again 1:4) the village retains its basic Norman layout: the castle (now in ruins), inn and church all stand around the triangular green (once the market-place).

Dorstone stands at the head of the lovely Golden Valley, which lies in the shadow of the Black Mountains of Wales. Anyone planning a separate expedition here should take a look at the interesting Norman churches at Peterchurch and Abbey Dore. In St Faith's church, Dorstone (much restored in Victorian times) an ancient tomb recess is thought to commemorate Richard de Briton, one of the four knights who murdered Thomas à Becket in Canterbury Cathedral (1170) and who lived here after serving 15 years in exile in Palestine.

③ To return to the Wye Valley, go past the church, then bear left on to unclassified road (signposted to Mynydd Brith) before dropping to Cusop (short detour to left).

Cusop
(detour)

The yew trees in the churchyard are reputed to be those mentioned in the Domesday Book. Nearby, the Martyr's Grave commemorates a

Methodist preacher who was stoned to death by a mob he was trying
to convert.

Hay-on-Wye On the border of England and Wales, this pleasant market town had
been burned down at least five times by the Middle Ages. The ruined
Norman castle was replaced by an Elizabethan mansion, now owned by
the man whose second-hand bookshops brought fame to the town; Hay
is still a Mecca for book lovers.

Two fine stone buildings grace the end of Market St. – the Cheese
Market (two storeys) and the single storey Butter Market. At the foot of
the steep slope below them is a rather splendid Victorian clock tower.

The town has several pubs and hotels including the Swan and the
Three Tuns (which is on the B4350).

Clifford The castle was sacked by Owen Glendower in 1402. The ruins tower
150 feet (46 m) above the Wye and are best approached along a
footpath leading off to the left at the point where the castle comes into
view. In the village, a steep road to the right leads to the parish church
which contains a medieval wooden effigy of a priest.

Whitney Toll Bridge The bridge has crossed the Wye on giant wooden pillars since the
1790s. Strangely, an Act of Parliament that freed it from taxes has never
been revoked. Toll charges are very low.

Whitney The windows of the Boat Inn jut out almost over the river. ④ *At
T-junction in Willersley, turn left on to A4111, then right on to A4112.*

Kinnersley St James's church, with its massive tower and interesting interior, fronts
the Elizabethan castle *(not open to public)*.

Sarnesfield In the churchyard (on a left-hand bend) the tomb of Herefordshire's
famous builder of black-and-white houses, John Abel, is engraved with
the epitaph he wrote for himself. Weathering has made it hard to read,
but there is a transcript inside the church.

Weobley Perhaps the greatest concentration of half-timbered houses and inns in
Herefordshire. A pocket borough until 1832, Weobley was famous for
its ale and its witches, but is now an opulent backwater. In 1943 fire
destroyed many buildings, providing surprisingly open views at the old
borough's centre.

The church, with its tall, 14thC steeple, contains a life-size statue in
white marble to Col. John Birch, promoted from travelling trader to
cavalry commander by Cromwell. (However, after the Civil War, Birch
became a Royalist.)

There is a good choice of old pubs, including the Red Lion, the Royal
Oak and The Throne (formerly The Unicorn), where Charles I stayed in

⑤ *At the top of the central square, turn left at The Salutation and then sharp right on to minor road signposted to Wormsley.*

Weobley –
Brinsop

The road climbs out of the lush valley towards the tree-clad summits of a chain of hills overlooking the Wye. From the golf course there are splendid views to the left. *Go over the crest of the Ravens' Causeway and turn right at junction, to Brinsop.*

Brinsop

The tiny church spans the centuries, from a Norman tympanum of St George and the dragon to modern stained glass in memory of the poet Wordsworth, whose family had connections hereabouts.

Mansell
Lacy

Worth making the short detour along the minor road to the right to see the village's spirited half-timbering, especially the former shop and post office which has a dovecot in the gable. ⑥ *Follow lane back to A480. At crossroads go straight ahead to Bishopstone.*

Bishop-
stone
(detour)

A short detour to the left at the crossroads leads to Kenchester, where archaeologists are still finding remains of the Roman fortress-tower known as Magnis. *Return to crossroads.*

Bridge
Sollers

The Weir, a National Trust garden on the right just beyond the village, is particularly splendid in spring. There are magnificent views up-river. *Open Wed-Sun mid-Feb-end Oct; Bank Hol Mon, 11-6.*

The Malverns

The sharp ridge of the Malvern Hills cuts up from the Severn plain, separating the flat brown soil of Worcestershire from the rolling red sandstone of Herefordshire. Rainwater which collects in the granite fissures and issues from the hillside is so pure that patients came from far and wide to take the 'cure'.

Today, the hills themselves are the main attraction, and this tour is designed to show their beauty and grandeur from all angles. Route One goes round them in a circle, while Route Two climbs close to the Worcestershire Beacon.

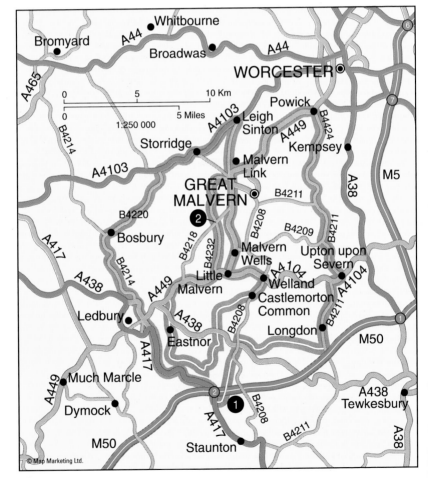

▬▬▬ ROUTE ONE: 50 miles (80 km)

Directions in sequence from: Great Malvern

Great Malvern

Hillside town, famous for the purity of its spring water. Developed as a spa in Victorian times, it now makes its living from high technology, education (Malvern College public school lies to the south of the town), and special products such as the Morgan sports car. *Tourist information: tel. (0684) 892289.*

Priory church, founded in 1085, still has its original Norman arches, although most of the structure is 15thC Perpendicular. A beautiful building, like a small cathedral, it is softly lit by daylight filtered through rare and lovely medieval stained glass.

Other sights include Abbey Gateway (in town centre), originally the gatehouse of the Benedictine Priory and now the home of the Malvern Museum (water-cure exhibits are most entertaining), *open Mar-Oct; closed Wed*; the Festival Theatre (formerly the Assembly Rooms), which opened in 1885 and where, during the Malvern festivals of 1929-39, Shaw was playwright-in-residence; and the handsome, listed railway station (1860). Beautifully restored in 1988 after a fire, it is worth a visit for its painted, cast-iron column capitals, each one a unique arrangement of leaves and fruit.

Leigh Sinton

This is a hops-and-fruit village. Stop at Norbury's farm shop for apples.

Storridge

On the way to this village astride the low pass through the foothills, look left for an impressive view of the northern end of the Malvern Hills.

Birchwood Lodge
(detour)

A 1-mile (1.5-km) detour along a narrow lane to the right *(signposted Birchwood)* leads to Sir Edward Elgar's summer cottage, Birchwood Lodge, now a farmhouse. *No admittance*, but the cottage (on right) is visible from the lane.

Stony Cross – Bosbury

B4220 goes through red-soiled farmlands and wire-railed hop-yards. From the road there are glimpses of the western slopes of the Malverns.

Bosbury

Pretty village deep in hop country. Near the church, the remains of a 13thC palace – once the country seat of the Bishops of Hereford – serve as a hop store. The mainly Norman church has a 15thC screen with fine fan tracery and interesting tombs. The massive, unbuttressed, separate tower, was a fortified refuge during border raids by the marauding Welsh.

Pub
(Bosbury)

The Bell Inn, a well-kept, timber-framed pub among timber-framed houses, serves good meals.

● *The footpath running from end-to-end of the Malvern Hills makes an easy 9-mile (14.5-km) walk. It offers some spectacular views, and, in the right conditions, almost incredible sightings; for example, the Mendips (south) and the Wrekin (north).*

Ledbury   Old market town with many architectural styles along both sides of the wide main street. The Market House, c.1655, is a fine example of chevron timber-framing. John Masefield, Poet Laureate from 1930 to 1967, was born in Ledbury, at Knapp House.

The parish church of St Michael and All Angels has a 13thC detached tower surmounted by an 18thC spire. The parents of Elizabeth Barrett Browning are buried here and she grew up at nearby Hope End. Church Lane is a notable medieval street, often used as a film location – even the loos are listed. Along the narrow, cobbled roadway, the Old

Grammar School (1480-1520) is now a heritage centre. Vari
show the evolution of timber-frame construction.

Hotel
(Ledbury)
The Feathers Hotel, a 16thC coaching inn, is a quiet place for a drink or afternoon tea in oak-beamed ambience.

① *Turn left along minor road signposted 'The Malverns'. At junction with A438 turn right, following signs to the Waterfowl Sanctuary.*

Upton-upon-Severn
Former port, now a residential town and pleasure-boat haven. There are good riverside walks. The heritage centre within the old lantern-topped church tower, known as the Pepperpot, has local history displays. Across the road, Cromwells sells luxury chocolates hand-made on the premises.

Pub
(Upton-upon-Severn)
At The Anchor Inn (1601), Cavalier bridge-defenders sought boozy comfort at the expense of duty and allowed Cromwell's men to surprise them. Ale (called Jolly Roger) is still brewed round the back.

Upton – Powick
Five miles (8 km) from Upton, pause for a stroll across the undulating common land known as the Old Hills (on left of road). From here there are fine views of the whole Malvern range and tree-tufted May Hill.

Powick
The old bridge over the River Teme (alongside the modern bridge carrying the A449) was the site of the first skirmish of the Civil Wars in 1642. The last battle of the wars (1651) was fought on the nearby river meadows. At the base of the tower of St Peter's church there are shot marks made by Cromwell's guns in 1651.

Powick – Gt. Malvern
While travelling along the A449, glance at the skies above the hills; sometimes the cloud effects are remarkable.

WORCESTER
A city that merits at least half a day to itself. Priority should be given to the cathedral, with its fine monuments, crypt and cloisters. Walk down the High St., past the eye-catching 18thC Guildhall (which houses the tourist office) to the Royal Worcester Porcelain Works (Severn St.) for factory tours, showroom, seconds shop, and museum. Visit the historic Commandery for a permanent exhibition on the Civil Wars. *Tourist information: tel. (0905) 723471.*

● *Malvern's Belle View Terrace, from the Priory Tower.*

ROUTE TWO: 27 miles (43 km)

Directions in sequence from: Great Malvern

Malvern Wells
As the original centre of the Malvern water cure, the village began to be developed as a resort during the 18thC. Elgar lived at 86 Wells Road.
For the Holy Well take turning to right off A449 (Holy Well Rd.). Water from this spring has been bottled for sale since 1622. The building around the fountain, where the public may drink, is in cottage *orne* style, 1843. *Continue along minor road which rejoins A449.*

Little Malvern
All that remains of the Benedictine priory established here in the 12thC, is the church and the guest hall, now part of Little Malvern Court. *Open Wed and Thurs afternoons, mid-Apr to mid-July.*
Sir Edward Elgar (1857-1934) is buried in the churchyard of St Wulstan's Roman Catholic church.

Castle-morton Common
Fine mid-range view of the hills. *After crossing common on minor road which leads towards the hills, bear left along the foot of the hill. Cross A438, then take first turning to right.*

White-leaved Oak
(Not on map.) Pretty, isolated hamlet at the summit of this minor pass through the hills. *Continue for 2 miles (3 km), then turn right.*

Eastnor
Early 19thC crenellated castle containing paintings, tapestries, carved furniture and armour. *Open Sun and Bank Holiday Mon, Easter to late Sept; Sun-Fri, Aug.*

British Camp
Also known as the Herefordshire Beacon, this superb example of an Iron Age hill fort has earthwork ramparts that are visible for miles. The

path to the summit (1,114 feet/340 m) starts near the large car park alongside A449.

Jubilee Drive B4232, a lovely contour road along the western face of the hills, was constructed in 1887; fine views.

Worcester-shire Beacon On a clear day the view from the summit (1,395 feet/425 m) extends across at least 12 counties. There are paths to the top from the car parks along the B4232.

② *Return to Great Malvern either by the short route through Wyche Cutting or along the road through West Malvern and North Malvern.*

Constable Country

The Vale of Dedham, immortalized by the artist John Constable (1776-1837), epitomizes the ideal English landscape in many people's minds. Ironically, modern farming methods have altered the look of East Anglia, but the Vale is still lovely, and many of the places Constable painted can still be recognized.

Elsewhere on this tour, the upland landscape of central Suffolk can sometimes seem like one vast wheatfield with occasional interruptions. However, these 'interruptions' include Kersey, Long Melford and Lavenham: outstanding survivals from the Middle Ages.

ROUTE: 73 miles (117 km)

Directions in sequence from: Hadleigh

Hadleigh
Delightful old market town, notable for its long High Street of low, leaning buildings. Church St. (just off High St.) has a 15thC town hall (formerly the Cloth Hall), 14thC church and the remains of a deanery in close proximity.

① At deflected junction on the new Hadleigh bypass take the Lavenham road (A1141). Pass mill on right, then take left turning to Kersey (unsignposted).

Kersey
Walk down the steep village street to the watersplash early in the morning, and it may seem that the medieval occupants of the old houses will rise and throw open their casements. Recent renovation has given some of the houses a 'film set' quality, but the village is justifiably famous.

Monks Eleigh
② Turn left and left again for Monks Eleigh, where a triangular, cottage-lined green rises, exactly as it should do, to the church. If the scene seems familiar, this is because it was once used on railway posters, although the railway *(now closed)* never came nearer than Lavenham.

Lavenham
Arguably the most perfect and unforgettable township of timber-framed buildings left in England. The Guildhall, dominating the market-place, dates from 1529. Today it houses a museum which includes a useful exhibition on the medieval cloth trade. *Open daily, late Mar-end Oct. Closed Good Fri.* The church (15th-16thC) is magnificent from the outside, with a massive, unfinished tower. Inside, the proportions are not quite as good as at the remarkable churches of Long Melford or Stoke-by-Nayland (see below).

The Old Tea Shop, opposite the church, does a traditional English tea with home-made cakes. Rather more sophisticated cake-making may be enjoyed at the Bank House Tea Shop, 95 High St.

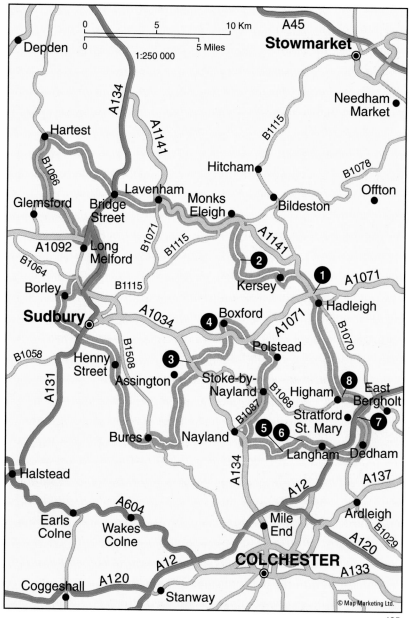

Bridge Street   Before reaching the main road note the splendid moated Hall to the left. *Go over A134, turning right then immediately left; then right to Shimpling.*

Hartest   In East Anglian terms, the road leading down into this pretty village is positively Alpine. Hartest has grown up around a large green; church and pub stand together at the southern end.

Long Melford   The High Street running southwards from the splendid green is broad and very long indeed. To park, turn left at The Black Lion pub.

The fine Perpendicular church has the spaciousness and height of a small cathedral, and the Lady Chapel, with its separate entrance, is an unusual and lovely additional feature.

Melford Hall is a mellow, mid-16thC red-brick house with distinctive pepper-pot turrets, massive yews in the garden and an octagonal gazebo. *Open afternoons, Sat, Sun and Bank Hol Mon, end Mar-end Apr; Wed, Thurs, Sat, Sun, May-Sept; Sat, Sun, Oct.* More romantic than its neighbour, moated Kentwell Hall (*c.*1564) is approached along a glorious avenue of lime trees. It is gradually being restored to something of its former splendour. *Open afternoons only, Wed, Thurs and Sun, early Apr to late June; Wed-Sun, late July to Sept; also open Bank Holidays.* The Crown Inn serves Adnams excellent Southwold bitter.

Borley   Notorious Borley Rectory, 'the most haunted house in England', was built in 1863 and destroyed by fire in 1939. Both the builder and his son died in the Blue Room; messages appeared on walls, disembodied voices were heard, bells were rung and, since the fire, a ghostly nun is said to have appeared on the site and in the churchyard. All in all, an ideal place for a picnic.

Beyond Borley, sweeping, sky-filled views of East Anglia at its best can be seen from the road.

Sudbury *(detour)*   A short detour leads to this old silk-weaving town, with its three churches (St Peter's is the best) and splendid Corn Exchange (1841) in the south-eastern corner of the market-place. The house where Thomas Gainsborough was born (46 Gainsborough St.) is now, appropriately, an art gallery. *Open Tues-Sat; afternoons, Sun and Bank Holiday Mon.*

Henny Street   Tiny village with an unpretentious little pub, The Henny Swan, right next to the river.

③ *Look out for the first unsignposted, single-track road to the right off A134.*

Boxford   A village of great charm. Most of the old timber-framed houses are still

● *Watermill on the Essex-Suffolk border: mills like this provided the important service of fulling to cloth towns such as Dedham: newly woven material was soaked in water, then beaten to give it density and strength.*

plastered over in the traditional Suffolk manner. The River Box, which gives the village its name, runs through the centre.

St Mary's church has an imposing, crumbling, 15thC stone porch on the south side, and a rare 14thC wooden porch to the north. The decorated, lead-capped spirelet on the tower is unusual, and the interior of the church is elegant, airy and plain. ④ *Return to the main road. Turn left, then take first turning to the right, signposted to Polstead.*

Polstead From the duckpond, a pretty, steep little street of thatched and tiled cottages rises to a triangular green. St Mary's church has Norman nave arcades built of brick which give the interior of the church an individual appearance. From the churchyard there is a good view of Stoke-by-Nayland's magnificent church tower. In 1827, the notorious murder of Maria Marten took place in a red barn (long since demolished) not far from St Mary's.

Stoke-by-Nayland The church is one of the most memorable and ethereally lovely Perpendicular churches in East Anglia. Constable often painted it – not surprisingly, since its tall tower of faded pink brick is strikingly prominent from the valley floor. Inside, the clerestory seems to float on piers of light golden stone and the tall, narrow tower arch suggests an entry to Heaven better than many a sermon. Note also the beautifully carved oak doors in the porch.

Nayland *At the 'Give Way' sign turn left to enter the square.* This is another highly individual little cloth-making township of plastered and openly half-timbered houses, some with oversailing upper storeys. Walk up Fen St. for a delightful juxtaposition of cottages and stream, with a plank footbridge to each front door. The church has a (not very good) painting of Christ by Constable.

(5) *Ignore the sign to Boxted School and take the next turning on the left signposted to Higham. After 2 miles (3 km) take turning right (before bridge), signposted to Boxted Cross, then follow signs for Langham.* (6) *Immediately after a white building (water works) turn left along a black-surfaced, unsignposted road. Turn right at T-junction after ¼ mile (0.5 km), then at next junction, fork left. At second T-junction turn right.*

Langham A private drive which is also a public footpath leads to the church and Church Farm, the subjects of Constable's painting *The Glebe Farm*. Walk past the farm and look back to see it from the artist's view point.

Dedham The near-perfect centre has changed only superficially since Constable's time, and possesses another grand (if rather austere) Perpendicular church, whose tower is a feature of many of the artist's paintings. In *The Cornfield* he moved it about ¾ mile (1 km) to the east and reduced it in size in order to improve his composition. The Vale of Dedham was referred to as 'Constable Country' not only within his lifetime, but within his hearing, as he was travelling by coach to London. *Tourist information: tel. (0206) 323447.*

Flatford Mill can be reached by car (see below) or on foot (½-hour walk) across the water meadows – the very stuff of Constable's landscapes. The footpath begins at the eastern end of the village street.

The Marlborough Head inn, at the crossroads in the centre of the village, serves first-rate bar food. (7) *Turn left at the church* (note its

bold flint and stone interior) *to join the A12 (follow Ipswich signposts).
After about ¾ mile (1 km) turn right.*

**East
Bergholt**

This is the village where Constable was born and lived. Of the
surrounding countryside he said: 'These scenes made me a painter.' The
church has a tower that was never completed and its bells hang upside
down in a timber frame in the churchyard.

**Flatford
Mill**
(detour)

*Follow the one-way system to the car park. From here there is a short
walk to the waterside.* Willy Lott's cottage is much as it appears in *The
Haywain*, but beyond it the fields have been transformed into a gigantic
gravel quarry. The mill is now a field centre, and is not open to the
public. For a pleasant saunter along the old tow path, cross the
footbridge next to the shop and tea room. *Closed, Mon, Tues.*

*Higham –
Hadleigh*

⑧ *At Higham take unsignposted turning to right before reaching centre
of village. (As the road goes down the hill, note the delightful, tiny oval
cottage on the left.) After about 2 miles (3 km) take turning left
signposted to Shelley, then follow signposts back to Hadleigh.*

The Shropshire Highlands

South-west Shropshire is a sparsely populated haven dominated by high hills and moorland ridges, but also includes gentle valleys, dreaming villages and many castles built by Marcher lords to hold back the Welsh. Although it is one of the highlights of the tour, the road across the Long Mynd should not be attempted in poor weather, and an alternative route has been suggested. Conversely, those who have time to spare on a clear day should drive a few miles east from Ludlow along the A4117 for stupendous views into Wales.

▬▬▬▬ ROUTE: 75 miles (121 km)

Directions in sequence from: Ludlow

Ludlow
Eight centuries of building styles line narrow medieval streets within the town walls. The centre is a jackdaw's nest of hidden treasures well explained in local guidebooks. Plenty of small shops and locally produced food, ranging from crusty bread and cakes to venison, pheasant and other game, which are sometimes on the menus of the town's many restaurants and pubs. *Tourist information: tel. (0584) 875053.*

The Norman castle, where Prince Arthur – Henry VIII's elder brother – died on honeymoon with Catherine of Aragon, became an Elizabethan palace known as 'the Windsor of the West'. *Open daily and Bank Hol weekends, Feb-Nov.* Instruments of torture found in the castle are on show in Ludlow museum, in Castle Street. *Open Easter-Sept.* St Lawrence's, the largest parish church in Shropshire, has a tall tower (136 feet/41 m), stained glass, masterly woodcarving and Tudor tombs. **①** *Follow Shrewsbury signposts along one-way traffic system. One mile (1.5 km) north of the town join A49 and continue to Bromfield.*

Bromfield
To reach St Mary's, a former Benedictine priory, *turn on to A4113 for a few yards, then turn left again.* Park by half-timbered priory gate house. Inside the church there is a naïve folk-art chancel ceiling of angels and clouds. *Return to A49.*

Stokesay Castle
A fortified manor house built by a wealthy Ludlow wool merchant in the 13thC, Stokesay is possibly the best-preserved example of its kind in England. In Tudor times the half-timbered gatehouse was added. *Open Wed-Sun, Mar-Oct; weekends, Nov.*

Cheney Longville *(detour)*
② *Go through Craven Arms then take second turning on left for detour to Cheney Longville,* a village deemed a conservation area because of its medieval street layout. *Return to A49. Turn left and then right almost immediately under a railway bridge.*

Wistanstow
This Saxon village on the old Roman road has a comfortable inn, The

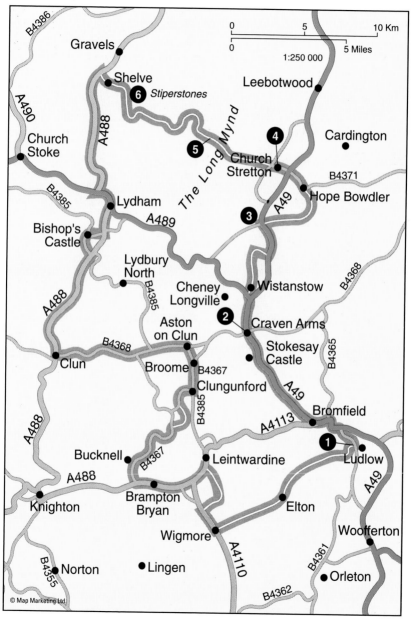

● *Stokesay Castle, fortified manor house, one of the earliest of its kind in Britain.*

Plough, which has its own brewery. A short distance further on, Holy Trinity church dates partly from the 12thC. *Continue along the straight road that later turns abruptly back to join the A49.*

Wistanstow – The view straight ahead is dominated by the southern end of heavily
Church wooded Wenlock Edge. The stone tower topping it is Flounders' Folly,
Stretton built in the 19thC to mark the boundaries of four estates. *At junction with A49 turn left. After about 1 mile (1.5 km) turn right at signpost to Acton Scott.*
  ③ *Continue through Acton Scott. After about 1 mile (1.5 km) take first turning to left (unsignposted). At T-junction turn left to Hope Bowdler and Church Stretton.*

Church This small spa town, built by the Victorians on the site of a much older
Stretton settlement, has a Norman church, sparkling air, pure water and plenty of opportunities for hill-walking. Cardingmill Valley (clearly signposted from crossroads at town centre) is a National Trust property and one of the best places for walks.

④ *At central crossroads take Burway road (1:5 gradient and cattle grid) to the steep uplands of the Long Mynd. If weather is doubtful, ignore this part of the tour and head south through Little Stretton; turn right at A49 and again at A489 and drive up the Onny valley (wonderful view of the Long Mynd to the right) to Bishop's Castle (see below).*

The Long Mynd
Vast National Trust-owned, ancient plateau (1,695 feet/518 m) where grouse whirr and sheep roam free through heather and whinberry bushes. The single-track road has plenty of passing places. Pause at car park on left for magnificent views. ⑤ *Where road divides, fork right to Ratlinghope. Descend to valley and fork right to Bridges. Just beyond the Horseshoes pub turn right then left (an obviously more important road), then almost immediately turn sharp right (signposted to Squilver) over cattle grid.*

Stiper-stones
Third highest hill in Shropshire (1,732 feet/528 m), with its craggy crest resembling the back of a prehistoric monster. The road goes across desolate moorland with enormous views. From the car park on right a path leads to the Devil's Chair, where Old Nick is supposed to sit exulting during thunderstorms.
⑥ *Beyond the summit, take right turning signposted to Shelve. Go past Stiperstones Field Centre, then turn right on to straight road signposted to Gravels and Minsterley. After ½ mile (0.8 km) turn left to Shelve. At T-junction turn left on to A488.*

Bishop's Castle
All that remains of the Norman castle (built by a Bishop of Hereford) are some stones in the car park of the Castle Hotel. Next to the town hall, the half-timbered 16thC House on Crutches has a projecting upper storey supported on two stout wooden posts. The Three Tuns has been brewing its own beer for centuries.

Bury Ditches
From the car park and picnic area to the left of the road, paths lead up the hill to the enormous Iron Age fort.

Clun
Go downhill (past land leading to the ruined 12thC castle) into the tiny square where the museum contains an outstanding collection of flint tools and weapons. *Open Tues and Sat afternoons and Bank Holidays, Easter-Oct.*
Sir Walter Scott stayed at The Buffalo Inn while writing *The Betrothed.* The Sun serves real ale and bar meals.

Aston on Clun
On the left, the tall tree decked with flags (or their remains) is the Arbor Tree, decorated every 29 May since 1786 to celebrate the wedding of the local squire. The Kangaroo Inn was named soon after Captain Cook discovered Australia. Note the unusual circular house next door.

● *Carding Mill Valley, near Long Mynd.*

Broome   The pub's name – The Engine and Tender – hints at the hamlet's origin; it grew up around the railway station when the line was constructed between Craven Arms and Swansea.

Clungun-ford   One of the four villages (the other three are Clunton, Clunbury and Clun) described by A. E. Housman in *A Shropshire Lad* as 'the quietest places under the sun'. The churchyard contains an excavated Bronze Age barrow. *Continue on B4367 (take care on bends). At point where road bends to right, go straight ahead on minor road to Beckjay.*

Beckjay   *(Not on map.)* The thatched cottage dates from 1296.

Bucknell   Looming over the village to the south-east is Coxall Knoll, reputedly the site of the final battle between the British chief Caratacus and the Romans. *Go over Lingen bridge and turn left on to A4113.*

Brampton Bryan   Scene of a Civil War siege, when Lady Brilliana Harley defended the castle while her husband was away serving Parliament. As wealthy Earls of Oxford, the family later gave their names to London's Oxford St. and Harley St. The castle remains were incorporated into the Hall and are best viewed from the grounds of the church.

Leint-wardine   The Roman town of Bravonium. The chancel of St Mary Magdalene's church is noticeably higher than the nave because part of an old Roman wall lies beneath it. The Lion, at the bottom of the long main street, is a famous fishing inn.

Leintwardine – Wigmore   The line of the river bridge points southwards to a narrow Roman road. One mile (1.5 km) along it is half-timbered Paytoe Hall *(not open to the public)*. The remains of Wigmore Abbey, with its handsome gate house, can be seen ½ mile (0.8 km) further on.

Wigmore   The remains of the 12th-14thC castle *(not open to the public)* can be seen from the approach road. The village itself, though peaceful now, was vibrant in medieval times when royalty came to visit.
   Opposite the church, on the other side of A4110, an unclassified and unsignposted road leads past The Compasses inn and through the heart of Mortimer Forest.

Mortimer Forest   *(Not on map.)* The road weaves past Norman churches at Leinthall Starkes, Elton and Aston. On the right after a long climb are car parks with access to paths. The road rolls over Maryknoll and down through conifers, with an exhibition centre and forest trail marked on the right.

Whitcliffe   *(Not on map.)* The view from a small lay-by on the left sums up Shropshire hill country. Below lies Ludlow in its fertile plain. To the left are the Stretton Hills; the wooded slopes to their right are outliers of Wenlock Edge; while the county's highest hills, the Clees, can be seen straight ahead.

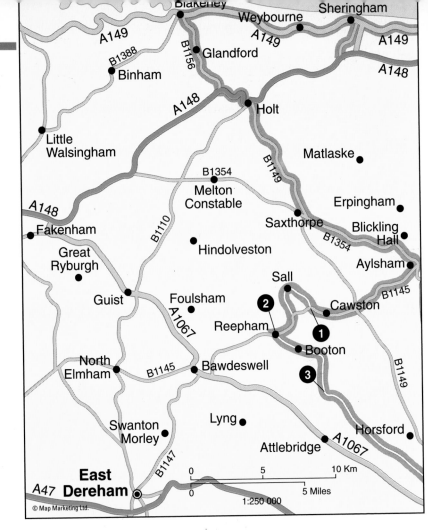

Norwich and the Norfolk Coast

At least three subtly different types of landscape are explored on this tour. To the north-west of Norwich, the farmlands are open and sweeping or enclosed by hedges and woodlands. South-east of the city, the Yare and Bure rivers wind through flat marshland which blends almost imperceptibly into the Norfolk Broads, one of the most popular sailing areas in the country. Although the Broads are notoriously difficult to see from the road, you may catch glimpses of sails moving between fields.

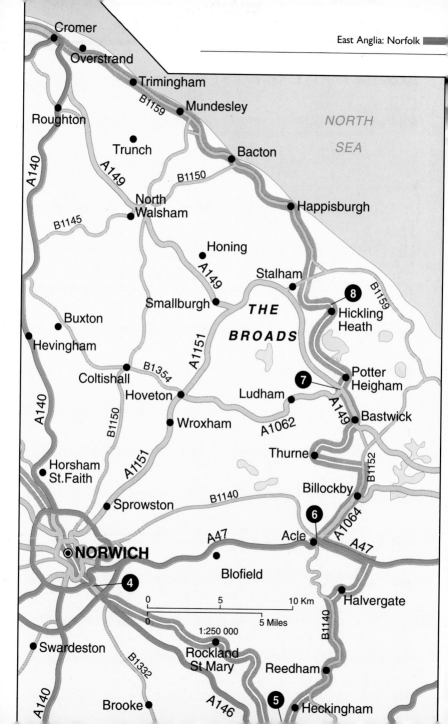

East Anglia: Norfolk

ROUTE: 112 miles (180 km)

Directions in sequence from: Aylsham

Aylsham
Pleasant little town with some good Georgian-fronted buildings in the market-place. Most of the houses are roofed with local, blue-glazed pantiles. Humphrey Repton, the great landscape gardener, is buried in the churchyard.

Cawston
On entering the village, fork left down New St., then go over crossroads. The 14th-15thC church of St Agnes possesses a glorious hammer-beam angel roof and a rood screen with painted figures in unusually good repair.

Salle
① *At a triangular junction, turn right for Salle (not signposted).* The church, almost isolated amongst the fields, is one of the grandest in Norfolk. Compared with Cawston, the nave is wider and possesses more elegant piers. The engineering of the roof is also more daring although the result is not quite so lovely.

Reepham
Dominated by its 18thC orange-brown brickwork, this small town has two churches, intriguingly joined together.

Pub
(Reepham)
The Old Brewery House, in the market-place, is a pub of great character. Bar meals are available.

② *Leave Reepham on the Norwich road, then take the second turning on left, signposted to Haveringland.*

Booton
St Michael's church, essential viewing for anyone with a taste for the more ostentatious flowerings of Gothic Revival architecture, has twin towers that have no equal, a massively tall tower arch, and bulky angels resembling ship's figureheads. St Michael's was designed by its rector, Whitwell Elwin, an amateur architect.

③ *Go through Swannington, then take left fork, signposted to Felthorpe. At crossroads go straight ahead, then turn left on to Norwich road at T-junction.*

Norwich
Go straight across first roundabout. At second roundabout follow signs for city centre. At third roundabout turn left. At fourth roundabout turn right. The cathedral and the castle are the obvious attractions, but reserve time to explore one of the largest open-air markets in Britain (the fish stalls sell samphire in season), and to stroll down medieval Elm Hill, Tombland and Bridewell Alley. *For details and directions, go to the Tourist Office (The Guildhall, Gaol Hill, by the market). Tel. (0603) 666071.*

The Cathedral is on a rather smaller scale than most, with Norman nave arcades and an exquisite 15th-16thC roof. There are enjoyable carved bosses in the cloisters, and The Close has a rich collection of domestic architecture.

The vast Norman keep of Norwich Castle houses an extensive museum and the best single collection of works by the Norwich school of painters including the paintings of John Sell Cotman (1782-1842), one of England's most original and under-estimated watercolourists. *Open Mon-Sat and Sun afternoon, closed Good Fri.* ④ *Leave Norwich on A146, signposted to Lowestoft, then turn left to Kirby Bedon.*

Rockland St Mary
Beyond the village the road descends to the level of the flat marshy meadows of the Yare valley. Look out for the ruins of a small castle on private land, to the left as you enter Claxton.

⑤ *At Hales, turn left on to B1136, then immediately turn left again at crossroads, along single-track road signposted to Heckingham. Follow signs for Reedham Ferry.*

Hecking-ham
Turn left off route to see the prettily situated church which has a thatched roof, an elaborate Norman doorway and an octagonal flint and brick tower. *Three hundred yards (274 m) beyond church, turn left along 'By-Road'.*

Reedham Ferry
Ring the bell to call the ferryman, who will take you and your vehicle across 200 yards (183 m) of water. *Daily service; there is a small charge.*

Halvergate
New 'suburbs' have encroached, but it still possible to identify the character of the old village. Just beyond the village a well-defined track leads out across Halvergate marshes, past two derelict windmills. The former marshland, stretching away eastwards to the horizon, is used for rough grazing but much of it is now threatened with conversion to arable use.

⑥ *In centre of Acle, turn right on to Caister-on-Sea road (A1064).*

Thurne
An untidy little village with two windmills and a busy mooring inlet off the River Thurne used by Broads boat people. Look out for the occasional 'quanting' boat, carrying cut reeds for thatching.

Bastwick
Turn left along A149 (no signpost), then left again after ½ mile (0.8 km). In summer, boats can be hired just beyond Potter Heigham bridge.

⑦ *Take turning to right (signposted Yarmouth) and go over main road. At T-junction turn right along road misleadingly marked 'No Through Road, Church Only'.*

● *The front at Cromer, a fashionable resort in Edwardian times, and still one of the most charming East Anglian seaside towns.*

Potter Heigham
The 14thC thatched church has a stone sculpture of a pagan god (the Old Man of the Woods) set incongruously into a niche above the porch. *Follow the unsignposted lane to the left of the church. At the T-junction turn right.*

Hickling Heath
Take right turning (signposted Hickling Broad) to the boat-yard and mooring area. Two hundred yards (183 m) further on a house-lined track leads to a cluster of old thatched boathouses, some with reed walls, and one of the best views of the water from dry land. ⑧ *Turn right (signposted Sea Palling). Just beyond the post office turn left along unsignposted lane. At T-junction, turn left.*

Happisburgh
Note the use of pebbles from the beach on houses in the village street. Perched on the cliffs, the church is a landmark for sailors.

Trimingham
Opposite the church, the side-road has a sign saying 'No Highway Beyond Barrier'. This was the old main road until the sea washed away the cliff from underneath it. One house stands perilously close to where the tarmac juts out into space.

Cromer
The oldest part of this small resort lies between the church and the sea. Do not miss narrow Jetty St. with its bow-fronts. Cromer's famous crabs can be bought direct from the fisherman at 15 New St. This is probably the most congenial of East Anglia's seaside resorts.

Sheringham Another pleasant, small resort with good bathing. Fishing boats are moored in a small inlet on the shingle strand.

Sheringham – The loveliest stretch of the Norfolk coast: rolling farmlands slope down
Blakeney to salt marshes cut off from the sea by a long shingle strand. 'Hides' are provided for bird-watchers.

Along the way, stop off at Cley next the Sea to look at the handsome windmill. In the main street, Cley Smoke House sells home-cured, oak-smoked fish.

Blakeney In spite of its popularity, this little port has retained most of its character. Park beside the quay, then walk up the delightful High St. A footpath which begins to the east of the quay goes across the salt marshes along the top of a dyke.

Glandford From the main street, a road marked 'Unsuitable for Motors' leads to an attractive ford with a footbridge over the river, here adapted into a mill race.

Holt Tidy town rebuilt after a fire in 1708.

Blickling The first view of this splendid Jacobean house at the end of its drive is
Hall breathtaking, and the interior – particularly the elaborate plasterwork ceiling in the Long Gallery – does not disappoint. *Open Tues, Wed, Fri-Sun and Bank Holiday Mon, Apr-Oct; afternoons only; closed Good Fri.*

Blickling The Buckinghamshire Arms Hotel serves excellent meals; *restaurant open evenings and Sun lunch only.* Uses fresh local produce.

The White Peak

The Peak District National Park is divided into two regions: the Dark Peak to the north and the White Peak, a limestone plateau intersected by deep gorges and narrow dales, bounded on the western side by the long line of the Gritstone Edge.

Apart from offering some of the best scenery in Britain, the White Peak has old mills, ancient stone circles and stately homes. (Chatsworth, the 'Palace of the Peak', lies just off the route to the north-east of Haddon Hall, and deserves at least half a day to itself.) Visitor numbers are high, yet there is still an air of timelessness.

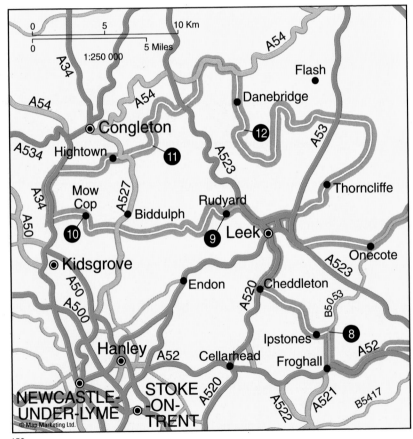

■■■ ROUTE ONE: 58 miles (93 km)

Directions in sequence from: Leek

Leek   The silk industry gave the town prominence 200 years ago, and still
flourishes here. There are many old mills and cobbled back streets. St
Edward's church (founded 1042) has a Saxon cross in its churchyard.
Tourist information: tel. (0538) 381000.
   Brindley Water Mill, Mill St., is a preserved, operational corn mill.
Upstairs, a museum commemorates James Brindley, 18thC canal
engineer. *Open afternoons, Sat, Sun and Bank Holiday Mon, Easter to
Oct. Also Mon, Tues and Wed afternoons in July and Aug.*

Hulme End   Terminus of the old Leek and Manifold narrow-gauge railway.

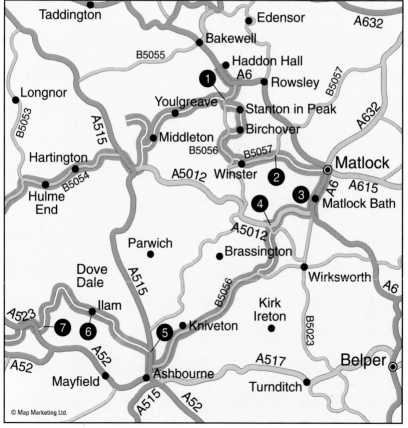

Hartington   This compact village, huddled around its green, has a duckpond, a 14thC church, and a Stilton cheese factory with a shop. Walking sticks and shepherds' crooks are a local speciality.

Hartington –   Limestone country at its best. The route follows sheer-sided, dry valleys,
Middleton   crosses ancient bridges over rivers which flow one week but are gone the next, and passes old lime kilns, lead mines and industrial remains now reclaimed by nature.

Arbor Low   A 2-mile (3-km) detour leads to this late Stone Age or early Bronze Age
(detour)   stone circle, the 'Stonehenge of the north'. An impressive sight, even though the stones are lying down *(entry fee)*.

Middleton   The village guards the entrance to glorious Bradford Dale, which can be glimpsed to the right of the road.

Youlgreave   All Saints' church has a unique Norman font. In June, the village's well-dressing ceremony draws large numbers of visitors.
On leaving the village, look left to see Conksbury's medieval pack-horse bridge, Raper Lodge and the end of Lathkill Dale, the most hidden and picturesque of all the Derbyshire dales.

① At junction with B5056, turn left for short detour to Haddon Hall, or right and then left almost immediately on to unclassified road to Stanton in Peak.

Haddon   Magnificent 14th-15thC fortified manor house, renowned for its
Hall   medieval tapestries and furniture and for being one of the best
(detour)   preserved medieval houses in Britain. The setting, above the River Wye, is attractive. *Open Tues-Sun, April-end Sept; closed Sun, Jul and Aug.*

Stanton in   Just beyond the village, there are distant views to the right over the
Peak   White Peak, Derbyshire and Staffordshire. Stanton Moor, to the left, has
(detour)   standing stones, 70 Neolithic barrows and a stone circle called the Nine Ladies.

Birchover   The chapel has a memorial to Joan Weaste, burned as a heretic in the 1550s, during the reign of Bloody Mary.

Winster   In the main street (which has been virtually untouched for 250 years) the Market Hall (15th-17thC) houses a National Trust information centre and shop.

② Go through Wensley on B5057, then turn right at signpost to Oker and Snitterton. At junction with A6, turn right to Matlock Bath.

Matlock Bath Clinging to the side of the Derwent gorge, the town became famous for its medicinal springs in the 17thC. Boat trips on the river and canal are the best way to see the surrounding scenery; the Heights of Abraham can be reached by cable car from the riverside. There are show caves, a model village, and a museum of lead mining *(in The Pavilion, which also houses the tourist office – tel. (0629) 55082).*

Riber Castle (built by Victorian hosiery manufacturer John Smedley) is now a ruin, but the grounds are a wildlife park for endangered European species. *Open daily except Christmas. ③ Leave Matlock Bath on A6, then turn right on to B5036, and right again on to A5012, past water mill and lodge.*

Via Gellia Famous for its trees, this valley was named after the local Gell family. *④ Turn left at Hopton signpost. Go over crossroads, then turn right on to B5035.* (After about 2 miles (3 km) there are extensive views over the Vale of Trent and the White Peak.)

Kniveton Worth pausing to see the tiny ancient church and massive churchyard yew tree.

Ashbourne One of the best small Georgian towns in England, Ashbourne is famous for its Shrovetide football game, its mineral water and its gingerbread. St Oswald's church with its fine spire should not be missed.

● *Hartington: Stilton and walking sticks.*

Pub　　　　The Green Man and Black's Head serves real ale. ⑤ *Leave town on*
(Ashbourne)　*A515, then turn left to Thorpe. Follow signposts to Dove Dale car park*
　　　　　　between Thorpe and Ilam.

Dove Dale　The most famous dale, an essential stop for exploration on foot.
　　　　　　Memorable sights include towering pillars of stone, gorges, hidden caves
　　　　　　and natural arches.

Hotel　　　The Izaak Walton Hotel is recommended for its food. ⑥ *Turn right at*
(near Ilam)　*the cross in Ilam, wind through village, then turn left down road*
　　　　　　signposted to Castern and Throwley. One mile (1.5 km) from Ilam, bear
　　　　　　sharp right before Rushley Farm. After short distance, route passes
　　　　　　through Throwley Hall farmyard. Turn left after first barn. Close yard
　　　　　　gates behind you.

　　　　　　⑦ *At T-junction in Calton, turn right then right again at fork. At*
　　　　　　Waterhouses, take left turning by Old Crown pub, signposted to
　　　　　　Cauldon Lowe and Cheadle.

Pub　　　　The Yew Tree Inn's drab exterior disguises an Aladdin's cave of working
(Cauldon)　polyphons, pianolas, pennyfarthings, and assorted curiosities including a
　　　　　　pair of Queen Victoria's stockings. Real ale, bar meals and table skittles.

Froghall　An industrial archaeologist's paradise, deep in the secluded Churnett
Wharf　　Valley. There tug-drawn narrowboat trips *(2 pm, Thurs and Sun, Easter-*
　　　　　　Sept) along the Caldon canal.

　　　　　　⑧ *At Ipstones, turn left and follow 'Leisure Drive' signs towards*
　　　　　　Cheddleton.

Basford　　The old railway station is now the Cheddleton Steam Railway Centre
Bridge　　and museum. *Open afternoons, daily, Easter-Sept; closed Thurs*
(Cheddleton)　*afternoons Jul and Aug.*

Cheddleton　Unique flint mill, with two massive water wheels, operates most
　　　　　　afternoons. *To reach mill, turn left along A520 towards Wetley Rocks.*

ROUTE TWO: 40 miles (64 km)
Directions in sequence from: Leek

Rudyard　Kipling was named after this compact village at the foot of the reservoir.
　　　　　　⑨ *Turn right at mini-roundabout. Bear left uphill, then turn left at*
　　　　　　signpost to Horton. Turn right at Horton Hall, then follow signposts to
　　　　　　Lask Edge. (Not on map.)

Lask Edge　Panoramic views extend across nine counties.

Mow Cop   Climb up the hill to the mid-18thC mock ruin for immense views from the fringe of the Gritstone Edge. ⑩ *Turn left out of car park at Mow Cop, then turn right down steep Top Station Rd. Go over level crossing, turn left then right over canal, then turn right again down Stonechair Lane. At A34, turn right (or left for detour to pub).*

Pub   A 1-mile (1.5-km) detour leads to The Bleeding Wolf inn (excellent bar
(Scholar Gn.) meals and Robinsons Ales).

Lt. Moreton One of the most perfect black-and-white half-timbered manor houses in
Hall   Britain. *Open afternoons, Wed-Sun, Bank Hol Mon, Apr-Sept; Wed, Sat, Sun in Oct.*

Hightown   *Go over traffic lights, then bear right at Coach and Horses pub.* About 2 miles (3 km) along the road, the Bridestones Neolithic burial chamber (on left) is accessible by footpath.

                 ⑪ *Bear left and follow road around the edge of The Cloud* (extensive views from the top), *then turn sharp right.*

Pub   The Ship Inn, dating from medieval times, is Cheshire's oldest pub.
(Danebridge)   ⑫ *Follow road around the edge of Swythamley Hall estate; bear left at telephone box, then turn left at junction by copse. Follow Meerbrook signposts.* (Spectacular view ahead of the Roaches and Hen Cloud.) *Turn left in Meerbrook in front of Three Horse Shoes pub. Close gates across road.*

Roach End   *(Not on map.)* Good place to stop and gaze across Cheshire (to the west) and Staffordshire (to the south).

Pub   The Mermaid Inn at Morridge Edge *(not on map)* is renowned for the quality of its food and beer. From the lay-by near the pub there are unrivalled views.

The Lincolnshire Wolds

A county of contrasts, Lincolnshire divides into three distinct regions: Kesteven, to the south-west, is attractively wooded; Holland, to the south-east, is the reclaimed fenland area famous for its bulb fields; while Lindsey, in the north, is dominated by the rolling Wolds.

Starting in Woodhall Spa, the little resort that grew up around its medicinal springs, this tour does a figure of eight through some of the Wolds' loveliest scenery. This is Tennyson country: the old Poet Laureate was born in Somersby, went to school in Louth, and derived much of his inspiration from the Lincolnshire landscape.

ROUTE: 96 miles (154.5 km)

Directions in sequence from: Woodhall Spa

Woodhall Spa

Small Victorian resort attractively set amid pine and birch woods and farmland. Both the mineral spring and the rheumatism treatment centre are now closed. *Tourist information: tel.(0526) 353775.* Near the championship golf course, the tall Tower on the Moor is thought to date from the 15thC.

To leave town, go through Jubilee Park then turn right at crossroads along route signposted to Old Woodhall. The Wellington Monument, to the left, is said to face Waterloo. Close by, Waterloo Wood was grown from acorns planted after the battle (1815).

Horncastle

① *Join B1191 then turn left for Horncastle (in sight down the hill).* The Romans named it Banovallum (the walled place on the River Bain) and traces of the old walls can still be seen around the town, incorporated into various buildings including the public library. St Mary's church has a brass to Sir Lionel Dymoke (1519). As King's Champion he defended the monarch against challengers. His descendant at nearby Scrivelsby Court still holds the title.

② *Leave town centre on A153 (signposted to Louth). After ¾ mile (1 km) turn right at signpost to Fulletby.* ③ *Turn right at T-junction in Fulletby (signposted to Belchford) then turn left and right again, towards Tetford.*

Fulletby

Just beyond the village there is a good view over 'Tennyson Valley'.

Tetford – Little Cawthorpe

④ *On reaching Tetford take turning to left, signposted to Ruckland.* The road rises to one of the highest parts of the Wolds with fine views all around of unspoiled country. ⑤ *Just beyond Ruckland turn right. At junction with A16, turn right to Burwell. Pass through village, then take turning to left and follow signs to Muckton.*

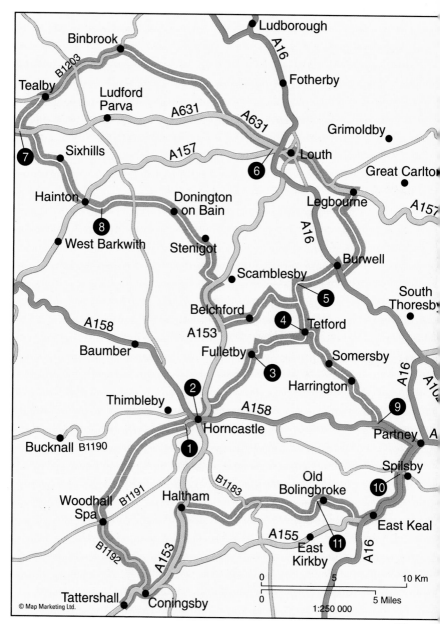

Little Cawthorpe Turn right past the duckpond to charming old pub called The Splash (good bar meals). *Carry on across the ford; if flooded, do a U-turn and go round the village to rejoin the road on the other side of the ford.*

Louth This busy, rambling market town with its confusing one-way system is dominated by the impressive tower and spire (295 feet/90 m) of St James's church. Dating mainly from the 15thC, the church has numerous stone carvings of animals, birds and humans; look out too for the Louth Imp. Well-preserved 17th-18thC houses can be seen in Westgate and Upgate in the town centre. ⑥ *Leave town on A157, then turn right on to A631. Just past South Elkington turn right on to minor road signposted to North Elkington.*

Binbrook Just south of this neat Wolds village lie old wartime airfields; to the north the massive, operational RAF base is all too conspicuous. *Turn left along B1203 to Tealby.*

Tealby Tennyson's grandfather lived in this lovely village and the poet spent much time here, at Bayons Manor (demolished 1964). There is, of course, a 'Tennyson Walk' around the village, starting at the church.

Tealby – Donington on Bain ⑦ *Turn left on to A631. At North Willingham, turn right on to unclassified road to Hainton. Pass through village, then go over A157 to South Willingham.* ⑧ *At South Willingham, turn left up hill (passing television mast) and continue on to Donington on Bain.*

Donington on Bain Tiny parish church where newly-married couples were pelted with hassocks – until one injured a vicar.

Belchford The long-distance walk known as the Viking Way goes through the village on its journey from Leicestershire to the Humber. *Keep left through village. After 1 mile (1.5 km), turn right at T-junction.*

Belchford – Tetford For a short distance the route goes along the old Bluestone Heath road which runs north-south across the Wolds. Not far from the T-junction there is a viewpoint with a map of the surrounding countryside. On a fine day it is possible (with binoculars) to see Lincoln Cathedral, more than 20 miles (32 km) to the west. *Continue to crossroads, then turn right and go down the hill to Tetford.*

Tetford *Turn left into the village, continuing past the church to The White Hart Inn, on right.* Tennyson once supped at this 16thC inn, and Dr Johnson is reputed to have drunk here. The old settle where both great men sat is preserved in the bar. Next door, the cabinet-maker's workshop is open to the public. *At T-junction turn left, then turn first right at signpost to Somersby.*

Somersby In 1809, Tennyson was born at the Old Rectory (the central house of the three opposite the church where his father was rector and where there is a memorial to the poet). The castellated house next door is attributed to Vanbrugh. *Follow signposts to Bag Enderby.*

Harrington Hall Turn left at T-junction to reach the mellow Hall. It recently burnt down and its future is uncertain.

Spilsby A statue in the market square commemorates the Arctic explorer Sir John Franklin, born in Spilsby. Worth looking inside St James's church to see the fine 14th-16thC tombs of the Willoughby family. In the town centre an old grocery has been converted into a restaurant where well-known painters display their works and top musicians play chamber music. ⑩ *Leave Spilsby on the A16. After about 2 miles (3 km), fork right on to A155, then almost immediately turn right at signpost to Old Bolingbroke.*

Old Boling-broke Opposite the tiny post office a short lane leads to the remains of the famous castle where Henry IV was born in 1367. *Return to post office and turn right (signposted to Hagnaby).* ⑪ *Turn left at T-junction, then take first turning to the right up the hill to the old windmill.*

East Kirkby *(detour)* Turn left down unclassified road for a short detour to Aviation Heritage Centre, a re-creation of a World War II airfield, complete with control tower and Lancaster bomber. *Open Mon-Sat. Retrace route to junction, turn right to Miningsby. Just beyond Miningsby, turn left at signpost pointing to the wonderfully named village of Claxby Pluckacre. Two cattle gates lie ahead (remember to shut them).*

Pub *(Haltham)* *Turn left on to the A153* to reach the only pub in England to be called The Marmion Arms. This 16thC hostelry was named after the Duke of Marmion, another King's Champion.

RAF Coningsby *(detour)* *Before reaching Coningsby, turn left along B1192* for a short detour to the RAF station where the operational Battle of Britain aeroplanes are usually kept. *Flight times on notice board on perimeter fence.*

Coningsby The clock on the 15thC church tower has only one hand (minute hands were not used until the 17thC).

Tattershall Castle *(Short detour along A153.)* The huge, red-brick, five-storeyed keep (all that remains of the 15thC castle) is an outstanding example of a fortified manor house. *Open daily except Christmas.*

The South Pennines

Gritstone dominates the South Pennines. It has created a wild, open landscape of moorland and sheep pasture, criss-crossed by dry-stone walls and dotted with farms. The same dark stone was used to build the terraced cottages that were erected near the textile mills during the Industrial Revolution. Today, many of the mills are silent, but towns such as Hebden Bridge and Todmorden have retained much of their nineteenth-century character. Other settlements originated as communities of hand-weavers, whose lives were ruined by the coming of the factories.

ROUTE ONE: 56 miles (90 km)

Directions in sequence from: Hebden Bridge

Hebden Bridge
The capital of the South Pennines, this busy market town has grown around the Tudor bridge across Hebden Water. Its streets are built in steep terraces along the hillsides, connected by stepped alleyways, and back doors are often a floor higher than front doors. The whole effect is reminiscent of a Cornish or Mediterranean fishing village. *Tourist information: tel. (0422) 843831.*

Hardcastle Crags *(follow signs on left of A6033 after ½ mile/0.8 km)* are a combination of rocks, woodland and steep Pennine valleys. A useful place for picnic areas and woodland walks.

'Automobilia'
(detour)
Take right turning off A6033 1 mile (1.5 km) from town, and follow signs to 'Automobilia'. A former mill houses a collection of early Austin and Morris cars, motor cycles and bicycles. *Open Tues-Fri and Bank Holiday Mon, Sat and Sun afternoons, Apr-Sept; Sat and Sun afternoons, Oct and Mar; Sun afternoons, Nov-Feb.*

Oxenhope
The Worth Valley Railway featured in such films as *The Railway Children* and *Yanks. Frequent steam train service to Haworth and Keighley; daily in July and Aug; weekends and Bank holidays, rest of the year, with some midweek in June and Sept.* The museum has more than a dozen locomotives from America, Sweden and Britain, including the Victorian 0-6-0 locomotive used in *The Railway Children*. There is also a picnic site beside the museum, which is *open when trains are running.*

Haworth
Famous for its Brontë connections, this bleak village has a cobbled main street, unaltered since the days when Charlotte, Anne and Emily were writing their novels. At the Parsonage, where the Brontës lived, their possessions are touchingly displayed. Even the furniture adds to the sadness of the story: visitors see the couch where Emily died, and the table round which the three sisters and their brother took their endless 'walks'. *Open daily except early Jan to early Feb and Christmas.*

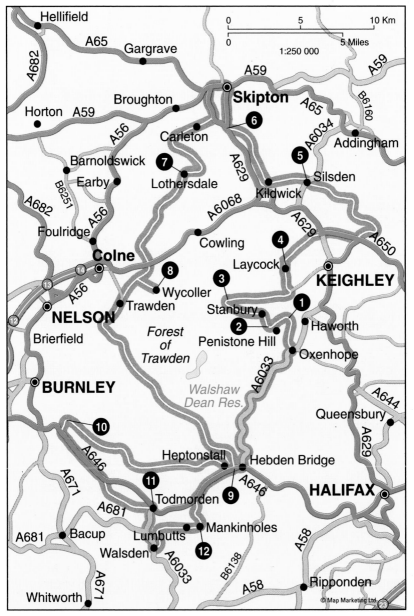

Pub *(Haworth)*	The Black Bull was where the notorious and unfortunate Branwell Brontë drank himself to an early grave.

① *At the top of the village, turn left on to Stanbury and Colne road, bear left at first fork signposted Penistone Hill Country Park.*

Penistone Hill Country Park	An area of open moorland dedicated to recreation. There are parking places, picnic areas and superb views. Excellent starting point for walks to the Brontë Falls (much loved by Emily) and Top Withens (the supposed inspiration for *Wuthering Heights*). ② *Continue along road past Penistone Hill; turn right over reservoir dam to road junction, then left to Stanbury village.*
Stanbury	This is a typical Pennine village which has 17th-18thC cottages and farmhouses, and two pleasant inns. *Continue directly ahead down to Ponden.*
Ponden	*(Not on map.)* The 17thC Hall, considered by many to be the original of Thrushcross Grange in *Wuthering Heights*, is now a craft centre. Nearby, Ponden Mill sells locally made textiles.

③ *Continue to next junction before taking sharp right turn to Oldfield and Oakworth. Soon after Golden Fleece pub in Oakworth, turn left and follow road signposted to Sutton and Laycock. Go past cemetery, then turn left to Gooseye.*

Gooseye	*(Not on map.)* This curiously named little mill hamlet crowds into a narrow gill. One of the old mill buildings is now a restaurant and club, and The Turkey Inn is celebrated for the production of its own excellent Gooseye ale.

④ *Continue up extremely steep, winding road to junction. Turn sharp right into Laycock. At Keighley, go straight ahead at traffic island and left at traffic lights along main street to next set of traffic lights. Watch out for Cliffe Castle car park sign on left.*

Cliffe Castle	*(Not on map.)* Built by a Victorian wool magnate, this ornate mansion is now a natural history museum. *Open Tues-Sun and Bank Hol Mon. Return to main road, turn left to traffic island, then right along Bradford main road to East Riddlesden.*
East Riddlesden Hall	Fine Jacobean house with strong Civil War associations and great atmosphere. Virtually unaltered, it has fine ceilings and fireplaces, rare rose windows and, inevitably, a ghost. The tithe barn, predating the house, has a collection of vintage farm vehicles. Its cruck-style roof dates from monastic times and is one of the finest examples in the north of

● *Heptonstall, once a focal point for weavers.*

England. *Open afternoons only, Sat-Wed, May-Nov; Thurs in Jul and Aug; weekends, Apr.*

Go up Granby Lane opposite the Hall. At junction, turn left. From this road there are views across Airedale, Keighley and into Worth valley.

(5) *At Silsden, turn right into main street; when road bends left keep straight on following Farnhill signs.*

Kildwick   The hall, a fine 17thC house with gabled façade and mullioned windows, is now a high-class restaurant.
At top of village bear right, following signs to Bradley. At junction with A6131 bear right to Skipton.

Skipton   Large, bustling market town with fully roofed medieval castle at the top of the High St. *The castle is open daily.*

(6) *Leave town on Keighley road (A629), then take third road right past bus station, signposted to Carleton. From Carleton follow Earby road uphill to junction, then turn left. Take right turning at second junction, signposted to Lothersdale.*

Lothers-   Beautiful, isolated valley which has more of the character of the
dale   Yorkshire Dales than the Pennine valleys. The village has a mill with a huge waterwheel, and a pleasant pub.

(7) *Follow signs to Colne, turning left on outskirts of town to Laneshaw Bridge beside The Emmot Arms. Cross A6068 and follow Wycoller signs to village car park.*

Wycoller   Wycoller is a medieval weavers' settlement that sank into decay after
Village and   the Industrial Revolution. With its pack-horse bridges and ruined hall, it
Country   is now the focal point of a country park. Cars are not allowed in the
Park   village, and visitors must walk about ¼ mile (0.5 km) from the car park; exceptions are made for the disabled.

(8) *Follow Trawden signs from Wycoller road end; turn left in Trawden, soon bearing right to follow Hebden Bridge signs over narrow moorland road via Widdop.*

Trawden –   The splendid views from this road are of a wild, desolate landscape
Hebden   reminiscent of the Scottish highlands. The Pack Horse, a comfortable
Bridge   traditional pub, has real ale, simple food and open fires in winter.

ROUTE TWO: 27 miles (43 km)
Directions in sequence from: Hebden Bridge

(9) *Leave town on A646; follow signs up hill to Hepstonstall.*

Heptonstall Hilltop village (originally a handweavers' settlement) with a ruined church, an octagonal Methodist chapel (built 1764 and still in use) and a Tudor cloth hall.

Heptonstall – Burnley Fine views along the entire length of this road which follows The Long Causeway, a major trade route in medieval times.

Mount Cross *(Not on map.)* An extraordinary, medieval wayside cross which reveals strong Viking influence in its design, and dates back to the period of Viking settlement in the south Pennines. *To reach the cross, turn left at Shore/Stone Cross sign. A quarter of a mile (0.5 km) along lane, park and walk along track on left. Cross is in field on left.* ⑩ *At Mere Clough, turn left at T-junction and go down to Holme.*

Towneley Hall *(detour)* *Turn right on to A646. At major road junction keep right towards Burnley. Turn into Country Park soon after junction.* Towneley Hall is a substantial art gallery and regional museum.

Cliviger Gorge *(Not on map.)* Superb views to be enjoyed throughout the length of this steep Pennine pass.

Todmorden The fine, neo-classical town hall dominates the scene, but the most charming building is the post office, a Jacobean house. As at Hebden Bridge, cottages and farmhouses cling to the hillsides often at fantastic angles; considerable driving skill is required to negotiate the steep lanes.

⑪ *Leave town on the Rochdale road (A6033). Just past Walsden post office, turn left to Lumbutts and Mankinholes, then bear right after ½ mile (0.8 km) to Lumbutts.*

Lumbutts This tiny village has an extraordinary relic of the textile industry: a tall water mill, which once held three water wheels, fed by water syphoned up from nearby dams.

Mankin- holes Half a mile (0.8 km) from Lumbutts, Mankinholes has several fine 17th- and 18thC houses and cottages. ⑫ *From Mankinholes, go down wooded road, turning sharp left at junction to joint A646, 3 miles (5 km) from Hebden Bridge.*

The Dales

Many of the Yorkshire Dales take their individual names from the rivers that flow along valleys carved out by glaciers. This tour of the eastern Dales begins in Wharfedale, where the lovely landscape can be seen magnificently from the road. On the way to Nidderdale, gritstone gives way to limestone: at Stump Cross Caverns there is an opportunity to explore the underground beauty of limestone caves, while High Stean Gorge reveals what the wind can do to limestone. But for many, the high point of the tour will be the ruins of one of England's greatest monasteries: Fountains Abbey.

▮▮▮▮ ROUTE: 80 miles (128 km)

Directions in sequence from: Ilkley

Ilkley Originally an important Roman fortress-town, Ilkley became a popular health resort in the 18thC because of its moorland springs. The museum tells the town's story. *Open Tues-Sun and Bank Hol Mon. Tourist information: tel. (0943) 602319.*

Immortalized by a traditional dialect folk song, the moor is a fine place for a bracing walk. White Wells, a restored 18thC bath-house, is only ½ mile (0.8 km) from town centre *(follow signposts to 'Moor').* ① *Take road over the river to Middleton and Langbar.*

Beamsley Beacon A short walk from the road leads to the summit, and superb views across Wharfe valley. Beamsley was part of a chain of sites across northern England where fires were lit to announce the arrival of the Spanish Armada. ② *Continue down to Beamsley, turn right at junction then left on to A59.*

Bolton Abbey These Augustinian priory ruins in a beautiful setting were painted by Turner and Landseer, and described by Wordsworth and Ruskin. The nave of the church escaped destruction and is still in use as the parish church.

There are two car parks, riverside and woodland walks (1½ miles/2.5 km to Strid Woods, where the river presses through a narrow gorge) and nature trails. The Grassington road is one of the most beautiful in England; fine views across Wharfedale all along.

Barden Tower A 17thC priest's house attached to a former hunting lodge of the Clifford family, lords of Skipton, is now a tearoom.

Burnsall This greystone village, lying in a great bowl of hills, has a village green on the riverside. The church has Viking hogback gravestones, and the attractive 17thC grammar school remains in use as a primary school.

The Red Lion, by the river serves real ale and is noted for its food.

Horsehouse

Well

B6267

Healey

Masham

West Tanfield

A6108

Scar House Res.

Middlesmoor

Grewelthorpe

Stean

Kirkby Malzeard

6

Ripon

5

Winksley

4

Ramsgill

Gouthwaite Reservoir

Wath

Fountains Abbey

Pateley Bridge

B6265

7

0   5   10 Km

0   5 Miles

1:250 000

3

Grassington

B6265

8

South Stainley

Summer Bridge

Linton

Burnsall

Dacre

B6165

Hampsthwaite

B6451

B6160

A59

A61

Blubberhouses

A59

Harrogate

Embsay

Bolton Abbey

Fewston

A59

Beamsley Beacon

B6451

B6161

kipton

A65

2

A658

Addingham

Askwith

1

9

A659

Weeton

A629

A6034

Silsden

Ilkley

A65

Otley

Pool

A659

Marketing Ltd.

Linton
(detour)

Tiny village dominated by a gracious, 18thC almshouse (thought to have been designed by Vanbrugh) and well worth the slight detour from the route.

Grass-ington

The capital of Upper Wharfedale has a fine cobbled square and many 17th- and 18thC cottages and houses built around narrow courts or 'folds'. In the mornings, a queue forms outside the baker's shop, drawn by the smell of freshly made pies and other Yorkshire specialities.

In the Upper Wharfedale Museum (in the Square) old farming equipment and domestic relics throw light on life in the Dales in the pre-mechanical era. *Open 2-4.30 Apr-Sept; weekends only in winter.*

A five-minute walk from the village leads to Linton Falls, which tumble impressively over limestone crags. The church, which dates from Norman times but is mainly 14thC, is a further five minutes' walk away.

Stump Cross Caverns

Remarkable limestone caves containing well-lit stalagmites and stalactites. Recent excavations have uncovered remains of prehistoric animals including bears, hyaenas and wolverine. There are many items of archaeological importance on display in the visitor centre. *Open daily mid Mar-mid Nov; weekends only in winter.*

Pateley Bridge

This unspoiled small town at the top of Nidderdale is a useful centre for riverside walks. From the ruined church of St Mary (follow signs to 'Panorama Walk') there are extensive views.

③ *Return along B6265 across river, then take right turning (by garage) signposted Lofthouse.*

Wath
(detour)

The 35-foot (11-m) high waterwheel at Foster Beck Mill was constructed in 1904 and powered a textile mill producing heavy yarn. It now forms a central feature of a popular pub and restaurant just off the route.

Gouthwaite Reservoir

The hamlet of Gouthwaite, and Gouthwaite Hall, were drowned to enable this beautiful reservoir to be constructed in the 1890s. Today it is also a wildfowl reserve, which can be seen from the road. It is especially interesting in winter when it is visited by migrant geese.

Ramsgill

An attractive village with a green which still boasts a horse trough. The Yorke Arms offers traditional English dishes at lunchtime. ④ *Continue to Lofthouse, then turn into first lane on left, signposted to How Stean.*

How Stean Gorge

A narrow gorge, where the limestone has been carved into strange and fantastic shapes, has been made safe with handrails to facilitate pedestrian access. The path winds thrillingly above foaming torrents, underneath overhanging crags and across footbridges. There is even a small cave which can be explored with the aid of a torch, but it is muddy underfoot.

● *Classic Dales landscape: rugged tops, with limestone outcrops, but a lush, green pastoral valley floor. In many such valleys, a rushing river enlivens the scene.*

(5) *Return to Lofthouse, taking the steep road left through the village, signposted to Masham. At Healey, turn right, following the Ilton signposts. The road goes through a steeply wooded gorge and over a bridge; turn left at next junction, then go along lane through woods signposted to Druids' Wood. There is a short walk from the car park to the Druids' Temple.*

Druids'
Temple

A miniature Stonehenge in the middle of a Yorkshire forest is an eerie sight. It was built *c.*1820 by William Danby, local squire and owner of Swinton Hall, as a means of creating employment. A plan near the car park outlines local walks.

Grewel-thorpe

An agreeable village with a long green and large pond, several 18th-and early 19thC cottages and two unspoiled pubs. Nearby, Hackfall Woods beside the River Ure were a major tourist attraction in Victorian times. Today, the sham castle and grottoes overlooking a steep wooded gorge are overgrown but still accessible by riverside footpath.

The Grewelthorpe Weavers' shop in the village has fine fabrics made on hand looms, and a selection of clothes made from their own fabrics.

Kirkby Malzeard

Situated at the crossing of many ancient trackways, lanes and paths, the town has a market charter which dates from 1307, and a medieval market cross restored in the 19thC. The church is particularly fine, with a great deal of Norman work, and a 13thC priest's doorway.

⑥ *Leave by lane signposted to Galphay and Grantley. At the fork, keep on the Grantley road to the right, but turn left shortly along lane signposted to Winksley. Continue through village; at T-junction turn left up narrow road, cross B6265, then follow signposts to Aldfield and Fountains Abbey.*

Fountains Abbey

Acknowledged to be one of the finest monastic ruins in Western Europe, this magnificent Cistercian abbey (founded 1132) lies on the sheltered banks of the little River Skell. Its wealth came from the growth of the wool trade; wool from the Yorkshire Dales was exported through the medieval port of York to the growing city-states of Renaissance Italy. The great cellarium with its elegant arches – one of the glories of Fountains – was where much of this wool was stored.

A model of the original abbey, with many recent archaeological finds, can be seen in the museum close to the Abbey. *Abbey and museum open daily.* A particularly fine view of the Abbey is to be found downstream on the opposite bank of the Skell.

Fountains Hall

Built with stones taken from nearby Fountains Abbey after the Dissolution, this is a fine example of Jacobean-Renaissance architecture.

Studley Royal

A ten-minute walk from Fountains Abbey leads to an estate which, in terms of 18thC formal and landscape gardens, is almost as important as the Abbey itself. Artificial canals and a lake reflecting temples and towers form a rare example of the neo-classical garden, while the deer park above the valley is more typically English parkland, with views across to Ripon Cathedral. *Open daily.*

⑦ *From Fountains Abbey car park, turn right on to the Harrogate road, then bear right at junction. Keep straight on avoiding right turns to Sawley. After climbing steep hill, take right turning, signposted to Brimham Rocks. Turn left at junction. You will shortly find Brimham Rocks car park on the right.*

Brimham Rocks On a headland above Nidderdale, a group of gritstone rocks have been carved by the wind and rain into weird and often astonishing shapes. Paths wander between the rocks, and there are fine views.

⑧ *From the car park, turn right and follow lane downhill. At cross-roads, go straight across on to B6451, signed Otley. After 1½ miles (2.5 km) take right turn signposted to Greenhow. At crossroads keep straight on to Thruscross Reservoir.*

Thruscross Reservoir Thruscross was built in the 1960s when the upper Washburn valley was flooded, covering the village of West End.

Fewston and Swinsty Reservoirs The second and third of the chain of reservoirs that forms Washburndale's little lakeland. There are good views of the reservoirs from the dam bridge, and a pleasant walk – about 3 miles (5 km) around Swinsty Reservoir.

Lindley Wood R'voir There are fine views from the steep switchback road leading from the woodland picnic site at Norwood down to the Lindley Wood Reservoir.

Otley This bustling market town (market day Fri) has managed to preserve its ancient courts and alleyways, old shops and inns. South of the town there are extensive views of Wharfedale from Chevin Hill. ⑨ *Go back across the river, then take the first turning on the left to Ilkley via Weston and Askwith.*

The North Yorkshire Moors

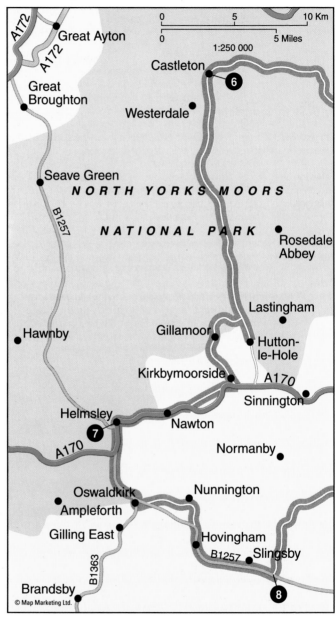

0   5   10 Km
0   5 Miles
1:250 000

A172

Great Ayton

A172

Castleton

6

Great Broughton

Westerdale

Seave Green

N O R T H   Y O R K S   M O O R S

B1257

N A T I O N A L   P A R K

Rosedale Abbey

Lastingham

Hawnby

Gillamoor

Hutton-le-Hole

Kirkbymoorside

A170

Sinnington

Helmsley

7

Nawton

A170

Normanby

Oswaldkirk

Nunnington

Ampleforth

Gilling East

Hovingham

B1257

Slingsby

B1363

Brandsby

© Map Marketing Ltd.

8

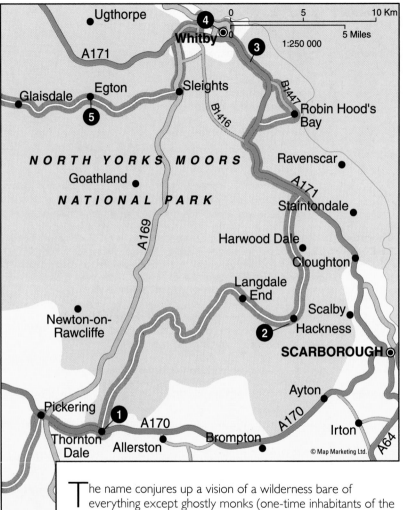

The name conjures up a vision of a wilderness bare of everything except ghostly monks (one-time inhabitants of the great abbeys at Whitby and Rievaulx). Yet below the high, heather-clad moors lie attractive stone hamlets, large forestry plantations and, to the south, the plain of Ryedale.

The tour begins at Pickering, the terminus of the old North Yorkshire Moors Railway. Those who ride on one of the steam trains could be met at Grosmont by drivers doing the complete route suggested below.

ROUTE: 100 miles (161 km)

Directions in sequence from: Pickering

Pickering   Market town with a pleasantly old-fashioned atmosphere, where a colourful market is still held every Mon in the main street. *Tourist information: tel. (0751) 73791.*

The Beck Isle Museum, beside the river, has interesting displays illustrating rural life in Yorkshire over the last 200 years. *Open Apr to Oct, closed Mon in winter.* Not much remains of the Norman castle where Richard II was held prisoner, but it is worth walking up the steps at the top for the splendid view. The medieval wall paintings in St Peter's church were hidden for centuries and are now the town's star attraction.

Steam train enthusiasts can travel from Pickering to Grosmont (about I hour) on the North Yorkshire Moors Railway, *open Feb-Oct, Sun only in Mar.* The railway was built by George Stephenson in 1836.

Thornton   Known as the 'prettiest village in Yorkshire', its old stone houses beside
Le-Dale   the Beck are most attractive, but try to avoid visiting them in high summer if possible. ① *In the centre of the village take road signposted to Whitby, up the hill. After about I mile (1.5 km) turn right into forested area. A toll barrier marks the beginning of the Forest Drive.*

Low Dalby This small village is about I mile (1.5 km) along the Forest Drive, a beautiful route through Forestry Commission plantations. *Follow signs carefully, leaving by Langdale End exit.*

Hackness   Set in a broad and lovely dale, this former estate village on the River Derwent has a church which merits a visit. Dating in part from the 11thC, it contains inscribed fragments of an even earlier cross. ② *Leave village on road signposted to Silpho. Beyond the village, fork left and, shortly after, turn left at crossroads. Just before Harwood Dale, turn left, then left again after about ½ mile (0.8 km) on to A171. Leave main road at turning to Robin Hood's Bay.*

Fyling-   From the approach road to the village there are fine views of the moors
thorpe   and the steeply shelving coastline. The village itself was a popular resort in Victorian times.

Robin   This famous old smugglers' haunt is an unspoilt warren of narrow streets
Hood's Bay and alleys. Be warned, however, that the village can only be reached on foot, down a steep hill; cars must be left in the car park at the top of the cliffs (some of the highest in Britain).

Whitby   ③ *Follow 'Town Centre' signs to the harbour/car park (beside bus station).* The ruined abbey dominates not only the town but religious history, for it was here in 664 that the Synod of Whitby agreed when Easter should be celebrated.

In the alleys overlooking the harbour there are several interesting antique shops. Whitby jet jewellery, made popular by Queen Victoria when she was in mourning, can still be found here. A flight of donkey steps leads from the harbour to St Mary's, an extraordinary church with a roof built like a ship's hull and a surprising Georgian interior well worth investigating.

To reach the sandy beaches and the promenade follow the one-way system leading up the 'Khyber Pass'. Park beside the garden overlooking the sea. The garden contains a statue of Captain Cook, who first went to sea in Whitby-built ships, and the huge jaw-bones of a whale. ④ *To leave town, drive along the front on the cliff top, then follow Scarborough/Teeside signs round a slightly complex traffic system. At T-junction, turn right on to A171.*

Grosmont   The terminus of the North Yorkshire Moors Railway (see Pickering.)

Egton   ⑤ *On entering Egton, take left fork for Egton Bridge, down a steep hill.*
Bridge   A tiny village, renowned for its vast, Victorian Catholic church and for its annual gooseberry fair. Villagers claim that the world's biggest gooseberry was grown and shown here. *Just past the church turn right for Glaisdale, then turn left at T-junction at the top of the hill.*

Glaisdale   Just before entering the village there is a pretty picnic spot beside an old stone bridge over the River Esk.

Lealholm   The stepping stones across the river – just one of the attractions of this delightful Esk Dale village – provide the name of the antique shop which has a large collection of second-hand books. *Turn left in village along the road to Danby.*

Danby   The Moors Centre at the edge of the village supplies information on the North Yorkshire Moors National Park.

⑥ *On leaving Castleton, fork left along road signposted to Rosedale.*

Castleton –   The road crosses wild moorland with magnificent views on either side.
Hutton-le-   After about 4 miles (6.5 km) a cross dating from Celtic times marks one
Hole   of the Moor's highest points.

Pub   A little further on, the isolated Lion Inn serves bar meals, and just beyond the pub the view stretches out for about 30 miles.

Hutton-le-   This remarkably pretty village has strong Quaker associations, but is best
Hole   known today for its Ryedale Folk Museum. Indoors there are lots of

● *Busy Whitby Harbour.*

country life exhibits; in the Folk Park several old houses and shops have been reconstructed. *Open Easter to Oct.*

On leaving the village turn back along route for a short distance, then turn left to Gillamoor.

Gillamoor   Mr Frimble's Country Store comes as a delightful surprise in this tiny village. It sells fashionable, locally made clothes, and a better than average selection of souvenirs.

Kirkby-moorside   Gay with stalls on market days, this friendly town has several fine old inns. *At the roundabout at the bottom of the main street, take the Helmsley road (A170).*

Helmsley   Delightful old market town built in warm stone. The ruined castle, which dates from the 12thC, is *open daily, except Mon in winter.*

Rievaulx
Abbey
(detour)

A worthwhile detour about 3 miles (5 km) west along B1257 leads to Rievaulx Abbey, another 12thC ruin, *open daily except Mon in winter.* Surrounded by hills, these substantial remains look superb from the Rievaulx Terrace; *open Apr-Oct.*

Hotel
(Helmsley)

The Spanish owner of The Feversham Arms has produced an unusual menu that puts Yorkshire specialities side by side with exotic dishes from his native country. He also offers an amazing choice of sherries. ⑦ *Leave town on A170 signposted Thirsk. Fork left on to B1257, signposted Malton, then left again on unclassified road that leads to Nunnington Hall.*

Nunnington
Hall
(detour)

Large 16th-17thC manor house built on the banks of the River Rye. It has fine panelling and a beautifully carved chimneypiece, but is best known for its collection of miniature rooms. *Open afternoons, Tues-Thurs, Sat, and Sun, Apr-Oct; also Fri in Jul and Aug. On leaving, turn left and return to B1257.*

⑧ *At Barton-le-Street turn left to Brawby.*

Kirby
Misperton

At Flamingo Land more than 1,000 animals and birds can be seen in natural surroundings from ground level or monorail. There are all sorts of extra diversions including Britain's biggest looping roller coaster. *Open Easter-Oct.*

Windermere, Eskdale & Coniston

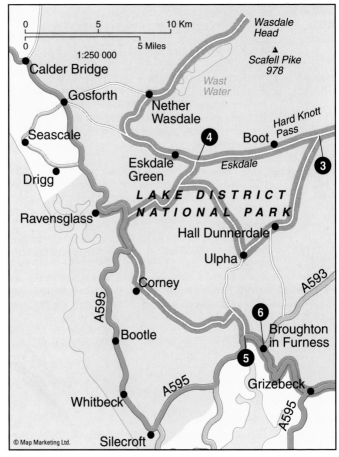

Starting in Windermere, the tour takes to the heights over mountain passes where roads are narrow and twisting and are often closed in winter because of snow and ice. On summer days those who make an early start will not only avoid most of the traffic, but will enjoy the pleasure of morning light on dramatic scenery.

For the energetic, there are opportunities for water sports and walks throughout the tour. For those whose love of landscape has been inspired by books, there are literary shrines: Wordsworth, Ruskin and Beatrix Potter all had houses locally.

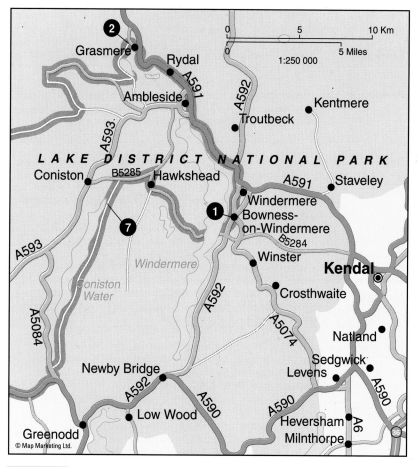

© Map Marketing Ltd.

ROUTE: 68 miles (109 km)

Directions in sequence from: Windermere

Bowness-on-Winder-mere

Bustling lake-side town with numerous hotels, shops and restaurants. From the pier, steamers ply to both ends of Windermere: Lakeside to the south, Waterhead to the north. Motor boats and rowing boats can be hired and there are motor-launch trips round the lake.

① *From the lakeside promenade take the road past 15thC St Martin's church, then fork left (the road is signposted Keswick). The Steamboat museum (open daily Easter-mid Nov) offers trips on the lake. Nearby, a car park with picnic area gives access to the lake shore.*

Hammar-bank   Park here to take in extensive views across Windermere to the central mountains. *At mini roundabout turn left (signposted Keswick).*

Brockhole   The National Park Centre has exhibitions, films, a cafeteria, a lakeshore walk and flower and shrub gardens.

Ambleside   This popular centre has hotels, cafés, shops, and an interesting mural in the church of St Mary. A ½-mile (0.8-km) walk leads to Stock Ghyll waterfalls. The road passes photogenic Bridge House, a tiny 17thC cottage on a bridge over Stock Ghyll.

Rydal   Rydal Mount, Wordsworth's home from 1813 to 1850, has portraits and many of the poet's personal possessions, as well as a lovely garden landscaped by the poet. *Open daily; closed Tues in winter.* By the church, Dora's Field (named after Wordsworth's daughter) is carpeted with daffodils in spring.

To the left, Loughrigg Fell rises steeply from the far shore of Rydal Water. (Park at White Moss Common just beyond the lake.)

Rydal – Grasmere   The road runs on through a wood. At a sharp bend Grasmere comes into view – when unruffled by the wind, the lake reflects the surrounding mountains. Silver Howe lies across the lake; ahead, Helm Crag is surmounted by the Lion and the Lamb – rocks with intriguing animal-like silhouettes.

Grasmere   Before the turn into the village, a road to the right leads to Dove Cottage (Wordsworth lived here from 1799 to 1808) and the Wordsworth Museum; *open daily except mid Jan-mid Feb. Tourist information: tel. (05394) 35245.*

② On leaving village, fork left at signpost to Langdales. The narrow, twisting road leads to Red Bank, a short steep hill (1:4). At top where road divides take the right turn signposted Langdales.

Descend into Great Langdale on open road over Elterwater Common with fine view of Wetherlam (2,502 feet/753 m) and to the valley head. Sharp left bend near bottom of descent signposted Colwith; at Elterwater crossroads in the valley bottom, turn right (signposted Great Langdale).

Langdale   Spectacular valley with the Langdale Pikes standing prominently ahead, their rocky outline against the sky. From the large National Trust car park at the New Dungeon Ghyll Hotel, walkers can explore the Pikes: the path climbs steeply beside rushing waterfalls.

The road takes a sharp left turn out of the valley head, then climbs a steep hill with tight bends to Blea Tarn. All around there is splendid mountain scenery. Just beyond the road's summit there is a small car park; walk from here to the edge of Blea Tarn (about ¼ mile/0.5 km) for a classic view of the Langdale Pikes, twin peaks with striking outlines rising to 2,403 feet (732 m).

Little Langdale

Descend to the head of Little Langdale on a steep narrow road across a boulder-strewn and juniper-scattered mountainside. *In the valley bottom turn sharp right, signposted Wrynose.*

Wrynose Pass

A long and sometimes extremely steep climb to the summit (1,281 feet/390.5 m) along a narrow road with an unprotected drop into the valley on the left.

The carved Three Shires Stone at the summit marks the former meeting place of Westmorland, Cumberland and Lancashire.

③ *At Cockley Beck, turn right over bridge for Hard Knott Pass (1,290 feet/393 m).*

Hard Knott Pass

Narrow and steep (1:3 in places), with severe bends, this is certainly the Lake District's most exciting road. However, there is a less taxing alternative route that is also interesting: *go straight on at Cockley Bridge, through beautiful Duddon valley. At Ulpha, turn right up steep twisting hill signposted to Eskdale. Cross Birker Moor* (superb views) *and rejoin route at George IV Inn (see Eskdale below).*

Hard Knott Castle (on the descent) is a partly reconstructed Roman fort in a magnificent situation with views across the upper Esk to England's highest mountains, Scafell Pike and Sca Fell.

Eskdale

There is only one road down this beautiful dale with its pink granite buildings, its walks, woods and rocky cliffs.

At Boot, a working water mill can be visited. Close by, at Dalegarth, narrow-gauge railway enthusiasts can take a train to Ravenglass.

Also near Dalegarth, Stanley Force waterfall (reached along a rocky path through a deep wooded gorge) is a fascinating sight after heavy rain. *Follow valley road* to junction at George IV Inn (meals available).

Wasdale
(detour)

A detour along the most dramatic valley in the Lake District, to Wasdale Head and back, adds 19 miles (30.5 km) to the tour. *At George IV Inn turn right, then go through the scattered hamlet of Eskdale Green to Wasdale.* The pastoral nature of the first few miles gives no warning of what is to come. Wast Water, the deepest lake in England, is dark and foreboding. Beside the lake the road is an open, narrow, undulating strip of tarmac, while across the water the great awe-inspiring fans of scree drop from black crags directly into the lake. High mountains stand about the valley head, Scafell Pike and Sca Fell to the right, and the conical peak of Great Gable in the centre.

Inn
(Wasdale)

Meals are served to non-residents at the Wasdale Head Inn (famous for its associations with early rock climbers) at the end of the public road.

● *Esthwaite Water is skirted by the route between Windermere and Coniston.*

Close by, St Olaf's church (16thC) is one of the smallest churches in England.

④ *At George IV Inn take road signposted to Ulpha and Broughton. After ½ mile (0.8 km) turn right, and take the narrow and twisting road running beside the River Esk to junction with A595.*

Ravenglass
(detour)
A short – 5-mile (8-km) detour takes in Muncaster Castle *(open Tues-Sun afternoons, Easter-Oct and Bank Hol Mon*, and well-known for its rhododendrons and azaleas) and Ravenglass village, where Roman remains have been found. This is also the starting point for the narrow-gauge railway. *Return to junction where detour began, and turn right on to Barrow road (continuation of A595).*

Corney Fell

After about 1 mile (1.5 km), turn left along 'scenic route'. The road goes over rolling moorland with Black Coombe stretching out into the sea on the right.

⑤ *Rejoin the A595; turn left over the bridge and follow signs into Broughton.*

Broughton in Furness

An attractive little town with a spacious market square and several interesting 18th-19thC buildings.

⑥ *Follow A595 up to Grizebeck (note slate quarrying on the right). At beginning of descent keep left, signposted Lancaster, and at next crossroads turn left, signposted Torver and Coniston. This is a curving minor road which goes past Lowick church.*

Cross A5084 and take road marked 'Nibthwaite and East of Lake', which then turns north to run beside the River Crake to Nibthwaite.

Coniston Water

The steam boat *Gondola*, originally launched in 1859 and now beautifully restored, takes passengers from Parkamoor pier near the south end of the lake to Coniston village and back. *Open Apr-Oct.*

The road, running close to the lake, has parking and picnic places and easy access to the shingly shore. There are dramatic views across to Coniston Old Man (2,635 feet/803 m); Peel Island, in the fore ground, featured in Arthur Ransome's *Swallows and Amazons* as Wild Cat Island.

Brantwood, home of art critic John Ruskin, 1872-1900) has paintings and memorabilia. *Open daily; Wed-Sun in winter.*

⑦ *Near the head of the lake where the road divides, take right turning to Hawkshead. No cars allowed in the village, but there is a car park off the bypass.*

Hawkshead

The village where Wordsworth went to school has quaint buildings, cobbled passages and narrow alleys, and there are several inns, cafés, gift shops and a gallery displaying Beatrix Potter's original paintings.

Leave the village by road signposted 'Windermere by Ferry'.

Hawkshead – Windermere

Hill Top, behind the Tower Bank Arms in Near Sawrey village, was the home of Beatrix Potter. Many of her original drawings have been moved from her small cottage *(open Apr-Oct, Mon-Wed, Sat and Sun)* to Hawkshead (see above) due to congestion in high season.

Windermere

The ferry service operates daily, every 20 minutes until 9 in winter and 10 in summer, and the crossing takes seven minutes. There may be queues, particularly around 5 on summer afternoons. The ferry takes ten cars so time of waiting can be calculated.

On disembarking, drive to the top of the ferry road, then take left turning to Bowness-on-Windermere.

Buttermere and Derwentwater

Ever since it was 'discovered' by nineteenth-century travellers, the Lake District has attracted waves of tourists. Most are content to follow the main roads that link the better-known sights, but this tour explores every aspect of the area: waterfalls cascading down mountainsides; forests; high bare peaks; tranquil lakes; and, in the valleys, cultivated fields contrasting with the untamed landscape of the great passes.

Although scenery is the main theme, the tour includes the small towns of Keswick and Cockermouth, and the Bronze Age Castlerigg Stone Circle.

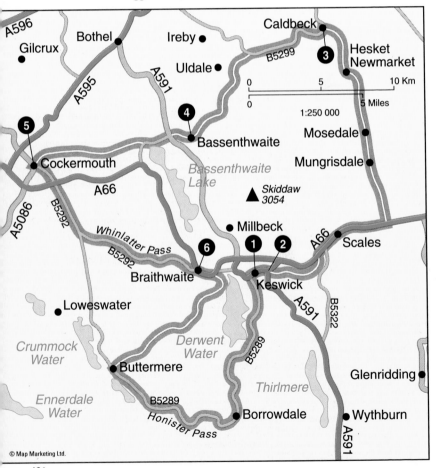

© Map Marketing Ltd.

ROUTE: 64 miles (102.5 km)

Directions in sequence from: Keswick

Keswick
The principal town in the northern Lake District has crowded, narrow streets, a Moot Hall (restored 1813) in the market-place, a theatre, a museum containing manuscripts and relics of literary luminaries who lived in the area and three other museums – of, respectively, railways, cars and pencils. *Tourist information: tel. (07687) 72645.* ① *Leave town by Penrith road and immediately after junction with Windermere road take minor road to right signposted Castlerigg Stone Circle.* About 1 mile (1.5 km) from the town, a short walk across a field leads to the Stone Circle, over 3,000 years old and the best example of prehistoric standing stones in the north of England. From here there is a magnificent mountain panorama, with Helvellyn to the south, and Skiddaw and Blencathra to the north. ② *Continue on minor road, taking right turn at two T-junctions, then turn right again on to A66.*

Scales
At the top of a long hill the White Horse Inn serves good bar meals, and is the most popular starting point for climbers ascending Blencathra. *Continue on A66 for about 4 miles (6.5 km). At crossroads, turn left to Mungrisdale.*

Mungris-dale
This tranquil village lying close under the hills has a tiny, white-washed church (1756) with a three-decker pulpit. The Mill Inn can be found set picturesquely beside the River Glenderamackin.

Mosedale
At the Friends' Meeting House (1702), coffee and cakes are served from May to September. A short detour can be made into the Caldew Valley (cul-de-sac) which has fine picnic places beside a rocky river. At the end of the road there are old mines and spoil heaps; the area was exceptionally rich in minerals, and specimens can still be found here.

Beyond the village the road runs over unfenced common with the steep boulder-strewn slopes of Carrock Fell on the left.

Hesket Newmarket
The village has many 18thC houses set about a green, and useful pub, The Old Crown.

Caldbeck
John Peel, the fox-hunting enthusiast immortalized in the well-known song, was born in this charming village in 1776. His grave can be seen in the churchyard. There are also craft shops, tea places and, of course, The John Peel Inn.

Over the bridge a small car park is the starting point for a 1-mile (1.5-km) walk to the Howk, a limestone gorge. ③ *Leave village on B5299 signposted Uldale and Bassenthwaite, then fork left after 3 miles (5 km) on to a minor road (signposted Keswick) and left again at turning to Orthwaite and Mirkholme.*

**Caldbeck –
Bassen-
thwaite**

At Orthwaite *(not on map),* the 17thC Hall, well seen from the road, declares its antiquity in its mullioned windows and architectural detail.

The spectacular Dash Falls can be glimpsed in the distance to the left. *Beyond Orthwaite Hall, take next turning to the right to Bassenthwaite.*

**Bassen-
thwaite**

Huge new farm buildings dominate the village, but a few old houses survive; note, near The Sun Inn, a stone over a cottage door which reads 'This house done by John Grave 1736'. ④ *Go through village then turn right on to A591. At crossroads near The Castle Inn, turn left to Bassenthwaite Lake,* the only lake in the Lake District (the others are 'meres', 'waters' or 'tarns').

Cross Ouse Bridge over the outflow, take right turning (signposted Cockermouth), then go right again at turning marked Golf Course and Higham Hall, along a quiet and elevated road to Cockermouth.

**Cocker-
mouth**

The wide, tree-lined main street has several old and interesting buildings, including the house where Wordsworth was born in 1770. *House open Mon-Fri, Apr-Oct.*

Fletcher Christian, mutineer on the *Bounty,* was also born in the town, in 1764.

The partly ruined castle, which dates from the 12thC, is still inhabited *(only occasionally open to the public).* ⑤ *Leave town on B5292 signposted to Lorton and Buttermere. Before Lorton when road divides take left fork signposted to Braithwaite and Keswick.*

**Whinlatter
Pass**

Near the foot of the pass Spout Force waterfall may be reached by a marked rough track (½ mile/0.8 km).

At the summit, there is a Forestry Commission's Visitor Centre.

The pass has extensive forest on both sides with marked walks; on the descent a picnic site affords a fine view over Bassenthwaite Lake to Skiddaw.

⑥ *Turn right in Braithwaite and look for signs to Newlands. Go over humpback bridge and in ½ mile (0.8 km) fork right.*

**Newlands
Hause**

Approached along the pastoral Newlands valley, the pass across Newlands Hause has hairpin bends.

Keskadale Oaks, on slopes to the right, are remnants of ancient forest cover. There is a steep final climb to 1,092 feet (333 m).

Buttermere

A grand backdrop, provided by the towering peaks of High Crag, High Stile and Red Pike, makes this modest lake (it is only 1¼ miles/2 km long) one of the loveliest.

Tiny Buttermere village has a fittingly tiny Victorian church which stands in a splendid position.

Turn left on to the Keswick via Honister road, which runs well above the lake giving extensive views. Ahead, with an exceptionally steep side silhouetted against the sky, is Fleetwith Pike. Rowing boats for hire at Gatesgarth Farm (end of lake).

Honister Pass

A twisting narrow road, steep near the summit (1,174 feet/358 m), runs between boulder-strewn mountainsides; Fleetwith Pike is on the right and Dalehead on the left.

At the top of the pass Honister slate quarries, recently closed, were in operation for more than 200 years.

The descent into Borrowdale is gentle at first, across open moorland, but the final drop into the hamlet of Seatoller is steep. Here, the National Park Dalehead Centre provides information about Borrowdale and mountain expeditions.

A diversion can be made to Seathwaite (1 mile/1.5 km), the wettest inhabited place in England.

Borrowdale

With its steep mountainsides, bare crags, clear river and abundant trees, Borrowdale contains the essence of the Lake District. The extensive oak woodlands are protected as they are of international importance and in them the red squirrel can still be seen.

Beyond Rosthwaite the road twists close to the river through the narrow pass called the Jaws of Borrowdale.

There is a car park among the silver birches at Quay Foot. From

• *Borrowdale.*

● *Boating on Derwentwater has not always been mainly for pleasure. The lake was once a significant commercial thoroughfare, with cargo boats carrying ore from mines around the valley for smelting at Keswick.*

here, a short walk is signposted to the Bowder Stone, a huge, precariously balanced rock; there is a wooden staircase to its summit.

At picturesque Grange, where an arched, 17thC bridge spans the wide river, you could pause for tea (there is a choice of places). In summer parking may be difficult.

A little further down the valley the Borrowdale Hotel serves excellent meals, while the Lodore Swiss Hotel provides a more luxurious setting, with matching prices. Behind the latter, the Lodore Falls are an impressive sight after heavy rainfall.

Derwent-water

With its indented shoreline and wooded islands, Derwentwater is considered by many to be the most beautiful of the English lakes.

Across the water, the ridge of Maiden Moor and Catbells rises above Brandlehow Woods, the first property acquired by the National Trust in the Lake District. (The Trust now owns a quarter of the National Park.)

There is a frequent public launch service which calls at various points around the lake.

Watendlath
(detour)

The rewards of this 3-mile (5-km) drive along a narrow, twisting, sometimes congested road include Ashness Bridge, one of the most photographed places in the Lake District, and Surprise View – a splendid view over Derwentwater from the edge of a vertical cliff.

Watendlath itself is a hamlet cradled in the fells, its picturesque qualities much favoured by artists.

D'wentwater – Keswick

Calf Close Bay is an excellent place for a picnic. The car park is in Great Wood to the right of the road.

WALES

Brecon Beacons and Black Mts

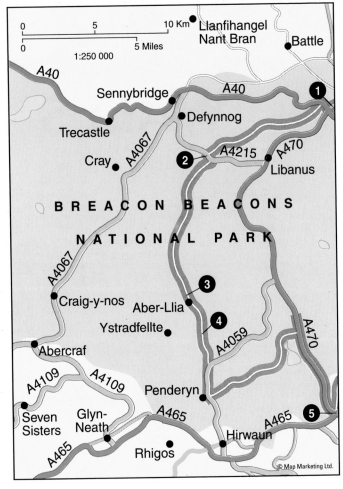

0   5   10 Km
0   5 Miles
1:250 000

Llanfihangel Nant Bran

Battle

A40

A40

1

Sennybridge

Defynnog

Trecastle

A4067

A4215

A470

Cray

2

Libanus

B R E A C O N   B E A C O N S

N A T I O N A L   P A R K

A4067

3

Craig-y-nos

Aber-Llia

Ystradfellte

4

A4059

A470

Abercraf

A4109

A4109

Penderyn

A465

Seven Sisters

Glyn-Neath

A465

5

Hirwaun

A465

Rhigos

© Map Marketing Ltd.

Route One takes in some of the most spectacular scenery in the Brecon Beacons National Park. There are grand views of the Old Red Sandstone range that dominates the area, and to contrast with barren mountainsides there are wooded valleys.

Route Two offers some of the best views of the long, whale-backed ridges of the Black Mountains. Driving into the heart of this range is tricky; most of the valleys are dead ends and the narrow, single-track roads become congested in summer.

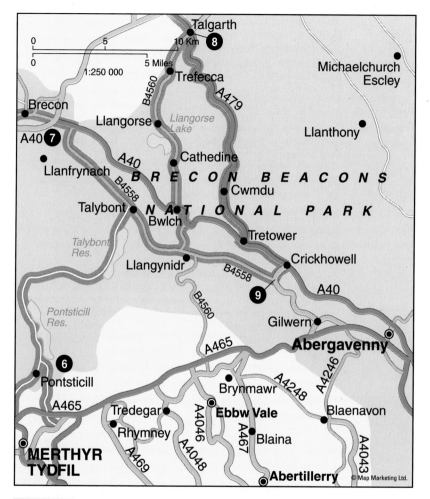

ROUTE ONE: 50 miles (80 km)

Directions in sequence from: Brecon

Brecon   The main centre for the National Park has a confusing one-way system. There are several handsome buildings in the centre, but the 13thC Priory of St John the Evangelist, which was given cathedral status in 1923, lies on the western edge of the town. Inside, note the unusual stone cresset for candles.

Tues and Fri are market days, when many of the pubs stay open for extended hours. There is a craft market in the Market Hall on at least one Sat each month. *Tourist information: tel.(0874) 622485.*

The Brecknock Museum has excellent local history displays and includes a reconstructed assize court. *Open Mon-Sat.* ① *Go over bridge, following signs for Mynydd Illtyd. Thereafter, follow signs to the Mountain Centre.*

The Mountain Centre

Built in 1966, the centre *(open daily)* provides information, picnic facilities, a cafeteria, slide shows and guided walks. Take the opportunity to buy a leaflet on Ystradfellte waterfalls (see Porth yr Ogof below), as none are available on site.

Twyn y Gaer, the site of an Iron Age hill fort, can be reached on foot (about 1¼ hours) from the centre. From the top of the hill there are good views of the Brecon Beacons.

② *At junction with A4215 turn left, then turn sharp right on the bend, following signs to Heol Senni. Before reaching village, take second turning on left near the bottom of the hill, signposted to Ystradfellte. The small sign is often overgrown in summer.*

At the top of the hairpin bends, pause for a magnificent view back across the Upper Senni Valley. Just over the pass (Maen Llig *not on map,*) and visible from the road is a large standing stone, 13 feet (4 m) high and 8 feet (2.5 m) wide. Standing stones dating from the early Bronze Age are common locally, but their function remains a puzzle. This one may have marked the pass which was later used by the Romans.

- *The River Usk at Crickhowell.*

According to local folklore, standing stones come alive on Midsummer's Eve and roam the countryside. Anyone who sees them is fated to an early grave. ③ *Either continue straight on to Penderyn, or fork right for detour to Ystradfellte and Porth yr Ogof. The narrow roads around Ystradfellte are often congested in summer.*

④ *Near the brow of the hill, turn right on to unsignposted lane immediately before forestry plantation. Drive down narrow lane to car park on right; be prepared to reverse to make room for oncoming traffic you are all too likely to meet.*

Porth yr Ogof   Here *(not on map)* the River Mellte goes underground for nearly 1 mile (1.5 km) and has worn away the limestone into a cave system. Look down on the entrance from the easily accessible viewpoint (only experienced cavers should venture inside). The area is famous for its spectacular waterfalls, accessible on foot only. Details of walks are given in the National Park leaflet; wear sensible shoes as wet limestone is dangerously slippery.

Penderyn   *Turn right immediately after the village sign and follow narrow road to the crest of the hill.* The church here is usually locked, but the graveyard is fascinating and there is a good view of the surrounding countryside. *Return to village and take left turning signposted Cwm Cadlan.*

Forest Centre   Garwnant Forest Centre has displays and information about the role of the Forestry Commission. *Open daily in summer; Sat and Sun afternoons in winter.*

Inn *(detour)*   At Nant-ddu Lodge there is excellent home-cooked food and real ale, worth the extra distance.

⑤ *At Cefn-coed-y-cymmer turn left before the main Heads of the Valley road (A465). Follow signs for Vaynor, Pontsticill and Talybont.*

Pontsarn   *(Not on map).* After 1¾ miles (2.75 km) park opposite the Pontsarn pub, near the top of the hill. Walk down the bank and under the road on to the fine stone viaduct (1866), which stands 90 feet (27 m) above the Taf Fechan River.

Vaynor   Follow the signpost to the church, to see the grave of infamous iron master Crawshay Bailey. Inscribed 'God Forgive Me', the huge granite slab was reputedly donated by locals who wanted to ensure that their old master and persecutor stayed underground. From the church there are views down the valley, back to Pontsarn viaduct.

⑥ *At Pontsticill, either make a sharp left turn signposted to Talybont, or turn right just past a derelict chapel for a detour to Pant, terminus of the Mountain Railway. Turn right at end of dam.*

Pant
(detour)

(Not on map.) The narrow-gauge Brecon Mountain Railway runs to Pontsticill (1¾ miles/2.75 km) but tickets must be bought and journeys started in Pant. The planned extension to Torpantau will include the highest railway tunnel in Britain. Trains run frequently in summer. *For details, telephone (0685) 722988.*

Torpantau

Look left for an impressive view of the three main peaks of the Brecon Beacons, with their flat tops and steep northern scarp slopes. Pen y Fan is the highest at 2,906 feet (886 m); Corn Dᶙ and Cribyn slightly lower.

Blaen-y-glyn

(Not on map.) At the bottom of the steep hill, park on right and walk along the forest path for about 400 yards (365 m) to see a pretty waterfall and fine views.

Talybont Reservoir

Newport's water supply and a nature reserve particularly noted for wintering wildfowl.

Talybont

Starting point for pleasant walks along the canal towpath. The village is renowned for its pubs: The Star offers at least ten different real ales and bar meals; The White Hart, dating from the 14thC, serves Felin Foel (real ale) on draught.

Pub
(detour)

The White Swan at Llanfrynach is worth a short trip to sample its excellent food.

◼◼◼ ROUTE TWO: 50 miles (80 km)

Directions in sequence from: Brecon

⑦ *Leave Brecon on A40, then turn right on to B4558.*

Cwm Crawnon

(Not on map.) Known locally as Upper Llangynidr. There are attractive walks beside the canal. Head towards Brecon and within half a mile (0.8 km) there are five locks, which change the water level by 48 feet (15 m). The Coach and Horses, by the canal, serves real ale and bar meals.

Coed yr ynys

The six-arch bridge over the River Usk dates from the 17thC and has a 7-foot (2-m) width restriction.

Bwlch

The name means 'pass' or 'gap' in Welsh. Over the crest of the hill look out for the war memorial on the right which marks *the turning on to B4560, signposted Talgarth.*

Cathedine

Good views to the right of Mynydd Troed and Mynydd Llangorse, an outlying spur of the Black Mountains. Llangorse Lake, to the left, is the largest natural stretch of water in South Wales. *Access to the lakes: follow signs past campsites and caravan park.* Rowing boats, windsurfers, canoes, splashcats and wayfarers may be hired.

Trefecca
The village is tiny; be careful not to miss it. *Turn right in village* to Coleg Trefecca, built in the 1750s to house the self-sufficient community founded by Howell Harris (1714-73), one of the leaders of the Welsh Methodist movement. *No admittance* to the building (now a theological college), but the early neo-Gothic exterior is worth seeing.

Talgarth
Former stronghold of temperance and Welsh Methodism. ⑧ *In Talgarth, turn sharp right, then bear left beyond the bridge, following signs to Crickhowell. Alternatively, turn left on to A479, for short detour to Bronllys Castle.*

Bronllys
(detour)
The tall round tower is all that survives of this 13thC castle, but there is a good view from near the top. *Open daily.*

Castell Dinas
Just past telephone box, turn left up lane marked 'No Through Road'. Park at end of lane, then walk along rough track and up steep hill to the summit. Although there are few visible remains of the Iron Age fort and 12thC castle built on this site, the views are magnificent.

Cwmdu
Take a close look at the exterior buttress of the church; it incorporates a 6thC Roman tombstone with Latin inscription.
 The Farmers' Arms serves draught cider and bar meals.

Tretower
Turn right at end of village, following signs to Tretower Court and Castle. Bear left past church and park on cobbled pavements beside 17thC barn. The medieval fortified manor house has been justly described as one of the most beautiful houses of its kind in the country, even though it is completely devoid of furniture or furnishings. Sensitive restoration has preserved its original atmosphere.
 In the field next to the house the cylindrical tower and castle walls date from Norman times. *Open Mon-Sat and Sun afternoon.*

Crick-howell
This interesting little town with its ruined 13thC castle, 14thC church and well-preserved 19thC buildings is best explored on foot. Leaflets are available from The Cheese Press in the square, which also serves coffee and home-made food. From the town there are excellent views of the Black Mountains and, in the foreground (to the north), the flat-topped Table Mountain. Crug Hywel, an Iron Age fort on the summit of Table Mountain, gave the town its name. ⑨ *Go over narrow bridge then turn right, following signs to Llangynidr. Return to Brecon along B4558, which follows the route of the canal.*

Cader Idris and Lake Vyrnwy

The dominating feature of the first part of this tour is the great mass of Cader Idris, a mountain area almost as popular as Snowdon. Opinions differ as to whether Idris was a warrior, king or poet, but his reputation was gigantic.

The second part of the tour – a loop round Lake Vyrnwy – begins at Dinas Mawddwy. From the Dyfi valley, the narrow road rises thrillingly over the highest pass in Wales, then winds it way round the lake, set in lovely wooded countryside, before returning to the A470. If weather conditions are at all doubtful, ignore this loop.

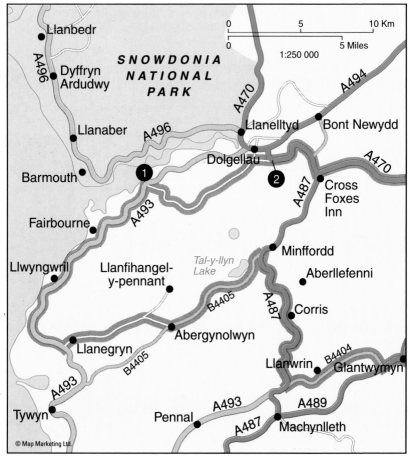

ROUTE: 82 miles (132 km)

Directions in sequence from: Machynlleth

Machyn-
lleth

A market town (market day Wed) in the Dyfi valley. The town centre is dominated by the large clock tower, donated by the Marquis of Londonderry in 1872.

The tourist information centre (tel. (0654) 702401) is housed in the 16thC Owen Glendower Centre; it is thought that a previous house on this site was where the Welsh parliament of Owen Glendower met in 1404, free of English domination.

The town's name is pronounced 'Mahun-leth' – approximately.

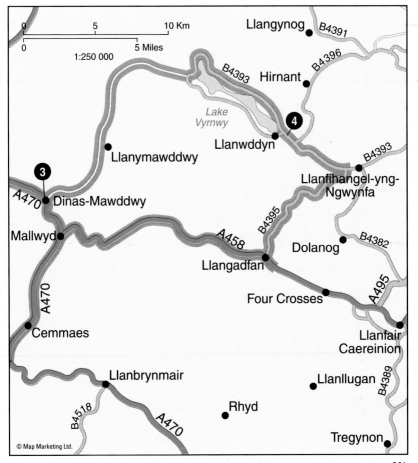

Llwyngwern The Centre of Alternative Technology was established in 1974 on the site of an old slate quarry. The dedicated group who run the centre have created a fascinating series of working exhibits illustrating possible alternatives to the accepted ways of producing energy and food with their harmful effects on our health and environment.

Many of the houses on the site incorporate the techniques advocated, including solar, wind and water power, and food is grown without the use of artificial fertilizers. *Open daily for tours around the site.*

Corris   At the Corris Craft Centre the central restaurant and information section is surrounded by workshops leased to local craftsmen who can be seen at work; jewellery, candle-making and picture framing are just some of the trades operating here. *Open daily.*

Corris Uchaf From the road running up the Corris valley there are fine views of Cader Idris with its great grey ridge.

Minffordd One of the routes up Cader Idris starts from here and has been popular since Victorian times, when tired climbers could relax in the refreshment hut which Richard Pugh, a mountain guide from Dolgellau, built at the top in 1830.

Many arctic alpine plants have their southern limit in this region. In summer pied flycatchers, wood warblers, redstarts and many other woodland birds can be seen amongst the trees.

Tal-y-llyn This little lake in the shadow of Cader Idris is surrounded by trees. Fishing permits are available from The Tyn-y-Cornel Hotel, which looks out over the lake and is a pleasant place for a meal.

Abergyn-olwyn The inland terminus of the Tal-y-llyn narrow-gauge railway, which has been carrying passengers up the valley from Tywyn on the coast for over 100 years.

In the village turn right up the steep hill. Care is needed on this narrow road.

Castell y Bere *At the crossroads, turn right.* The castle ruins, in a fine setting at the top of a wooded hill, are an easy walk from the car park.

Built in 1230 by Llewelyn ap Iorweth, Prince of Wales, Castell y Bere marked a high point in Welsh independence from England. However, it was captured by Edward I in 1283.

Llanfi-hangel-y-pennant The village, which lies a short way beyond Castell y Bere, was the home of Mary Jones. Born in 1784, she is famous for having walked barefoot across the hills to Bala, 25 miles (40 km) away, to buy a Bible from the Reverend Thomas Charles. Her long walk stimulated the formation of the Bible Society.

● *At 2,928 feet (892 m), Cader Idris is 431 feet (131 m) lower than Snowdon.*

Craig-yr-Aderyn
Return to the crossroads then carry straight on. The huge rock which stands out ahead is known as Bird Rock. This spectacular hill has a sheer drop of 200 feet (61 m) on its north-west face, with a further several hundred feet of steep scree to its base. It is the only known inland nesting site for a colony of cormorants, whose predecessors may have selected the site centuries ago when the sea came up the valley. Today, the West Wales Naturalists' Trust protects the 20 to 30 nesting pairs.

Llanegryn
This small village is typical of the few that are found in this sparsely populated area. It is worth pausing to look inside the church, which has a beautifully carved rood screen, thought to have been brought from Cymer Abbey, near Dolgellau, when it was disbanded in 1537.

Fairbourne
A popular seaside resort with sandy beaches, safe bathing and fine views of Barmouth and the Cambrian Coast Railway's wooden viaduct across the Mawddach Estuary.

203

*● Near
Dollgellau.*

Running along beside the sea, the miniature narrow-gauge railway uses both steam and diesel locomotives. The 4-mile (6.5-km) round trip lasts 1 hour. *Trains run daily Easter-Sept.*

① Half a mile (0.8 km) beyond Arthog there is a sharp U-turn to the right, signposted to Cregennen. Drivers wishing to avoid this steep, narrow, gated road should take the A493 to Dolgellau, picking up the route at The Cross Foxes Hotel, on the A470, to the east of the town.

Llyn Cregennen *(Not on map.)* A memorable spot: the great mass of Cader Idris forms a backdrop to the little lake which is surrounded by National Trust land.

Ty Nant *(Not on map.)* The pony track that goes up Cader Idris from here is still in use. (Pony trekking establishment nearby.)

Llyn Gwernan *(Not on map.)* The hotel by the little lake provides fishing permits, and is a delightful place for a drink.

Dolgellau The old county town of Meirionnydd has, for at least 100 years, been the centre for exploring Cader Idris, but there are also excellent short walks in the area. *Tourist information: tel.(0341) 422888.*

② Take the A470 out of Dolgellau (passing The Cross Foxes Hotel).

Dolgellau – Dinas- Mawddwy Great rounded hills rise up on all sides of this magnificent road as it crosses the Bwlch Oerddrws pass.

③ Turn left on to unclassified road signposted Dinas-Mawddwy.

Dinas-
Mawddwy

The road leading out of the village and up the valley becomes extremely steep with spectacular views.

Bwlch y
Groes

At nearly 1,800 feet (549 m), this is the highest point that can be reached by car in the whole of Wales. The view extends for miles across open moorland.

Fork right at junction, for Lake Vyrnwy.

Lake
Vyrnwy

This man-made lake, 5 miles (8 km) long, supplies Liverpool with water. Built in 1880, it can provide 45 million gallons a day. The lake is part of a vast nature reserve, and many woodland and water birds can be seen here.

The old village of Llanwddyn now lies beneath the water, but a new village has grown up beyond the dam. The visitor centre in the old chapel has an exhibition illustrating the natural and social history of the Vyrnwy estate.

High up on the hill overlooking the reservoir, the Lake Vyrnwy Hotel serves meals to non-residents.

④ *Leave Lake Vyrnwy on B4393, and follow route back to Machynlleth.*

Bala and Harlech

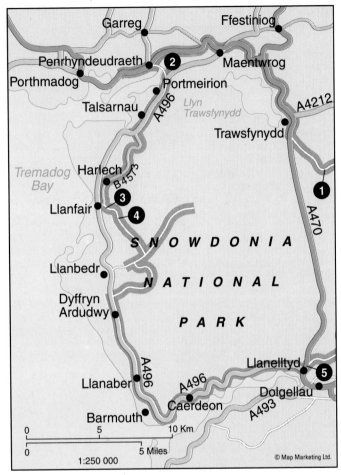

Snowdonia National Park includes not only Snowdon itself, but also land to the south, through which this tour runs. Between Bala and the coast lies some of the Park's loveliest scenery: secluded, wooded valleys and stretches of high hill country. Along the route ancient Stone Age sites and a medieval castle contrast with the stark modernity of Trawsfynydd nuclear power station and the Italian-style village at Portmeirion.

Some of the roads on this tour are not only narrow and steep, but gated as well – please shut gates after you.

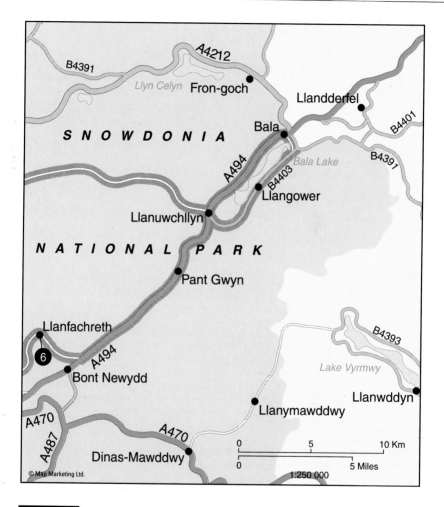

© Map Marketing Ltd.

1:250 000

ROUTE: 85 miles (136 km)

Directions in sequence from: Bala

Bala This pleasant country town, situated at the end of the largest natural lake in Wales, has a busy, friendly air. In the past it was an important centre on the route to England from the west and many ancient trackways converge here. *Tourist information: tel. (0678) 520367.*

From the large car park at the end of the lake, there is a fine view across the water to the mountains beyond. There is canoeing, sailing and

207

fishing for a variety of species at this end of the lake. The famous gwyniad, unique to Bala, is rarely caught by rod and line. It is a fish similar to the herring in appearance and origin.

Bala Lake

Along the lakeside road there are several large lay-bys where drivers can pause to take in the view. *Beyond the end of Bala Lake and before reaching Llanuwchllyn, take the road to the right, signposted Trawsfynydd.* Note the very large chapel, originally built in 1746 but restored and enlarged in 1810 and 1871. It is the oldest surviving Nonconformist chapel in Wales and is a symbol of the life of this area over the last two centuries.

From the lake, the old road winds up through the hills, initially amongst low oak woods, then out on to higher open ground, passing the occasional isolated farm, then leaving even these behind.

This high country with only the sheep, views of far distant peaks and dry-stone walls, is an unchanging world, with only newly planted forests breaking the old patterns. The many gates across the road mark the boundaries of the various sheep walks over these hills.

The Harlech Dome

This is the name given by geologists to the whole of this area of great arched rocks, 20,000 feet (6,096 m) thick. Frost, wind and rain have worn them away over millions of years, exposing the hard and craggy rocks below.

Foel Boeth rises above the forest of Coed-y-Brenin (wood of the king). Old copper mining spoil heaps can also be seen around here, relics of past industrial activity.

(i) *At the point where Trawsfynydd is signposted to the left, continue on the higher road.* There is a fine view of the nuclear power station (see below) and its lake from the brow of the hill before the road drops down to the A470.

Trawsfynydd

Designed by Sir Basil Spence, the power station stands at the far end of the lake. The first to be built inland, it was opened in 1965 and is the only freshwater cooled nuclear power station in Britain. There are public viewing areas and guided tours can be arranged.

Across the A470 from the power station lies the site of the Roman fort, Tomen-y-mur, the most remote outpost of the Roman Empire in Britain. Built in 78 AD, it is unique in having had an amphitheatre attached to it – a possible morale boost for the troops stationed at this fort on the outer fringes of the Empire. A Norman castle mound stands on the site of the old west gate. Only the outlines remain of the fort and its amphitheatre.

Hotel
(Maentwrog)

Lying in the beautiful Vale of Ffestiniog below the 19thC mansion of Tan-y-bwlch, the Oakley Arms is a convenient place to stop for a meal.

● *Harlech – granite, narrow streets – and dominating castle with its bloodstained notoriety.*

Port-meirion   *Passing through Penrhyndeudraeth, turn left to Portmeirion.* This unique, Italianate village was created by architect Sir Clough Williams-Ellis, who died in 1978. Lying on a wooded promontory beside the broad estuary of the River Dwyryd, the village has many curious features and is a cheerful antidote to the rather plain-faced architecture of most Welsh villages. Portmeirion has in addition been the location of several films. *Open all year, though restricted hours in winter.*

② *Returning to Penrhyndeudraeth, take the road to the right sign posted Harlech Toll Road. This road crosses the river on a narrow toll bridge. Proceed to Talsarnau. Just beyond the village take the B4573, the road to Harlech.*

Talsarnau –   From this road there are fine views of Harlech castle, looking much as it
Harlech   does in the picture painted by Turner around 200 years ago.

Harlech   The 13thC castle, built by Edward I as part of his grand plan to subdue the Welsh, stands on a high rock and dominates the small town set on the side of a steep hill. Six hundred years ago the sea came right up to the base of the castle (hence the watergate), but today it is more than ½ mile (0.8 km) away.

The castle has been the scene of much fighting. In 1294 it withstood a determined siege by Madoc ap Llywelyn; in the early part of the 15thC it was the main base of Owen Glendower's rising against the English; and in the Civil War of 1642 it was held by the Royalists until the very end. *Open daily, but closed Sun morning in winter.*

③ *Turn sharply up the hill by Barclay's Bank in the main street. Those who do not wish to go up this narrow and very steep road should take the main road southwards to Barmouth.*

At the top of the hill there are magnificent views of the coast to the south, and of the Lleyn Peninsula to the north. Inland lie the Rhinogs, a part of Snowdonia noted for its rough and broken landscape.

④ *On reaching crossroads go straight ahead. At the next T-junction turn left to Cwm Bychan, a lovely wooded valley.*

Cwm   In the summer, pied flycatchers and redstarts can be seen in the valley,
Bychan   and the surrounding area. Lake Cwm Bychan is also noted for its wild flowers and butterflies. Near the far end of the lake are the wrongly named Roman Steps. These rock slabs, set in the hillside to form a long series of steps, are part of a medieval track that went from Harlech to Bala. *Return down the same road to continue on to Llanbedr.*

Llanbedr   The Royal Aircraft Establishment have an airfield here for test flying. Close by the aerodrome a road runs down to Shell Island (it is only an 'island' at high tide). As its name implies, this sandy stretch of coast is well known for its sea shells; around 200 varieties have been found.

The Maes Atre Tourist Centre just outside the town has craft workshops, a model village and a children's adventure playground.

Barmouth A sunny, mainly Victorian seaside town on the Mawddach estuary. The Cambrian Coast Railway runs between the long sandy beach and the centre of the town, then crosses the estuary on a wooden viaduct. (At present the viaduct is undergoing repairs, having been attacked by unexpected vandals – Toredo boring worms). Wordsworth sang the praises of the view from the viaduct's footpath.

Caerdeon Fine view of the Mawddach Estuary with Cader Idris behind.

Llanelltyd ⑤ *At Llanelltyd, turn towards Dolgellau, then just over the new bridge turn left to Cymer Abbey.* Ruined walls are all that remain of a Cistercian monastery founded in 1209. In its time it wielded great influence over this part of Wales. *From the Abbey, take the road sign posted to Llanfachreth.*

Nannau The 18thC house seen from the road at Nannau was once the home of the Vaughan family, who were responsible for planting a great number of trees locally.

The house, one of the best in Wales, has been converted into self-catering apartments, but non-residents can drink (and eat) in the bar.

⑥ *Pass through Llanfachreth* (the road is lined with huge cedar trees). *At the crossroads beside telephone box, carry straight on. Go downhill and across the crossroads; the narrow road eventually joins the A494.*

Llan-uwchllyn Before the water level fell, Bala Lake came right up to this village. The narrow gauge Bala Lake Railway runs between Llanuwchllyn and Bala, along the south-eastern side of the lake. The 5-mile (8-km) round trip takes about 30 minutes. *Open daily, early Apr-early Oct; closed some Fris.*

Hotel *(Bala Lake)* The Bala Lake Hotel, restaurant and golf course is open to non-residents.

Lleyn and Snowdon

Apart from one group of high hills which includes the twin peaks known as The Rivals, the Lleyn Peninsula is restfully pastoral, with small farms and grass-covered stone walls dividing the fields.

The second part of the tour, from the old slate-exporting town of Porthmadog back to historic Caernarfon, could scarcely be more dramatic. The road goes through the lovely Aberglaslyn Pass, along Nantgwynant with its splendid views of Snowdon, to the Pass of Llanberis. At Llanberis itself there is the opportunity to ascend Wales's highest mountain in comfort – by train.

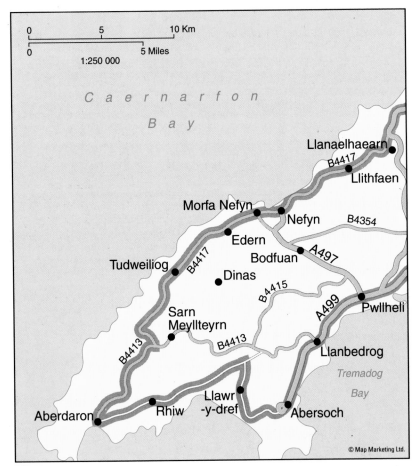

0   5   10 Km
0   5 Miles
1:250 000

Caernarfon Bay

Llanaelhaearn
B4417
Llithfaen

Morfa Nefyn
Nefyn   B4354

Edern
Bodfuan   A497

Tudweiliog   B4417
Dinas
B4415

Sarn
Meyllteyrn   A499   Pwllheli
B4413

B4413   Llanbedrog

Tremadog
Bay

B4413
Aberdaron   Rhiw   Llawr
-y-dref   Abersoch

© Map Marketing Ltd.

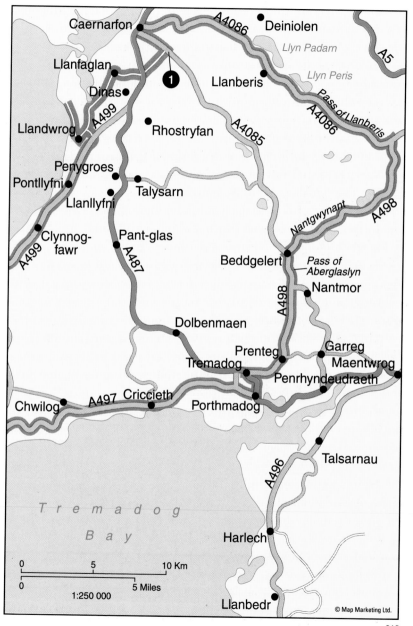

Caernarfon
Deiniolen
A4086
Llyn Padarn
Llanfaglan
Llyn Peris
Dinas
Llanberis
A5
1
Pass of Llanberis
Llandwrog
Rhostryfan
A4085
A4086
A499
Penygroes
Pontllyfni
Talysarn
A498
Llanllyfni
Nantgwynant
Clynnog-fawr
Pant-glas
A499
A487
Beddgelert
Pass of Aberglaslyn
A498
Nantmor
Dolbenmaen
Prenteg
Garreg
Tremadog
Maentwrog
Penrhyndeudraeth
Chwilog
Criccieth
A497
Porthmadog
Talsarnau
A496
T r e m a d o g
B a y
Harlech
0   5   10 Km
0   5 Miles
1:250 000
Llanbedr

© Map Marketing Ltd.

ROUTE: 106 miles (170.5 km)

Directions in sequence from: Caernarfon

Caernarfon The administrative capital of Gwynedd is dominated by its huge, late
13thC castle.

The castle was designed to be the main fortification of the ring built
by Edward I to subdue the Welsh (Conwy, Harlech, Flint and Beaumaris
are some of the others in this circle around Snowdon).

The first English Prince of Wales (later Edward II) had his title
conferred at an investiture held here, and both Edward VIII (later the
Duke of Windsor) and Prince Charles followed in this tradition. Within
the castle there is a display of investiture items, and an excellent Royal
Welsh Fusiliers regimental museum. *Open daily (but closed Sun morning
in winter).*

The yachting quay is a relaxing place to watch the world go by.
Tourist information: tel. (0286) 672232.

Leave Caernarfon on the A4085, signposted to Porthmadog. Just
outside the town lies the Segontium Roman Fort, built to defend this
part of the shore against attack from Ireland. No high walls are left but
the layout can still be seen from the stone foundations and there is a
small exhibition of excavated relics. *Open Mon-Sat and Sun afternoon.*

①︎ *At Caeathro, turn right to Bontnewydd (new bridge). Cross the
A487 and follow signposts to Saron and Llandwrog. Turn right for a
short detour to Dinas Dinlle.*

Dinas Dinlle The name stems from the pre-Roman hill fort (dinas means fort in
(detour) Welsh). From the airfield on the flat, marshy ground beyond the village
pleasure flights can be taken over Snowdonia and Anglesey.

Further down the road, Fort Belan is an old defensive fort at the
entrance to the Menai Straits. It houses a maritime museum and a
pottery, and the owner will organise a ceremonial firing of cannon on
request.

Clynnog- From the village the peaks known as Yr Eifl (The Rivals) can be seen to
fawr the south-west. Those who take to the hills on foot will see views of the
Lleyn, Anglesey and the mountains of Snowdonia.

Nefyn and Renowned in the past for the number of men they sent to sea, these
Morfa small towns are now quiet resorts. From the large car park at the
Nefyn entrance to the golf club at Morfa Nefyn there is a pleasant walk to Port
Dinllaen, which nestles in a sandy cove.

The Ty Coch Inn lies almost on the shore but is sheltered from the
westerly gales by the headland. Inland, at the crossroads where the
A497 meets the B4417, the Bryncynan Inn specializes in seafood dishes.

Morfa Nefyn – The B4417 gradually becomes more undulating and there are many little
Aberdaron   side roads leading down to rocky coves, such as Porth Ysglaig, Porth
Colmon, and Porthoer, each with its own individual character.

Aberdaron   Picturesque resort with a good beach. For a fine view of Bardsey Island
at the tip of the peninsula, take the narrow road to Uwchmynydd and
Mynydd Mawr. Boats for Bardsey Island by arrangement.

Y Rhiw   Coming over the brow of the hill there is a panoramic view of Porth
Neigwl or Hell's Mouth, 4 miles (6.5 km) of beach where big breakers
come rolling in from the south-west. Access to this popular surfing spot
is from the far end (signposted).

Abersoch   Once a small fishing village, this is now a smart sailing centre with several
hotels and a fine beach.

Pwllheli   The largest town on the Lleyn. In summer the sheltered harbour is
crowded with yachts, but in winter it is a good place for bird-watching.

Llany-   Lloyd George lived in this idyllic village which is reached along a minor
stumdwy   road signposted from the bypass (A497). A small museum houses items
devoted to the memory of one of the most famous prime ministers of
this century. *Open Easter-Sept (except Sat and Sun mornings).* There is
also a pleasant riverside walk much favoured by Lloyd George.

Criccieth   A delightful, south-facing seaside town with good swimming in clean,
clear water, and fine views of the Cardigan Bay coastline and the hills
inland. Queues form at Cadwalader's home-made ice-cream shop near
the beach.
    The 13thC ruined castle on the hill was a Welsh fortification which
Edward I adapted as part of his plan to encircle the area.

Porthma-   A great attraction here is the Ffestiniog steam railway, which runs across
dog   the Glaslyn Estuary and through the wooded hills of Snowdonia to
Blaenau Ffestiniog, a distance of 15 miles (24 km).
    The Maritime Museum by the harbour reflects the town's slate-
exporting history, while the local pottery (near main car park) has guided
tours and visitors can try their hand at 'throwing' a pot. *Open Mon-Fri,
Easter-Oct; also open Sat and Sun in high season and Bank Hol Mon.*

Tremadog   Attractive 19thC architecture.

Glaslyn   In the early 19thC William Maddocks reclaimed this area by building the
Estuary   causeway which now carries the Ffestiniog Railway and the toll road
across the estuary. The low-lying meadows to the right of the road are
good for bird-watching.

● *Heart of Snowdonia – Llanberis pass.*

At one time the sea ran up the estuary almost as far as Beddgelert, as can be seen from the name of the little village of Nantmor (which means 'stream of the sea').

Pass of Aberglaslyn One of the most beautiful passes in Wales. At the point where the River Glaslyn rushes through a narrow gorge lined with pines, there is no parking, but cars can be left further up the road. Walk back either down the track of the old Welsh Highland Railway or by the river.

Beddgelert A picturesque village lying at the junction of the Glaslyn and Colwyn rivers. A short riverside walk leads to the grave of Gelert, faithful hound of Prince Llewellyn. According to legend, Gelert saved the prince's baby son from an attack by a wolf. When the prince returned from hunting he saw blood on the dog, leaped to the wrong conclusion and killed him. In remorse the prince built a small cairn here. Cynics say the whole story was invented by an 18thC innkeeper, in order to attract more visitors to the village.

Nantgwy-
nant
The road rises steeply up the pass, beside Llyn Dinas and Llyn Gwynant. At the lay-by near the top fine views of Snowdon and nearby peaks.

Pen-y-Pass
The starting point for two of the main walking routes up Snowdon – the Miner's Track and the Pyg Track.

Pen-y-Pass lies at the head of the Llanberis Pass, a dramatic valley scooped out by slow-moving glaciers about ten to twenty thousand years ago. The road, which runs between towering cliffs of dark rock, is at its most impressive on a wild, wet day.

Llanberis
The terraces and workings of the huge Dinorwic slate quarry, which once employed over 3,000 men, can be clearly seen from the road. The slate has a lovely purple tinge to it. Under the mountain of slate now lies the Dinorwic hydro-electric power station, recently completed. The entrance can be seen at the bottom of the terraces where an arched tunnel goes into the mountain.

The Snowdon Mountain Railway takes passengers to the summit of the highest mountain in Wales (3,559 feet/1,085 m). On a clear day the views are unrivalled; half a day should be allowed for the trip. A ride on Llanberis Lake Railway, alongside Llyn Padarn, takes less time.

This tour includes one of the most beautiful roads in the whole country, the B5113 from Colwyn Bay to Pentrefoelas. From this ancient thoroughfare there are panoramic views in all directions: to the coast in the north; to the rugged eastern edge of the Carneddau range in the west; across the rolling Denbigh moors to the east; and south to the hills guarding the wild area of the Migneint.

The second half of the tour has interesting contrasts (Blaenau Ffestiniog is a slate-mining town, Betws-y-coed is situated in lovely wooded countryside) and culminates in a drive down the Conwy Valley to Conwy and its castle.

◼◼◼◼ ROUTE: 80 miles (128 km)

Directions in sequence from: Llandudno

Llandudno Planned solely as a holiday resort in the mid-19thC, the town has many fine examples of Victorian architecture and wrought-iron work and a pier built in 1879. *Town trail guide available from tourist office, Chapel St., tel. (0492) 876413.*

The town was built beside the massive headland of Great Orme (Norse for sea-monster) whose summit can be reached by a steep road, or by tramcar or cablecar. The Marine Drive is a toll road with an anti-clockwise one-way system (entrance beyond pier gates). On this 4-mile (6.5-km) drive around the Great Orme headland there are views of cliffs, coast, Anglesey and the Conwy Estuary. There is also the chance of seeing wild goats, ravens, falcons and several rare plants.

Back in town, Gogarth Abbey Hotel incorporates the house where Lewis Carroll stayed for summer holidays and wrote parts of *Alice in Wonderland.*

The Mostyn Art Gallery (Vaughan St.) specializes in contemporary art and often exhibits work by artists living in Wales. *Open Mon-Fri during exhibitions.*

ⓘ *At end of Marine Drive return down tree-lined avenue to the promenade. Drive round the bay and over the Little Orme towards Colwyn Bay.*

Colwyn Bay *On entering the town take B5113 signposted Llanrwst.* The Welsh Mountain Zoo, clearly signposted to the right at the crossroads, has an interesting collection of animals, including chimpanzees and sea-lions. On summer afternoons there are free-flying falconry displays. *Open daily.*

Colwyn Bay – B5113 is the old high road to Llanrwst and the south. Initially it goes
Pentrefoelas through pastures criss-crossed with hedges, but note how the hedges are gradually replaced by dry-stone walls as the road rises and enters more remote regions. Soon good views of the Conwy estuary, the

Great Orme and Llandudno open up. At the crossroads there are views of the Carneddau hills to the west and the expanse of the Denbigh moors to the east. (The River Conwy runs down a geological fault-line dividing the rugged Ordovician rocks of Snowdonia from the younger Silurian rocks of the Denbigh moors. This is the explanation for the difference in scenery on either side of the road.) The Welsh sheep seen in this area are bred to withstand the harsh winter climate, and the Welsh black cattle are equally hardy.

From the lay-by there are fine views across the valley above Betws-y-coed to Gwydir Forest and the Llugwy valley.

Hotel
(Pentrefoelas) At the junction of B5113 and A5, The Voelas Arms Hotel makes a good stop for a bar meal.

② *Turn left for 23-mile (37-km) detour to Llyn Brenig, or continue straight across A5 to Cerrigydrudion (see below).*

Llyn Brenig
(detour) *From the A5, turn left almost immediately on to A543.* This road crosses the wild grouse moors of Mynydd Hiraethog. An area famous for its natural beauty, it is dotted with the remains of Stone Age settlements and has been home to many Welsh poets. There are views of distant lakes, and the brooding Clocaenog Forest.

The huge man-made reservoir of Llyn Brenig was completed in 1977 and is used to control the level of the waters of the River Dee. Fly fishing permits are available, and there are nature and archaeological trails, picnic sites in the woods (take fly repellent), a children's adventure course and playground, and an interpretative centre at the southern end of the reservoir.

Cerrigy-drudion Old staging-post village on Thomas Telford's London to Holyhead road (A5). In the early 19thC horse-drawn coaches took 30 hours to complete the journey on fine days.

Pub
(Rhyd-lydan) The Geeler Arms, standing back somewhat from the main road, serves bar meals.

③ *turn left off A5 on to unclassified road and drive past Geeler Arms. After 1 mile (1. 5km) turn left at T-junction.*

Ysbyty Ifan The River Conwy runs through the centre of this picturesque, typically Welsh village with its slate-roofed stone cottages. Sadly, no remains have survived of the 12thC hospice which gave the village its name (Ysbyty means hospital in Welsh). The hospital cared for travellers passing to and from the holy island of Bardsey at the tip of the Lleyn Peninsula.

Migneint This area of bogs and moorland to the left of the B4407 is famous for its

● *The River Llugwy rippling through Fairy Glen Ravine near Betws-y-Coed; other attractions nearby are the beautiful Swallow and Conwy Falls.*

rare plants and, in summer, for its upland birds. The source of the River Conwy is at Llyn Conwy, just to the right of the road.

Blaenau Ffestiniog

Once a flourishing slate-quarrying town, it is now known for its show caverns and as the terminus of the narrow-gauge Ffestiniog steam railway.

At the Llechwedd Slate Caverns, just north of the town, a battery-operated electric train takes visitors 400 feet (122 m) underground into the heart of the slate mine. Guides explain the methods used by the miners, and the conditions in which they worked 100 years can be clearly seen. On the surface there are craft workshops. *Open Feb-Oct.*

At Manod, S of Blaenau, are underground quarries which were adapted to house National Gallery paintings in the Second World War.

221

● *Rhos-on-Sea harbour and the view towards Colwyn Bay.*

Dolwyd-delan

In 1247 the castle was the birthplace of Llewelyn, the last Welsh Prince of Wales. It was built in the 12thC to guard the pack-horse route down the Lledr valley and to withstand the repeated English invasions.

Betws-y-coed

The name, meaning 'chapel in the woods', refers to the old church of St Mary (near the station) which contains a fine effigy of a 14thC Welsh prince.

Although the village is crowded in summer, there are numerous opportunities for peaceful walks, either beside the river or further afield, perhaps to the lovely Swallow Falls (2½ miles/4 km), which are approached through ancient woods. *Details of walks from the tourist office opposite Royal Oak hotel.*

In the village itself there are shops, hotels, cafés, a small railway museum and several distinguished bridges, including Thomas Telford's Waterloo Bridge (1815).

Anyone intrigued by architectural oddities should make a 2-mile (3-km) detour to the west, along the A5, to see The Ugly House, built in the 16thC.

Llanrwst

On entering this old market town, take the road to right, to Gwydir Castle. The 'castle' – a restored 16th-19thC house with a 14thC hall – has an interesting garden: different areas were planted to commemorate historical events. *Open Easter-Oct.*

From Gwydir Castle, go over narrow, arched bridge (designed by Inigo Jones in 1636). In the centre of the town, the church of St Grwst

(15thC) and the Gwydir Chapel (17thC) are both worth a visit; the latter, possibly designed by Inigo Jones, contains the enormous stone coffin of Llewelyn the Great, the Welsh prince who died in 1240.

Near Inigo Jones's bridge, Tu Hwnt i'r Bont is a 15thC courthouse, now a café.

④ *Take B5106 back over bridge and travel up the valley to Trefriw.*

Trefriw   At the woollen mills, the whole process of making traditional Welsh cloth can be seen free of charge, Mon-Fri. The shop *(open daily)* sells all kinds of woollen goods including tweed made at the mill.

⑤ *At Tal-y-Bont turn left on to unclassified road which goes up hill to Llanbedr-y-cennin.*

Pub   Dating from the 13thC, the Olde Bull Inn at Llanbedr-y-cennin has fine views of the valley and a cosy atmosphere.

Conwy   Walled town famous for its 13thC castle. One of a series built to subdue the Welsh, it is still more or less intact and is considered one of the finest in the country. There are superb views from the ramparts. *Open daily (but closed Sun morning in winter).*

On the quay, visitors can squeeze into the smallest house in Britain; *open Easter-Oct.* In the High St., Plas Mawr (easily identified by its crow-stepped gables) is a fine example of an Elizabethan mansion. *Open daily. Leave town on the A55, which goes across New Bridge.* From here, two interesting engineering feats can be seen: Telford's suspension bridge (1826) and Stephenson's railway bridge (1848).

SCOTLAND

The Scottish Borders

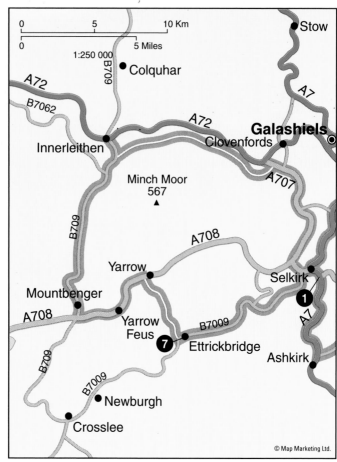

0   5   10 Km
0   5 Miles
1:250 000

Stow
Colquhar
A72
B7062
A72
Galashiels
Clovenfords
A7
Innerleithen
Minch Moor
567
▲
A707
B709
A708
Yarrow
Selkirk
Mountbenger
1
A708
Yarrow
Feus
B7009
A7
7
Ettrickbridge
Ashkirk
B709
B7009
Newburgh
Crosslee

© Map Marketing Ltd.

This is the trail of Sir Walter Scott, the land where he grew up, collected ballads, set the scenes of novels; and died. The eastern loop of the figure-of-eight covers well-wooded agricultural country and touches at Scotland's most famous medieval abbeys. The western loop embraces Ettrick Forest.

ROUTE ONE: 51 miles (82 km)
Directions in sequence from: Selkirk

Selkirk   An ancient royal burgh of twisting hilly streets, with tweed mills and mill shops. *Tourist information: tel. (0750) 20054.*

226

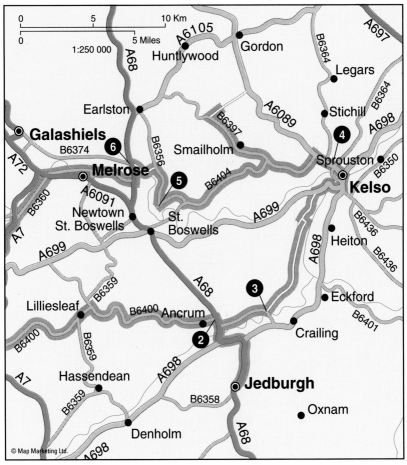

In the market-place stands a monument to Sir Walter Scott, sometime Sheriff of Selkirkshire, and in High St. a statue to locally-born Mungo Park, the African explorer. Near Market Place, Halliwell's House Museum includes re-creations of the building's past role as home and ironmonger's shop. Audio-visual and displays relate to Selkirk's history. *Open Mon-Sat and Sun pm, Apr-Oct; also am, Jul and Oct.*

Selkirk Glass, famous maker of paperweights, is open to visitors, with shop and coffee-shop, *open daily; afternoons on Sun.*

① *Leave Selkirk by the A7 signposted Hawick and in 4½ miles (7 km) turn left on to B6400, signposted Ancrum.*

● *The River Tweed curves gracefully through the Border country.*

Selkirk –
Ancrum

Leaving Lilliesleaf, a view of Eildon Hills opens out, left. They say the triple peaks (about 1,300 feet/400 m) were split in a night by the familiar devil of 12thC wizard, Michael Scot; however, the Romans called this place Trimontium (three hills). Two-and-a-half miles (4 km) beyond Lilliesleaf a wide view of the Cheviot Hills opens on the right. The hills form the natural boundary between Scotland and England and the 'Border Fence' runs along their crests.

Ancrum   The name of this undistinguished village serves as the courtesy title of the heir to the Marquess of Lothian, principal landowner hereabouts. The village is a centre for exploring the local woodland (spring flowers) and the Teviot riverbank.

Ancrum –   (2) *Half a mile (0.8 km) beyond Ancrum, turn right on to the A68*
Monteviot   *Edinburgh-Jedburgh road, then sharp left, signposted Nisbet.*

Jedburgh   A detour of 3½ miles (5.5 km) down the A68, takes you to another
(detour)   historic Border town which, like Selkirk, bears scars of Anglo-Scottish wars. The town houses of typical Jacobean Scots architecture with crow-stepped gables include a former lodging, now museum, of Mary, Queen of Scots. The ruined abbey in red sandstone dates from the 12thC, with a fine north transept surviving from the 14thC. The new visitor centre gives an insight into lives of the monks. *Open daily, afternoons on Sun in winter.*

Monteviot   *(Not on map.)* Signs ¾ miles (1 km) from Ancrum indicate Hairestanner Countryside Visitors Centre, on right. *Open daily Easter-Oct.*

Monteviot –   (3) Route continues through pastoral Vale of Teviot. *At Nisbet leave*
Roxburgh   *B6400 for bumpy, unclassified road signposted to Roxburgh.*

Roxburgh   The row of sleepy farm cottages gives no hint that Roxburgh was once a royal residence, a town which minted coins and a citadel which, along with Edinburgh, Stirling and Berwick-upon-Tweed, formed Scotland's defensive 'quadrilateral' against England.

Roxburgh   Steep grassy mounds at the roadside (right) on the A699 where Teviot
Castle   meets Tweed are the remains of a once-powerful Border stronghold, six times English and seven times Scottish. On the left, across the Tweed, is a view of Floors Castle (Duke of Roxburghe) and river terraces or 'floors' where James II of Scotland, while besieging Roxburgh Castle in 1460, was killed by a cannon which 'brak in the shooting'.

Kelso   Enter town by John Rennie's bridge over the Tweed, built 1803. Two lamp-posts are from Waterloo Bridge in London, created by the same engineer.

Kelso is a market centre for the lower Tweed district with a spacious town square. The 12thC abbey in the centre suffered badly in the last English assault in 1545, but part of the tower and façade survive, and the intricate Norman and early Gothic detail is worth a look.

The Waggon Inn, at 10 Coalmarket, is the place to eat and a 'Taste of Scotland' member. (4) *Leave Kelso by Edinburgh road (A6089) with the 'Golden Gates' of Floors Castle on the left. Turn left on to the B6397, signposted St Boswells. Public entrance to Floors Castle on left.*

Floors Castle Started 1718 by William Adam, with later additions by Playfair. The family home of the Duke of Roxburghe, it has a portrait gallery, period furnishings, garden centre, shop and restaurant, and was location of a Tarzan film, *Greystoke*. *Open Easter; Sat-Thurs, end Apr-end Oct; daily in Jul and Aug.*

Mellerstain Hse. *(detour)* A short detour from the junction of the B6397 and B6404 brings you to one of Adam's grand mansions. It boasts exceptional plasterwork, fine gardens with lake, gift shop and tearoom. *Open afternoons, Easter and May-Sept; closed Sat.*

Smailholm Tower A 16thC keep and viewpoint on the right of the B6404, was sentimentalized by Scott, and painted by Turner. A stiff climb, but the view is worth it.

Dryburgh Abbey Here is the most beautiful of the Border abbeys in a ghostly setting beside the River Tweed. It contains tombs of Scott and Field-Marshal Earl Haig, whose descendants live at Bemersyde next door.

Dryburgh – Leaderfoot ⑤ Back-track 1 mile (1.5 km); follow signpost for 'Scott's View'. Panoramic indicator at Scott's View helps locate 43 (according to Scott) places famed in Border legend and history. At this point, in 1832, Scott's horses, leading his funeral cortège to Dryburgh, stopped of their own accord.

⑥ Follow signposts for Melrose in the network of lanes, then turn right at signpost for Edinburgh and sharp left on to the A68. Cross the River Tweed and turn right under impressive (disused) Leaderfoot railway viaduct.

Newstead Here the Roman Dere Street crossed the Tweed. Large boulder marks site of Trimontium, where a major archaeological dig is planned for 1989-92. Roman artefacts are on view in their temporary home at Melrose Station (see below).

Melrose The 12thC abbey in the town centre is the best-preserved of all Border abbeys.

Road south to the golf course skirts Eildon Hills. Footpath to summits (40 mins) from clubhouse.

The disused railway station has been superbly restored, and houses a restaurant with home-cooking. *Open daily. Restaurant: open daily, except Mon.*

Marmions, in Buccleuch Street: a continental-style brasserie, with vegetarian dishes, which is fully licensed. Booking not esssential.

Abbotsford Custom-built pseudo-baronial home of Sir Walter Scott, stuffed with relics and heirlooms. *Open Mon-Sat and Sun afternoon, Mar-Oct.*

■■■■ ROUTE TWO: 37 miles (59 km)

Directions in sequence from: Selkirk

Selkirk　*Leaving by A707 and turning left on the B7009,* is a fine view of Bowhill (Duke of Buccleuch); entrance on the A708; *open July, Mon-Fri, 1-4.30 pm and Sun, 2-6 pm.*

Ettrick-bridge　⑦ *At the end of village take steep, tortuous, unclassified road on right across Ettrick-Yarrow watershed; single lane with passing places (don't park in them).* Wide all-round views at 1,187-foot (362-m) summit. Descend to the rushing Yarrow Water.

Between Yarrow and Gordon Arms, fenced-in beside the road, is the 6thC Liberalis stone, a monument to ancient British warriors.

Gordon Arms　*(Not on map.)* On this old drovers' inn a plaque records the last meeting of Scott and his friend James Hogg, poet, the 'Ettrick Shepherd'.

'Paddy Slacks'　This is the local name for the B709 through another hill pass, with views at the summit.

Traquair　The gates of Traquair House on the Peebles road ¼ mile (0.5 km) left of this route were locked in 1745 against the day when a Stuart monarch returns. Dating from before the 13thC, the house is popularly believed to be the oldest inhabited in Scotland. It has a brewhouse (ale from which is marketed commercially), craft workshops, tearoom and gift shop, and there is a programme of events throughout summer, such as falconry displays. *Open afternoons, Easter and May-Sept; all day in Jul and Aug.*

Walkerburn　Scotland's principal (though small) wool museum stands ½ mile (0.8 km) to the left of the route after the Innerleithen turning. *Open daily; mill-shop: open all year including Sun, Apr-Nov.*

Before the junction with the A72, on the road from Walkerburn to Selkirk, this Tweedside backroad offers picnic spots in pleasant woodland setting.

Argyll

Here is an exploration of the wilds of the Clan Campbell domains. Their hereditary chief is the Duke of Argyll, and the roughest, hilliest part of this area is known ironically as 'the Duke of Argyll's Bowling Green'. But you pass quickly from the grandeur of chopped summits to the civilized botany of sheltered places. Long fingers of both sea and inland lochs probe the hills: in spring their shores are carpeted with daffodils and primroses; in early summer they blaze with rhododendrons and azaleas – in fact there is colour in the landscape all year.

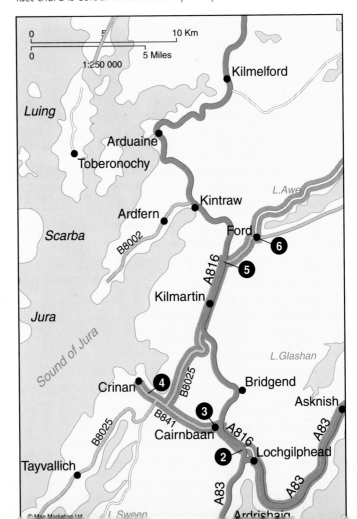

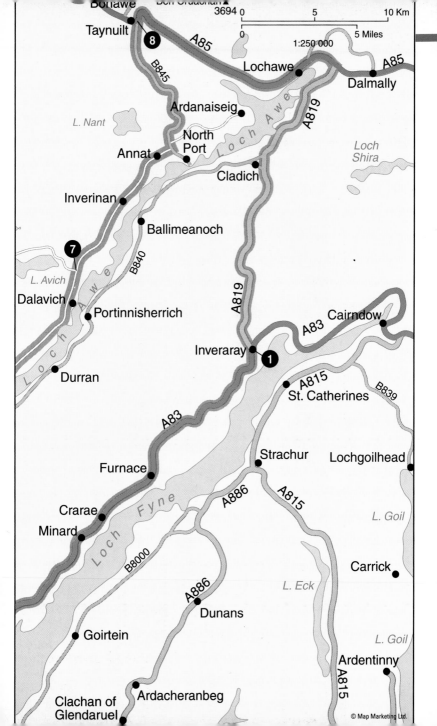

● *Kilchurn Castle stands on marshy ground that was once encircled by water.*

ROUTE: 90 miles (145 km)

Directions in sequence from: Inveraray

Inveraray

This royal burgh is often called (*pace* Inverness) the capital of the Highlands. It was built from 1753 onwards at the direction of the third Duke of Argyll, the population of the original village being relocated, and was the first 'planned' town in Scotland. *Tourist information: tel. (0499) 2063.*

The recently opened Inveraray Jail, former prison and courthouse, contains tableaux of reconstructions of trials, furnished cells and a crime-and-punishment exhibition entitled 'Torture, Death and Damnation'. *Open daily.*

Inveraray Castle

The splendidly ugly pseudo-Gothic seat of the Dukes of Argyll, chiefs of Clan Campbell, was for ages almost a royal palace, so influential was the family in national affairs. The present Duke and his family still live here, surrounded by historical treasures: silver, paintings, plasterwork, furniture and arms. Here Dr Johnson tasted his first glass of whisky. The castle is a major tourist attraction, but some people consider it over-commercialized. *Open Mon-Thurs, Sat and Sun afternoon, Apr-June and Sept to mid-Oct; Mon-Sat and Sun afternoon, July and Aug.*

In the castle grounds the Combined Operations Museum has World War II memorabilia, including a unique exhibition of models and photographs. *Opening times as for castle.*

① *Leave on road signposted Campbeltown.*

Argyll Wildlife Park
(Not on map.) Two miles (3 km) along this road, the park consists of 53 acres of habitat for badgers, wild cats, foxes and rare species of deer and owls. There is a woodland picnic area on the loch shore, a tearoom and gift shop. *Open daily.*

Auchindrain
The Museum of Farming Life depicts the lifestyles of farmers and crofters in bygone days. There is a display centre, shop and picnic area. *Open Sun-Fri, Easter-May and Sept; daily June-Aug.*

Furnace
A tiny port which *Para Handy* fans will remember as one of the sea-loch harbours served by the old-time 'puffers' or coal-burning coastal vessels. Neil Munro, creator of Para Handy was born at Inveraray.

Furnace – Crarae
The road hugs the Loch Fyne shore with spectacular views towards the Duke of Argyll's Bowling Green. The laird of the castle across the water, and his address, make a good tongue-twister for English visitors: Lachlan MacLachlan of Strathlachlan, Castle Lachlan, Strathlachlan, Loch Fyne.

Crarae
On right, Crarae Lodge has one of the finest gardens in the west. Rhododendrons and azaleas in May and June are the speciality and there are many exotica.
Crarae helps to explain why, in novels and plays about country-house life in England, the gardener was so often a Scot. *Open daily; plants sold 10-4.30.*

Minard – Lochg'phead
Beautiful views open up over the broadening Loch Fyne and on the distant hills of Knapdale and Kintyre.

Lochgilphead
Another tiny west coast fishing town. The best kippers (Loch Fyne herring) were traditionally cured here. Many fish shops and fishing-tackle shops: sea angling is a growth industry. ② *Keep right at roundabout at end of town and follow sign for Oban.*

Cairnbaan
A staircase of locks takes the Crinan Canal to its summit level. The 9-mile (14.5-km) canal, built for fishing craft, 1793-1801, is now used chiefly by motor-cruisers and yachts. ③ *Continue along B841 and follow the canal to Crinan.*

Crinan
A village and yachting centre with a remarkable rock garden rising from Loch Crinan: from the rooftop restaurant of the Crinan Hotel there are memorable views over the Firth of Lorn, especially when the sun goes down in a clear sky, which does not happen every day. ④ *Backtrack 1 mile (1.5 km) and turn left on to the B8025.*

Kilmartin 'Kil' usually signifies a church or burial place and this neat village lies in a glen littered with Bronze Age monuments and chambered cairns. The sculpted grave-slabs and 8thC carvings displayed at the church, on the left opposite the hotel, are well worth looking at. Kilmartin Cross, the decorated pillar behind the Memorial Gateway, is one of the great Celtic relics.

(5) *Turn right, signposted 'Ford'.* (6) *Continue along unclassified road signposted Dalavich.*

Ford – Numerous picnic spots on this minor road and several marked trails.
Inverinan You may see herds of Highland cattle hereabouts – they are fierce-looking but mildmannered. On left, after Dalavich, the signposted track to Loch Avich and Avich Falls is a pleasant and not too strenuous walk of 1¼ miles (2 km). (7) *Straight on after Dalavich, signposted Kilchrenan.*

Annat The mountain range which fills the northern horizon culminates in Ben Cruachan, 3,695 feet (1,126 m), the highest peak in Argyll. It gives its name to the war-cry of the Campbell clan: 'Cruachan!'
  The minor road on right leads in ½ mile (0.8 km) to Taychreggan, one of Scotland's most delightful lochside hotels. This upmarket establishment provides admirable attention to detail in all its services and supplies bar or Danish buffet lunches and gourmet dinners.

Ardanais- *From Kilchrenan a minor road on right goes to Ardanaiseig in 2½ miles*
eig *(4 km).* Georgian baronial house, colourful trees and shrubs. *Open daily*
(detour) *Apr-mid Oct.*

(8) *Turn right, signposted to Crianlarich.*

Bonawe *Turn left* and on the outskirts of Taynuilt is the Bonawe Iron Furnace, an
(detour) important industrial-archaeological site, largest and longest-surviving Highland blast furnace fuelled by charcoal and producing cast-iron 'pigs'. It was built in 1753. *Open daily Apr-Sept.*

Falls of Waterfall and footpath to reservoir are on the left as you emerge from
Cruachan the romantic pass of Brander. On the right, an underground hydro-electric station offers visitors an exhibition and a mile-long (1.5-km) minibus trip through tunnel. *Open normal working hours end Mar-Oct.*

Lochawe After right turn for Inveraray at head of Loch Awe, the much-photographed Kilchurn Castle is on the right. It was built by Colin Campbell, first of the Argyll dynasty, in 1440. Much knocked about in clan feuding, it has now been partly restored and is *open to the public (roadside car park) at all times.* There is a view of the castle from the road between Lochawe and Inveraray.

Glenaray   *(Not on map.)* Two miles (3 km) from Inveraray on the left, the fish farm is well signposted. Here are trout ponds (with fish which eat from your hand) and fishing lakes with a tearoom, children's play area, fish hospital and a toy village on stilts, inhabited by small mammals: entertaining and educative in a modest way. *Open daily.*

The East Neuk of Fife

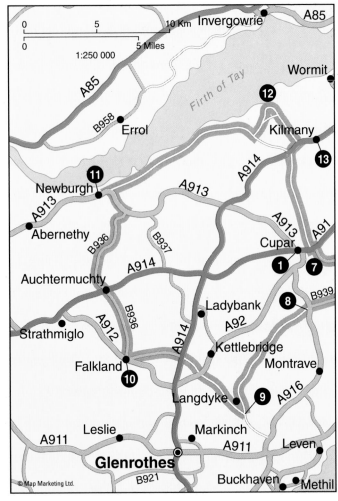

The fishing harbours of the 'East Neuk' are famed in Scottish history, yet tourists often overlook the seaward corners of this area – formerly the Kingdom of Fife. The Stuart king's description of Fife, 'a beggar's mantle fringed with gold', hardly applies today for the mantle (the once-useless swampland) is richly agricultural while the gold (the harvest of the sea) has become tarnished with the decline of the herring fisheries.

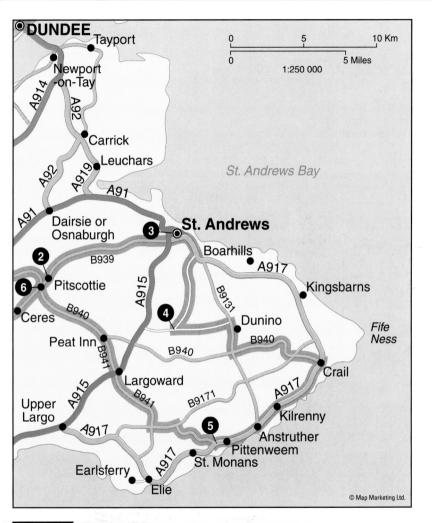

0   5   10 Km

0   5 Miles

1:250 000

© Map Marketing Ltd.

▬▬▬▬▬ **ROUTE ONE: 45 miles (72 km)**

Directions in sequence from: Cupar

Cupar   County town and ancient royal burgh with a bustling Regency air. The parish church, with early 15thC tower, is one which escaped the Reformation. There are some quaint inscriptions on the gravestones.

     Duffus Park contains the Douglas Bader Garden for the Disabled, an unusual kind of pleasure-ground adapted for the blind and handicapped.

① *Leave town by the St Andrews road and in ¼ mile (0.5 km) turn right, signposted Pitscottie.*

Pitscottie   The minor road labelled Dairsie enters a beautiful ravine called Dura Den, known to geologists as a rich source of fossils.
② *Turn left on to the B939 for St Andrews.* In 2 miles (3 km), an excellent view of this 'little city, worn and grey' (Andrew Lang).

St Andrews   *Enter town by South Street.* On the south side is part of Scotland's oldest university, founded 1411. Other University colleges are on the north side of North St. At the junction of South St. and North St. stands Scotland's oldest cathedral. Also at this junction (one-way system), Castle St. leads to St Andrews Castle, founded 1200. The ruins are widespread, with good views seaward. They include a Bottle Dungeon where John Knox was imprisoned, a secret passage and a ghost. *Open Mon-Sat and Sun afternoon. Tourist information: tel. (0334) 72021.*

The Scores, on seafront, leads to Golf Place, the Links and the Royal and Ancient Clubhouse. Anyone can play over the celebrated courses, including the Old Course, but some balloting for tee-off times is necessary in summer. The Clubhouse, ruling house of golf worldwide, is open only to members. The British Golf Museum close by, telling the story of the game from its ancient origins, open daily.

On West Sands near golf course, signposted, is the newly-opened Sea Life Centre. Octopuses, lobsters, sting rays and seals can be viewed at close range through multi-level windows. Restaurant, gift shop. *Open daily 9-6, June-Nov.*

③ *Turn right off South St. and leave town by Abbey Walk, signposted Crail, or by the vaulted Gothic 'Pends' (gatehouse). In one mile (1.5 km) bear right, signposted Grange (not on map).*

④ *Turn left at T-junction, signposted Dunino. Turn right at next junction and after 2 miles (3 km) left at crossroads.*

Crail   Some of the ancient, crow-stepped cottages in this oldest of East Neuk fishing ports have been sensitively restored by the National Trust for Scotland. In Crail's palmy days, a hundred boats crowded into the diminutive harbour. A small museum recalls local history. A 20-minute walk takes you to Fife Ness, the 'Kingdom of Fife's principal headland'.
Leave by coast road, signposted Kilrenny. In ½ mile (0.8 km) on the left, is a wide view of the Firth of Forth, Bass Rock and May Island.

Anstruther   Locally 'Anster', this is the largest East Neuk port, but a village for all that. Here is located the Scottish Fisheries Museum, highlights of which are an aquarium, the log-books of oldtime whaling skippers, examples of traditional fishing boats, and (moored alongside) the North Carr lightship.

● *Crail, oldest of the 'East Neuk' fishing ports, was made a royal burgh by Robert the Bruce in 1310, with a charter that conferred upon it the privilege of Sunday trading.*

Pittenweem Just beyond the village on the left there is another brilliant panorama of the Firth.

⑤ *In ¼ mile (0.5 km) bear right for Kellie Castle.*

Kellie
Castle
(detour)
Detour 1 mile (1.5 km) on right for this interesting old house. The tower dates back to Macbeth's time. *Open daily afternoons May-Oct. Return to B942 and take next right turn, signposted Cupar.*

⑥ *Continue on B941 for Cupar or turn left, signposted Leven, and join Route Two at Ceres.*

ROUTE TWO: 41 miles (66 km)

Directions in sequence from: Cupar

⑦ *Leave by South Rd. and after crossing railway take the fork to the left, signposted Ceres.*

241

Ceres   A jumble of 18thC cottages in this quaint little community has been
transformed into the award-winning Fife Folk Museum. *Open daily;
afternoons only, Fri.*

At the corner of High St. in centre of village, the photogenic 'Provost'
sits with his tankard and keeps an eye on things. This comical stone
statue was unearthed from a local garden. Its origin is unknown.

⑧ *Turn left on A916 then right on unclassified road which is signposted
Chance Inn.*

Craigrothie – An attractive hilly road with views north to Firth of Tay and south to the
Falkland   Firth of Forth. You can see Arthur's Seat (a volcanically-formed hill) in
Holyrood Park, Edinburgh. ⑨ *Successive turns: left (no signpost), right
(Cults), right (Burnturk) and straight on (Freuchie).*

Falkland   A compact, old-fashioned township full of country shops and Jacobean
'wynds'. It has a kiltmaker's, violin-maker's, art gallery, craft shop,
tearoom, pub and restaurant, all charming.

Embedded cosily in the heart of the town, the Palace was the
childhood home of Mary, Queen of Scots. Its French Renaissance and
Scots baronial architecture symbolize the 'Auld Alliance' of Stuart and
Bourbon. *Open daily Apr-Sept, afternoons only, Sun; weekends in Oct.*
⑩ *Exit by road on right and follow signs to Auchtermuchty.*

Auchter-   Just off the road but worth turning into for a glimpse of the archaic
muchty   simplicity of rural Fife life. The jokey place name is usually shortened to
'Muchty'.

Between here and Newburgh, fine views open out of Perth and the
upper Tay estuary.

Newburgh   A neat greystone village on one street, ancient despite its name. The
Mugdrum Cross in the churchyard dates from early Christian times.
⑪ *Exit by the unclassified road at the east of village, signposted
Gauldry.* In one mile (1.5 km) on the left are spread the barely-
identifiable ruins of Lindores Abbey, founded 1178. More interesting
architecturally is the water-mill.

Newburgh – Several points along this peaceful Firth-side road offer good views of
Balmerino   Dundee and its backcloth, the Sidlaw Hills. Six miles (10 km) from
Newburgh the two Tay bridges, road and rail, come into view.

Balmerino The ruined abbey on the left, atmospheric in its tranquil setting, has
recently celebrated its 750th birthday.

All the house-fronts on the row of cottages facing the Firth bear
inscriptions recalling the Scots Guards' colonel's address to his troops
before the Battle of Anzio, 1944.

⑫ *Turn right at junction ¼ mile (0.5 km) past abbey and in 400 yards cross another minor road. Follow signs to Rathillet.*

⑬ *Cross the A914 and head for Cupar.*

Speyside

This route runs through part of the 'Malt Whisky Trail', where the pagoda-like distilleries of world-famous brand names are constantly in sight. Several distilleries have their own visitor centres, where groups and individuals are welcome for guided tours at stated times.

The circuit is centred where the Glens of Livet, Fiddich and Grant, and the rivulets of the Cromdale Hills all join Strath Avon and Strathspey. Here are the sites of the innumerable illicit 'sma' stills' of bygone days; and apart from being of consuming interest to devotees of the 'single malts' (the unblended Scotch whiskies), the drive takes in some of Scotland's wildest scenery.

ROUTE: 81 miles (130 km)

Directions in sequence from: Elgin

Elgin

A market-town of character and a popular touring centre. *Tourist information: tel. (0343) 542666.*

The cathedral which makes Elgin one of Britain's smallest cities stands in roofless decay on the banks of the River Lossie. When new in 1270 it was accidentally burned out and one hundred years later deliberately destroyed by fire. Later on the steeple fell down and the then Earl of Moray helped himself to all the lead on the roof to pay off debts. In 1711 the central tower collapsed and for many years the place was a stone quarry. But a surprising amount of graceful architecture has survived in the nave, choir and chapter house.

① *Take Inverness road and bear left at hospital, signposted Dallas. Straight on at roundabout and at ½ mile (0.8 km) bear left then right, both signposted Pluscarden.*

Elgin – Pluscarden

Two miles (3 km) from Elgin on the left is a large store for malt whisky in cask. The road enters Monaughty Forest: picnic spots, footpaths.

Barnhill

At Pluscarden church the route bears right and then left, no signposts. (Detour straight on to Pluscarden Abbey, ½ mile (0.8 km)). The Cistercian priory is well restored and once more lived in. On request the monks will show the 'Burgie Necklace' (a jet Bronze-Age diadem).

Barnhill – Dallas

Turn left on to the B9010, no signpost. Sign for Highland cattle and a good view to the right over Macbeth's 'blasted heath' and the town of Forres.

Dallas

A hamlet on an innocent stream, as different as it could possibly be from the Texas city to which it gave its name.

The Dallas Hotel offers a cheerful undemonstrative welcome and serves simple fare at all hours.

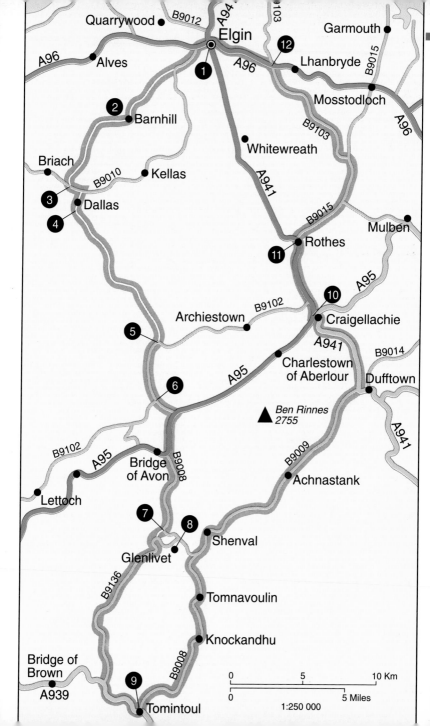

● *The Spey, second longest river in Scotland, and Mecca for salmon fishermen.*

④ *Leave Dallas by unclassified road on left, which climbs towards the source of the Lossie river.* Here begins the spectacular scenery.

⑤ *Turn right at junction.*

⑥ *Down into Strathspey. In 3 miles (5 km) from previous junction turn left and cross old railway line, now Speyside Way and River Spey.*

Marypark –
Ballindalloch   After one mile (1.5 km) a wide view of Strathspey and the braes of Moray opens up on the right.

Ballin-
dalloch   Two miles (3 km) from Marypark, on the right *(not on map)*, are the baronial-style lodge and gatehouse of Ballindalloch Castle, a 16thC tower house. *Open daily, Easter-Sept.*

⑦ *At a mini-spaghetti junction of mountain roads turn right, then immediately left. In ½ mile (0.8 km) there is a good view ahead of the Livet Water in its narrowing glen. In another ½ mile (0.8 km) is the Glenlivet distillery.*

Glenlivet Distillery

The best-known of the first licensed distilleries (1824, but operating illegally for a century before that date) has the privilege of describing its product as *The* Glenlivet, though half a dozen different malt whiskies depend on the River Livet for their water. *The reception centre opens Easter-Oct, Mon-Sat.* The guided tour, which includes hospitality, takes 40 minutes. No young children.

⑧ *Exit by turning right at the Blairfindy Lodge hotel, then in one mile (1.5 km) left at next junction.*

Glenlivet – Tomintoul

In one mile and two miles (1.5 and 3 km) are two useful picnic places, with amenities. Across the River Avon, the hills rise to the heights of Cromdale, a 2,400-foot (730-m) ridge whose short sharp torrents help give Scotch malt whisky its magic formula.

Tomintoul

The highest village in the Highlands (but not in all Scotland) at 1,150 feet (350 m). There are fine views to the south on entering the village; picnic area on right.

The main-street shop called Whisky Castle is an emporium of local crafts and of the produce of the region, including whisky. ⑨ *Exit village by road on left, signposted Braemar, then straight on signposted Dufftown. (Road on right surmounts the Lecht and goes to Cock Bridge. At 2,100 feet (640 m) it used to be a notorious snow-trap, but it is now kept open for winter sports, except in harsh weather.)*

Knockandhu

Splendid views on right to the Ladder Hills and ahead to Ben Rinnes. Bare granite and deep glens make this a dramatic route all the way, as far as Dufftown.

Dufftown

A model village of four streets meeting at a clock tower, founded in 1817 by Lord Fife (family name Duff) to provide work for soldiers returning from the Napoleonic wars. The clock tower has been gaol, council house and assembly room in its time and is now a museum and tourist information centre. The clock is 'the clock that hanged MacPherson' – a reference to a local villain condemned to death last century. Public opinion demanded a reprieve, but the sheriff of Banff advanced the clock to the time of execution, forestalling the arrival of the document.

Glenfiddich distillery, where the world's best-selling malt whisky is produced, off the Elgin road, *open Mon-Fri all year and Sat and Sun, Easter-mid Oct.* It is one of seven malt distilleries which surround the

● *Glen Avon, near Glenlivet.*

little town. Another is Mortlach, off Fife St., the first licensed distillery in Scotland (1823), *not open to the public.*

Mortlach parish church, at the end of Church St., has a strangely-carved Pictish cross and a symbol stone, also Jacobean graves and effigies. This has been hallowed ground since 566 AD, when St Moluag established a chapel. *On the exit road A941, ¼ mile (0.5 km) past Glenfiddich distillery, is the empty shell of Balvenie, a spacious courtyard castle known to Edward I, the 'Hammer of the Scots' and later to Mary, Queen of Scots. The outstanding feature is the 'yett' or iron gate. Open Mon-Sat and Sun afternoon, Apr-Sept.*

(10) *Take right turn, signposted Elgin. After crossing Spey, straight on at crossroads, signposted Elgin.*

Craigell-achie

On the left of the bridge over the Spey is the handsome former road bridge, built in 1814 by Telford from local granite with a Welsh pre-fabricated cast-iron span. At 8,000 it was the costliest civil engineering job in the Highlands.

Rothes

On the left is another showplace distillery, the Glen Grant, with visitor centre and hospitality (no young children). *Open Mon-Fri, Easter-Sept.* The large factory at the north end of the village turns distillery dreg and effluent into high-protein animal feed.

(11) *Take the B9015 from the village, signposted Orton.*

(12) *In 11 miles (17.6 km) from Rothes, turn left on to the A96, signposted Inverness. In 3 miles (5 km), enter Elgin.*

Index

Picture credits

Colwyn Leisure Services: 222; Fotobank/English Tourist Board: 171; Highland Islands Development Board: 246; Tom Wright: 184; Gloucestershire County Council: 120; Susan Griggs Agency/Rob Cousins: 119; Antony Howard: 224; Simon McBride: 52, 84; Michael St Maur Shiel: 124, 228; Patrick Ward: 23; Adam Woolfitt: 18, 30, 35, 150; Noel Habgood/Derek C Widdecome: 70, 107, 221; Robert Harding Picture Library: 137; International Photobank/Peter Baker: 77; Sarah King: 42, 58, 88; Lake District National Park Authority: 189; Andrew Lawson: 196; Colin Molyneaux: 114, 130, 192, 203, 209, 216; Norman Mays: 132; Moray District Council: 248; National Trust: 101, 108, 144, 204; Scottish Tourist Board: 241; John Sims: 46; Patrick Thurston: 102, 178; Charlie Waite: 65; Simon Warner: 165; Trevor Wood Library/Peter Phillips: 155; Trevor Wood: 1, 2-3, 142, 190, 234.